The Seven Ages of the Theatre

by the same author

★

STAGE-SETTING: FOR AMATEURS AND PROFESSIONALS
PROSCENIUM AND SIGHT-LINES
CHANGEABLE SCENERY
THE OPEN STAGE
THE MEDIEVAL THEATRE IN THE ROUND
etc.

THE
SEVEN AGES
OF THE THEATRE

by
RICHARD SOUTHERN

*with line drawings
by the author*

A DRAMABOOK

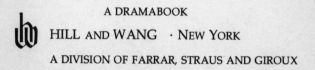

HILL AND WANG · NEW YORK

A DIVISION OF FARRAR, STRAUS AND GIROUX

THEATRE IS AN ACT

'His *Acts* being seven ages.'
AS YOU LIKE IT, II, 7

Contents

9

CONTENTS

CONTENTS

Illustrations

ILLUSTRATIONS

Acknowledgments

Plate 1 is reproduced from *The Illustrated London News*, 26 Dec. 1936 (all copyright records of this paper were destroyed during the war).

Plate 2a. Information Service of India.

Plate 2b from *Harvest Festival Dramas of Tibet* by Marion H. Duncan, 200 E. Luray Ave., Alexandria, Va., U.S.A.

Plate 3 from *Bali* by Philip Hanson Hiss, by permission of Duell, Sloan and Pearce, Inc., N.Y. (copyright 1941 by Philip Hanson Hiss).

Plate 4. Copyright Fotocommissie, Rijksmuseum, Amsterdam.

Plates 7 and 9 permission of Drottningholm Theatre Museum, Sweden.

Plate 8 permission of Theater-Museum, München.

Plate 10. Foto Harder, Celle.

Plate 12. Verlag Gundermann, Würzburg.

Plate 13. Bayer: Verwaltung der Staatl: Schlösser, Gärten und Seen.

Plate 14 from *Chinese Theatre* by Kalvodova Sís Vaniš, Books for Pleasure Ltd., Spring Place, London.

Plate 15. Japanese Centre of the International Theatre Inst., Tokyo.

Plate 18. Photo Paukschta, Berliner Ensemble.

Plate 19. André Villiers.

Plate 20. Studio Theatre Ltd. and Stephen Joseph.

Plate 21. Arena Theatre Productions and John English.

Plate 22. Stratford Shakespeare Festival Theatre, Canada.

ACKNOWLEDGMENTS

Plate 23. Ann Jellicoe.

Plates 5, 6, 11, 16, 17, 24 and Figs. 24 and 34 are from examples in the Author's Collection.

Grateful acknowledgments are made to all authors quoted in the text and are due also to the following: Messrs. W. H. Allen and Co. and George Braziller, Inc. (N.Y.) for quotations from Sean O'Casey's *The Green Crow*; Penguin Books Ltd. for quotation from H. D. F. Kitto's *The Greeks*; Suhrkamp Verlag, Berlin, and Methuen and Co. for quotations from Bertolt Brecht; L'Association des publications de la Faculté des Lettres de Strasbourg for quotations from Gustave Cohen's *Le Livre de Conduite* . . .; Curtis Brown Ltd., The Bodley Head and Charles Scribners (N.Y.) for quotations from Kenneth Grahame's *The Golden Age*; Curtis Brown Ltd., Robert Hale and Duell, Sloan and Pearce, Inc. (N.Y.) for quotations from Philip Hanson Hiss's *Bali*; The Clarendon Press, Oxford, for quotations from Sir Arthur Pickard-Cambridge's *The Theatre of Dionysus at Athens* and *The Dramatic Festivals of Athens*; Lund Humphries for quotations from P. G. O'Neill's *Early Nō Drama*; Marion H. Duncan, 200 E. Luray Ave., Alexandria, Va., U.S.A. for quotations from *Harvest Festival Dramas in Tibet*; the publishers of *Bauen und Wohnen*, Zürich, for quotation from Oscar Fritz Schuh's letter on the Teatro Olimpico; M. André Barsacq for quotation from 'Lois Scéniques'.

To My Readers

I said in my Foreword to *The Medieval Theatre in the Round* that that book would not be followed by another proceeding more remotely still into historical research. The present book is no denial of that. *The Medieval Theatre in the Round* was a piece of historical research; this book is not. But it has a particular reason for its existence, as the following will make clear.

In the Foreword I have just mentioned, I went on to say that there was, to me, a need more urgent still than the need for deeper theatrical research—'namely, the establishment of a body of information upon which the planning of new theatres can proceed with understanding'. In my view theatre practice is that one degree more important than theatre history.

Having such thoughts in my mind, I read with some doubt an invitation in February, 1960, from the American firm of publishers, Hill and Wang, Inc., to write for them 'a short history of the theatre from Greek times to the present'—a book that might be readable by college students as well as the general reader and that might eventually be sold as a paperback. This seemed at first sight a typical task of theatre research once more, even if only of research into existing writings and, as such, offered little inducement to me to draw my interest from the laborious and puzzling present.

But then I saw that at least from one point of view a very congenial task could come out of it if the 'history of the theatre' could be turned into an account of the development of the *forms* which theatre has taken. Such a review could serve very helpfully towards establishing a small part at least of that body of information upon which the planning of new theatres could proceed with understanding. I then asked if a review in these terms might be acceptable, and added that if it were I should like to make it touch all periods (not only from the Greek onwards, but before) and all countries—in short, an attempt to survey the whole development of theatre form throughout human society. The reply from America was, 'The book you have in mind is indeed one that we would like to publish.' And so I became committed.

I was committed, however, not to research (or not to very much research, for some of the material on Tudor Interludes is in fact quite newly thought out) but to setting in order a considerable body of informative ideas on theatre form that I had met in past reading, but never set down.

The reader, then, should understand that this is a much more general survey than any of my earlier books but, on the other hand, a survey of a much bigger subject—something which a little more nearly brings him to the problem of what theatre really is. And that, if one comes to look at it, is one of the essential basic problems to study if one undertakes to design a theatre today.

I would add one further thought. This book opens, as I hope, wider subjects than the use of grooves, or the method of presentation in a 'Round', and certainly wider subjects than the fitting-up of simple stage settings; and one might be concerned to ask, 'Where is it all going to lead?' In my view it is already clear that the essential thing to which everything in theatre finally boils down is the performance of the living player, and what is of assistance to that performance. In the end we can subtract so much of the technical refinements, but we cannot take away the centre of it all, the living player, and his one indispensable technical adjunct—his costume. To this we must come at length.

Pittsburgh and London 1961

The Second Edition

This second edition remains substantially like the first. A few misprints have been corrected, two or three figures redrawn for greater accuracy, and a passage brought up to date.

Southampton 1964

PRELIMINARY

The Essence of Theatre

PRELIMINARY

The Essence of Theatre

Stripping the Onion

If anyone takes the theatre, as Peer Gynt did the onion, and tries to peel off its accretions one by one to get at the heart of what Theatre really is, he can begin easily. He will no doubt find that the most recent accretion is Scenery. Scenery is here today but was not there three hundred and fifty years ago.

Thereafter, the peeling is progressively harder. Probably the Auditorium would be next to go; the theatre is then out-of-doors. Next might follow the Stage as a raised platform to act upon; take that away and the player is on the ground. Going relentlessly on, that player would next have to be stripped of his Costume and Mask. Remove these and there will probably fall apart two separate pieces, leaving nothing inside; those two pieces would be the Player and the Audience. Take these apart and you can have no theatre.

If the above is true it should be possible to begin at this point and trace the growth of the theatre forward from its beginnings. This book is one attempt to do so.

The story has complications. Instead of a simple development, there seems to be a succession of intrusions from outside upon what would otherwise appear as a self-contained, modest, and not unpopular human act; the act, that is to say, of performing something before a group of other people. There are no additions or trimmings to this at first, save the Player; it is something on its own. Yet it is remarkable to see the eagerness—one might almost say jealousy—with which, from time to time, certain outside interests have seized upon this modest act of theatre and exploited it for their own ends, or made it a peg to hang their own work upon. These interests have imposed upon the theatre an immense

21

amount of paraphernalia that fundamentally has nothing whatever to do with the root intention of theatre people—that is with the human and social act of a person or persons performing something before a group of other people.

It is thus important to make clear at the beginning just what is the original act upon which these intrusions, and the whole subsequent development, operate. What is the essence of theatre?

ART AND COMMUNICATION

If we set out to estimate what the essence of theatre is—at any rate sufficiently to help reader and writer to start from a similar point of view—we might begin with the following proposition—

> Any work of art
> is an address (in some form)
> by an individual
> to a number of people.

This way of putting it brings us at once within sight of the act of theatre; but instead of going on to the theatre immediately we should pause to remark something that follows from this proposition about art in general.

It is that there can be two ways of addressing a public. The one is by making something, and the other is by doing something. If you *make* something—an object, a picture, a story, a musical composition—you can embody in it whatever it is you have to say to the public; then you leave this 'thing' to its fate, to be read as may be by the separate individuals that compose the public according to their opportunity.

If you *do* something or *perform* something—speak, move, play an instrument—you can embody in that action whatever you have to say. But it is important to emphasize at the beginning that the secret of the theatre does not lie in the thing done but rather in something that arises from the manner of doing. Drama may be *the thing done*, but theatre is *doing*. Theatre is an act.

To give some sort of an example of this; Bertolt Brecht's primary contribution to the theatre was not the ideals and opinions he put in his scripts, whether of society or of humanity, nor the poetry he made to express them; these may have been his primary contribution to literature, but they were secondary contributions to theatre. His primary contribution to the theatre lay in the effect which he inspired his acting group, the Berliner Ensemble, to make upon those who saw them perform. This was theatre.

But whether we choose to address the public through something we make, or to address them through something we do, there are certain consequences we have to accept and they are somewhat different in the two cases. An address through 'making' involves work which however exacting can be perfected whenever one chooses. An address through 'doing', however it is prepared, depends on a concentrated effort on one *particular occasion*; moreover your audience is limited to the group present on that occasion. A creation, then, you can perfect in solitude before the people see it; but an action is done before them once, and is finished—the only chance of perfecting it if it has failed lies in an opportunity of trying it all over again on another occasion.

Though there is much to add to this, we may at this point distinguish between the Arts of Making which we may call the creative arts, and the Arts of Doing which we may call the executive or performing arts; remembering that in the creative arts no direct contact between the individual and the people need ever occur at all, while in the executive arts it is absolutely essential that the individual comes into direct personal contact with his public. You can enjoy Picasso at an exhibition in Stockholm while Picasso himself is on the coast of the Mediterranean, but you can only enjoy Sir Laurence Olivier when Sir Laurence himself performs in your presence, before you and an assembled audience in the self-same building. This coming into direct personal contact is part of the player's art and, with the relentless element of the One Occasion, must be appreciated for any true understanding of the essence of the theatre.

I realize we have to go some way farther yet with our original proposition before we can begin to be satisfied with it. For instance, it may be inquired where in this framework can we place those strange, new products of the modern age, the recorded or transmitted arts (the cinema, radio, television)? But in a history that is itself so short this question must, alas, be put aside.

Something more to the immediate point is that our proposition that art is an address to people, does not distinguish it from any ordinary communication of ideas between man and man—such as a casual conversation about the weather, or even an oath occasioned by hitting your thumb with a hammer. Each of these is an expression of ideas or emotions. What is it that distinguishes such communications from a work of art?

The difference simply stated is that in an ordinary communication the meaning is single and apparent. In the work of art there are always two meanings, and the apparent meaning is not the essential one but is only a symbol for a hidden meaning. (It might indeed much increase the understanding of art for many people if they could but see the truth in such a statement as 'art is really saying something and meaning something else'. Hence, of course, its link with dreams and with jokes and with symbolism—and hence too the existence of the odd word 'artfulness'.)

Nervousness

There is another matter arising from our proposition. In any study of the performing or executive arts the subject of *nervousness* must enter into especial consideration. Let us see what is involved here.

A single individual may of course address another individual without nervousness; but even between individuals, if the one addressed is more influential or more powerful than the one addressing, or can destroy him, then an element of nervousness, or at least deference, may colour the address. When instead of two single individuals we consider an individual and a group, then we realize that a group is always more powerful than an individual, and always capable of destroying him, or at least his reputation. Whenever an individual addresses a group—even the most easy and complacent group—then he is facing a strength that is capable of overpowering his own, and this is true not only from a physical point of view but also from a psychological point of view.

To handle a psychical power greater than one's own opposite to one, and to obtain and keep the direction of it, must entail feeling—a high-keying of perception and an instantaneousness of response which we call nervous. It must be understood that this kind of nervousness is something quite distinct from timidity. Indeed an audience itself is a nervous thing in that its reactions can be more delicate and more extreme than those of the individuals composing it; but an audience is never timid. It may be panic-stricken, but not timid. It is possessed of mass strength, and it feels this. This very strength is the power which the individual can, provided he has the personality and the skill, take to his advantage. It is a power indeed which makes all the difference to his technique of addressing a crowd. It is a psychical element; and in the performing arts the individual has to evoke and handle this psychical group-reaction.

That is why, behind all the essentials of technique which should be in his equipment as regard voice, gesture, costume and the rest, there lies one deeper essential still, the essential of feeling that audience-reaction and of responding to that feeling, but of also being able to engage it to convey to the public whatever happens to be the subject of his address to them. The feeling is a nervous response. One of its manifestations is 'stage fright', which is not fright but a high 'nervous key' in the presence of something capable at any moment of an unpredictable attack on you.

There is also a sort of nervous response or element of 'feeling' in the arts of indirect address such as painting and literature. Here it is a feeling for the effect of colour, of form, of tone, of rhythm and the rest. It is, I believe, not unlike the nervous response to the power of an audience, for it is a feeling for power or potentialities. As I see it, the element of nervous choice exerted by a painter in employing those potentialities—selecting this or that form, or colour, or combination—constitutes the medium for the expression of his art. The same kind of choice is open to a player to employ or reject this or that potentiality of audience-response and similarly make it the medium for the expression of art.

If this be allowed then we may draw an incidental conclusion in passing this point; namely, that an act of theatre is capable of being a work of art. Obviously it is not inevitably so, any more than a painting is inevitably a work of art. But it seems not unlikely that that deepness of communication (however hard to define) which marks an accepted work of art is the same sort of deepness of communication that can mark an act of theatre.

An act of theatre, then, may be a work of art; the medium through which the art is conveyed to the public is the manner of the individual's addressing that public; the achievement of the art is the reaction of the public; it is this which is the essence of theatre. Thus:

The essence of theatre does not lie in what is performed.

It does not lie even in the way it is performed.

The essence of theatre lies in the impression made on the audience by the manner in which you perform.

Theatre is essentially a reactive art.

In the theatrical art all the elements count for nothing whatsoever—elements such as playwriting, rehearsing, production, characterization, scene-design, costume-design—without the culminating and fusing experience of performance before a public. Without this, theatre whether good or bad has not come into being.

It will be seen from what we have said that the ground which is best suited to germinate the seeds of theatre is the public assembly, or originally the tribal gathering. Here can accumulate that reservoir of what is comprehended under the term 'group psychology', which provides the power upon which the player can draw; the carrier-wave as it were on which he can impose his communication.

THE TRIBAL GATHERING

There is one thing we should remark about this 'tribal gathering' before we begin, and this is that it is quite capable of some sort of elementary theatre all by itself. Provided it meets on a Particular Occasion, the elements of theatre are there—or can be called into being. We have seen that the essence of the theatre lies in communicating something to the people. So that if the gathering meets on a particular occasion, the subject of this occasion may be what is communicated to the people. And it can almost communicate itself—with the people's help.

Let us imagine a burial ceremony, or a 'rite of spring', or a harvest festival. That which has to be communicated to the people is already present. The fact that its exact nature is deeply hidden and difficult to isolate makes no difference. Without precisely knowing in detail, we can feel what is the essence of a burial ceremony—through its mourning, perhaps. Or of a spring rite—perhaps through its sense of primitive desire. Or of a harvest festival—through its tragic sense of fulfilment, and gathering, and death.

Here, under all these things, behind the drums and the dancing and the drinking and the fires, we may feel a deeper thing, a need of the people.

A need for what? We cannot hope to define it fully; but it will be the need for good fortune, assurance, a happy omen, a belief, the affirmation of a mystery. 'Behold, I shew you a mystery . . .'; 'that which thou sowest is not quickened, except it die.' I can pretend to do no more in a short history than touch on such things. But I am certain of this from practical experience: at a gathering, the honouring of an occasion can either be left to the instincts of the crowd or, on the other hand, an individual can rise in the middle of the crowd and refer to the occasion. And the results are different.

It would indeed be strange if this were not so, for shrewd men in the tribe will feel the great opportunity that is here. It is a two-fold opportunity; the opportunity to *take* the power of a gathering to oneself and to dominate; this is a proud and selfish motive, and it is very characteristic of a player to show himself off. Or the opportunity to *give*, to seize the power of a gathering to convey to them . . . what? A vestige of the godhead. This, curiously, is a very humble motive; and even more curiously it is equally characteristic of the player—to give of himself without return.

Thus we have the roots of the player's two major characteristics; his selfishness and his generosity. These will affect the theatre for ever.

In just the same way, since so much of these things is concerned with fighting against death, and with birth and resurrection, so the player will unleash another characteristic, that of his or her vitality as a man or woman. And he will be licentious. This, too, will affect the theatre for ever.

Our gathering, then, can intoxicate itself with the essence of the occasion, or it can experience the devilish thrill of being called to pause by an ideal leader rising from it, and of watching in his person the performance of the drama of its heart more expertly than it could hope to do it by itself.

It can experience this through a single player or through a group of players; and one of the problems of the primitive theatre is, which came first—the witch-doctor or the troupe interplaying with a leader? Maybe they sprang together from a common source, the witch-doctor leading towards organized religion and the troupe towards organized theatre. But the source was common to both.

A curious thing is that you will always find this dichotomy about the theatre. At all periods the theatre may manifest itself in either of two forms; in the form of a performance by a troupe of players, or in the form of a performance by a single individual, quite alone and yet capable by himself or herself of giving a full entertainment completely satisfying to the people, although bereft of almost all the paraphernalia of more complicated theatre —in short the one-man show.

THE PLAYER'S RESOURCES

It may or may not be, then, that the Common Source was the individual who rose, faced and addressed the assembled crowd on a particular occasion, taking advantage of its mass power to say or give something of omen to it or to the occasion, and who used that power with *all his resources* to reinforce his telling and to turn what he had to say of the occasion from a communication into a work of art. But, however it be, it is precisely at this point, with the mention of the word 'resources' above, that we begin the study of theatrical technique. We shall find in our study, that we can divide the resources into two kinds—a player's *personal* resources are:

> his voice
> his gesture
> his appearance (mask, costume)
> his instruments (properties, drums, etc.)

and his *external* or *secondary* resources are:

> his 'place' (the place where he acts)
> his stage
> his background (including his scenery).

In considering the resources of a player, we should approach with this observation: that Theatre can come into being whenever an individual arises in a crowd and turns to address that crowd, but that it does not automatically come into being with this alone; one other thing is required. If to gain effect the individual modifies his manner, or his voice, or his appearance, from the normal as he addresses the crowd, then an element of theatre has entered. In short, if he does anything deliberately to impress the crowd, he has to some extent made a demand upon the techniques of the theatre.

Now we may very well take a simple example of such an individual acting in this manner, and we may note certain of these resources at work, but yet at the same time we may have the idea that something of full theatre is missing. For instance; we can picture his voice being raised above the normal, its periods being given a more telling emphasis than normally, his gesture taking a broader sweep than the normal—in short the whole figure being informed with a passion above the every-day, commanding and dominating without question. And yet we may feel that we have come little farther than let us say a specimen of oratory. What is lacking of the theatrical?

We may proceed by steps. First, we may find the voice rise to rhythm and even to singing; then the gestures grow to movements amounting to dance. Both of these are quite non-naturalistic modifications of the normal resources and are capable of producing a deeper effect and opening the way for theatre. But there remains a third modification, a complete readjustment beyond the normal, a truly horrible power; and with it we pass quite beyond oratory and enter the realm of the technique of theatre unmistakably.

To appreciate it let us imagine our individual retiring from his worked-up audience for a short space after a period of singing and dancing. He can be pictured as going into a hut, with the ensuing moments of suspense, the proto-type of the 'dramatic pause'. Then picture his figure appearing again at the door of the hut but with a *mask* upon his face.

We touch here one of the most powerful elements of theatrical technique; it is clearly not for nothing that the one symbol of theatre which above all others has come to be accepted through the world is a mask. What does a mask do to the man?

Two things; it takes away the person we know (it can even take away humanity). And it invests the wearer with something we do not know but which is aweful and non-human, a god or a devil.

The mask rehabilitates the player's face.

Now let us consider the player's face throughout history. In a short outline of the theatre such as this we can do it very quickly.

Fig. 1. A mask from New Guinea
Fig. 2. A half-mask from the Commedia dell' Arte

Fig. 1 is a primitive African mask.

Fig. 2 is an 18th-century Commedia dell' Arte mask.

Fig. 3 is the make-up (still almost a mask) of the great clown, Grock.

Fig. 4 is any star of stage or screen.

Here is an unbroken chain. In every link there is the same fundamental purpose; the suppression of the man Abeyinka (let us say), or the man Fiorillo, or the man Adrien Wettach, or the woman Miss Felicity Smith—and the assumption of the personality of the God of Thunder, the roguery of Scaramuccia, the whimsy of Grock, or the character of the Queen of Beauty—or a Beauty-queen.

In all examples it is the assumption of something beyond the human individual, an ideal—to put it shortly, the vestige of a godhead.

It is worth noting how the assumption of even greasepaint (despite its seeming such a simple and naturalistic device) can in fact depersonalize almost as much as a mask. The Chinese theatre, for instance, has made a classic art of this (*see* Plate 14), but even on our own stage the same applies exactly.

The magic of the mask, and of its delicate substitute, make-up, remains as a mystery in our theatre to this day, but the player in a mask, powerful as a mask is, may yet be partially betrayed; most obviously by his hands, next by his feet, next by his arms and legs and last by his trunk. These at least are human and familiar.

Take now an 'extension' of his mask, and with it let the hands be gloved, the feet shod, the arms and legs clad, and the body invested, and you have a complete concealment of the world and a complete revelation of the supernatural.

Fig. 3. The conventionalized clown make-up of Grock
Fig. 4. The conventionalized make-up of a film star

And you have the origin (and can appreciate the significance) of theatrical costume.

Let us pause here and ask: How far can the player go in theatre with these things alone? With mask (or make-up), with costume, with singing voice (or special speaking voice), with dance (or significant gesture)?

When we reflect, it is clear that he can go all the way. There is no height to which he cannot reach. The most developed drama of a civilization is within his touch. He can appeal even to the sophisticated playgoers of the modern world. For proof we have to look no farther than Bali.

The Phases of Theatre

It is also clear, however, that the player may add to these personal resources, and develop *another phase* as it were of theatre in which he brings to them other resources from external things, that is things outside his own person and costume (for instance, his background), and organizes these to become additional to his personal technique. He may sometimes appear reluctant to do this; but the long pageant of theatre history gives an impression of a succession of such phases in which, one by one, the resources external to the player are added to and developed, and his show consequently made more complex and more highly organized and more 'civilized'.

There is nothing to show that his performance is made any better or more significant by these extensions—except perhaps in so far as the show is thereby fitted more expressively into the idiom of his age, and to the changing fashions of his civilization. It may be called evolution if you please, yet it is evolution in a spiral sense round a centre rather than evolution along a straight path from something imperfect to some eventual perfection.

I have, then, divided this survey of the development of the theatre into *phases* rather than dated periods, for the simple reason that the development of the theatre seems to happen by phases and not by dates. One country may cling to one phase for many centuries and perhaps develop it highly, yet have no occasion to go beyond it. Another may pass in a hundred years through two or more phases in response to the changing course of its civilization. But mere dates have nothing to do with this, and it is unprofitable to relate world theatre history to any framework of dates.

Thus a great local advance in one phase (as for instance in classical Greece) may take place as far back as 500 B.C., while most of the surrounding world is waiting for the 16th-century A.D. before bringing the same phase to its height. But the Greek civilization collapses, while its neighbours slowly persevere onwards into further phases.

Japan may reach a developed stage of another phase in the 1300s, and England in the 1600s. At Tardets in the Pyrenees they still use today a stage very similar to that of the Jacobean period in England. In a given country, one particular manifestation of the theatre may become fixed at an early phase and stay there while the rest will advance with the latest contemporary fashions.

These phases we may attempt to define as follows:

The first phase in the development of the theatre is the presentation of the costumed player; or the player's presentation of his costumed self—costumed so as to act as some other self. At this stage he has the assistance of no other technical element whatever, beyond himself and what he wears or carries.

This phase can run through the whole gamut of theatre; it is possible to achieve some of the highest, the purest and even the most sophisticated heights of theatre with this alone—that is to say without the addition of stages or playhouses or scenery or any of the other things that we today are so apt to think of as the essence of theatre.

The second phase sees the organization of this simple, player-in-costume performance to as elaborate a scale of great festival performance as one can reach, but still all acted under the same open sky as the first phase. There may be preliminary essays in the use of raised stages; there may be developments on quite a large scale of arrangements for the placing and seating of spectators; there may be the writing of scripts for the performance which already reach all the heights and profundities of poetry. But still the shows are open-air shows, and still they are performed only on special, ritual occasions in the year. There is still a dominating (but changed) religious element. There is no, or very little, professionalism, save 'on the side'.

Next follows an incursion of the secular; the shows decrease in scale, the performers decrease in number, elaboration gives place to simplicity, but a more specialized note creeps in. Professionalism begins. The seasonal element recedes; the religious gives place to the satirical or the philosophical—at any rate to the secular. And the show is designed for a far smaller and more particular audience, an audience which is sometimes indoors. This is the third phase.

Next follows a new tendency—the stage is invented. These reduced troupes of professional players begin to organize the area they play upon and the background they play against, so as to offer themselves certain regular facilities. As we have said, some civilizations get on quite happily in theatre without ever discovering this need, let alone proceeding beyond it. But for others it forms the fourth phase of their theatrical development, the phase of the organization of a practical tool out of their stage. Sometimes in this phase the stage continues to be out of doors, and seems reluctant at first to take to a fully-roofed building; but there is one branch of this organized-stage phase where particular attention is paid to the possibilities of the 'scenic background' and the development of it into a special kind of new adjunct to the visual effect of the show. It is here that scenery as we know it is born, and this particular development of the organized-stage phase *must* take place indoors.

The fifth phase is a revolution; it sees the regular and total retreat indoors of the theatrical performance. There are many reasons—primarily because scenery takes a popular hold of the performance, and painted scenery cannot easily survive the weather, nor be effectually displayed without the glamour of lighting. Also because performances are becoming more frequent —even taking place daily—and opening later in the day, so that protection is needed for the audience from the elements. Perhaps also the purely emotional evocation of early theatre is becoming more and more supplemented by an intellectual evocation, and this reduces a spectator's resistance to low temperatures. You can watch a football match in cold and rain and resist them with the heat of your excitement, but to concentrate your mind on the intricacies of a drama you prefer fine weather, or a roof.

In this phase, the first specifically-designed, roofed playhouse buildings are born. They are born, to begin with, as princely rooms for a new sort of aristocratic, musical theatricals, and then are followed by public buildings of a similar shape but run for commercial profit.

The sixth phase of the theatre is (perhaps more noticeably than the others) an artistic development. In sympathy with the trend of society of the time, the indoor public scenic show develops into a spectacle of illusion. Or, to speak more accurately, it now becomes this predominantly; many aspects of the theatre which characterized earlier phases still go on, such for instance as the development of style in acting, but dominating all in this phase is the peculiar idea of the theatre as the place of illusion. This is a new idea, never exploited before this phase.

And the last phase in this eventful history is shaped again primarily upon an artistic idiom characterizing the whole of the world of its age, it is (not unnaturally) a reaction from the preceding phase. It is the phase of anti-illusion.

ONE-MAN THEATRE

A footnote must be added to the notion of phase-development. There is one irregularity, or strain of theatrical manifestation, that seems both to transcend period and to run independently of any phase, taking a free course of its own but liable at any point to coalesce and become part of a phase, or break away again, perhaps only to assist in the institution of a fresh phase. This is the strain of the single player—the performer who carries his (or her) whole show, be it minstrelsy or music or character or acrobatics or conjuring or dance, on his own personality.

He and his class frequently preserve a tradition through a period of decline till a fresh awakening, or they may even occasion a new turn in the course of a vigorous phase. They remain an unpredictable and eternal element in our story.

FIRST PHASE

The Costumed Player (Part One)

THE BAVARIAN WILD MEN

THE PADSTOW HORSE

THE BRITISH MUMMERS' PLAY

THE OCCASION

THE COSTUME

THE WORDS

THE ACTIONS
  (a) *The Killing*
  (b) *The Processional Element*
  (c) *The Circle*

SUMMARY

FIRST PHASE

The Costumed Player (Part One)

*The numerals in square brackets in the text are in all cases
references to the Book List on p. 297. They do not refer to
notes and may be ignored by a general reader.*

THE BAVARIAN WILD MEN

Looking at a West-End theatre, or a theatre on Broadway, or
in Paris, or Bombay, or Osaka, at night with the names in
lights and the audience going in past the box-office, it is
really not believable that this all started out of a 10th-century
Christian Church liturgy. It is no more convincing to place its
origin on the threshing-floors of Ancient Greece. Would it then
be any more satisfying to say that the beginning lies in Primitive
Ritual?

Let us take an example of primitive ritual; turning from the
lighted theatre let us go into the Bavarian Mountains.

There a fairly simple, ancient ceremony survives. On the eve
of St. Nicholas' Day (6 December) certain masked men come out
of the snowy woods on skis and approach a village. An atmosphere reigns over the houses. The older, more experienced
inhabitants and the children remain indoors, and peer through the
windows into the night (Plate 1) not without apprehension for what
they will see. Horns of elfland blow. The 'wild men' wear voluminous distorting costumes of animal skins, and heavy concealing
headdresses with horns or antlers (Fig. 5). They knock at doors
and windows and claim kisses of the girls or catch them in the
street and rub them with snow. The reign of the Wild Men lasts
till daybreak [31].

Now, can we properly call this 'theatre'? Can we decide even
that the origins of theatre lie here?

Fig. 5. A Bavarian Wild Man

It seems to me that we shall have to say that the answer is both Yes and No. There are no words; there is no play. There is no particular place of performance; no stage; no scenery; no playhouse; and no rehearsal. Here there is not even—and this is perhaps the most noticeable lack of all—any assembled audience as such. True, there are many who furtively watch, and a few who brave the elements and the eeriness for, more or less, the devil of it. But what there is, is the masked group of men and the action itself—the thing they do. Resuming in two words we have the *Costumed Player*.

But how far can this be called theatrical action in the sense of being a prepared performance of something with the intent to make an effect on people? At first one might say, 'In no sense at all!' But then there is the putting on of the costumes and masks. There is no rehearsal; but there may be (it is hard to say) a quality of *improvisation*, for not one of these 'performers' can know just what will happen or how the night will go. And we shall admit, on reflection, that that very uncertainty is an experience which no player ever escapes even in a modern theatre; that particular quality of the unpredictable, and its accompanying demand for a quick ability to improvise, is a quality of all theatre.

Beyond this it is just possible to see the germ at least of three other things that may grow into positive theatre elements; procession, visitation in disguise, and the animal.

First; we have the notion of *processional theatre* because the Wild Men go through the streets from house to house. They do this, almost certainly, for the reason that is the original reason for all processional theatre; namely, to spread the magic about a whole community. This may perhaps be an earlier idea even than the public assembly gathered for the same purpose. However, the reason for both the assembly of people at an act of theatre and for the procession from house to house among the people's homes is to effect a communal spreading of the magic of a ritual act.

It is not difficult to see the origin of this. When we realize that much of primitive theatre consists in giving—the distribution of Good Omen—we may well see that a primitive people would wish the omen to be communicated not only to themselves personally but to their flocks, to their crops, to their very hearths and homes for the coming year. And thus it is not surprising to see the act of Good Luck performed at one house and then at another, just as the waits or carol singers pass from door to door at Christmas. Indeed there is more than a similarity, there is an identity of purpose, for the waits travelled to take the Luck to the homes of the community. The waits did not primarily call for coppers. (In many cases where a collection of money is made today, we find that there originally existed a ritual not for receiving but for giving. What the waits bring was once more significant than what they now receive.)

Thus then there is a processional element in early theatre. Not only is something enacted, but the virtue of the enactment is communicated by a led procession to houses, to fields and to flocks. This leads on to the next point.

Second: We shall meet again in our story the idea of a *visitation* by masked men or men *in disguise*. 'Mummings' or processions of disguised riders at night to a house with the purpose of bestowing a Gift, constitute the source from which derives the court masque in English theatre history.

Third: We have the animal element present in this ritual in the skins and horns of the Wild Men. This is not the place to trace the significance of this animal element back to see where it came from for that would take us certainly out of the realms of theatre; but we may trace it forward and we shall find that it can take on a significance so great as to become the very centre of certain performances—and it would not be too curious to see its survival even today in the fantastic horse of the pantomime.

But we can scarcely find in all the above any element that could go on the stage of one of those modern theatres we were looking at and hold a modern audience under its spell.

Have we indeed any justification to expect so much of the primitive theatre—namely, that it should hold a modern audience? Strangely enough, I think we have. Given that the audience has an open mind, a piece of great primitive theatre should make as profound an effect today as a piece of great sophisticated theatre: its language is the same.

This is not really surprising. We should all be familiar by now with the idea that art is not a thing that grows nearer to perfection the more civilized society becomes. A cave painting can evoke a similar satisfaction to that offered by the Classic Masters and the Great Moderns; and so also great theatre is great theatre whatever its period, and primitive theatre is neither crude nor ineffectual merely because it is primitive.

But we have not satisfied ourselves that in the Bavarian Mountain ceremony we can claim a true example of full theatre so let us go on to another example.

I take this time a British rite, which will witness that memorials of primitive and savage elements still lurk in the background of the English.

THE PADSTOW HORSE

This ceremony shows a step forward in comparison with the Bavarian, and the step is theatrically a significant one. In it we are again concerned with an animal mask, but one now used in an action capable of that double layer of meaning that we saw was characteristic of a work of art. The action itself expresses something on the manifest level about Death and Birth, but in the doing of the action there is also expressed in concealed language something about the ideal of Living.

The animal signified by the mask is, though it bears no positive resemblance to any living creature, the Horse.

Padstow is a town on the north coast of Cornwall. In the stables of the Golden Lion is kept what Miss Violet Alford speaks of as

Fig. 6. The Padstow Horse

'an alarming coal-black object crouching against the wall' [3]. And her description is very true.

On the evening of 30 April this object is taken out and paraded round the town to the accompaniment of 'The Night Song'. There is much concerning this, and the ritual that is to follow on the next day, that is lost or disappearing, but let us look at the object.

It is a black mask with a tall, pointed headdress. On the headdress are white lines. White lines encircle the eyes. A bow or knot of hair crowns the point of the headdress. A red tongue hangs from the mouth. There are heavy grey eyebrows and beard of hair. Great 'ears' project (Fig. 6). The appearance of the mask is so similar to a mask from the gulf of Papua (Fig. 7) that one is confounded at the glimpse of the primitivity of origins.

When this mask is assumed by a man, there spreads out from its neck a circle of black material some five feet in diameter, stretched horizontally on a hoop at the level of the wearer's shoulders. From the hoop again depends a sort of great skirt, also in black, covering the wearer right down to the ground.

Fig. 7. A mask from Papua

From the front of the hoop projects a small, carved, grotesque horse's head, with a movable jaw and a mane made from a cow's tail. Behind, on the opposite side, is a crude, gay horse-tail. This strange, this 'alarming, even diabolical' object is led or cajoled by a Mayer (a May man), or Teaser, with a club. The horse ambles after him. . . .

On Mayday the ceremony begins. In this, at certain moments, and to the accompaniment of accordion, mandoline and drum, the Horse dances (Fig. 8.)

It is when the Padstow Horse dances that we see a remarkable example of the fact that the essence of the theatre resides in the effect made on an audience by the way what is done is done. The diabolical, creeping crinoline becomes a completely unrecognizable swirl of shining black magic, for which the words 'awe-inspiring' are merely fitting. It creates its own background of primal jungle. It is savage and terrible. It tips its great circle up into a waving disc that transcends any relation to the shape of horse or man. Its skirts swirl round following the wind of its going, and just that particular command that the great player seeks, with his technique, to exert over an audience is imposed on us as we watch, with a tribute untouched by grudge or criticism. This mask, in a ceremony deriving from the springs of civilization, is as potent in theatrical effect today as an enchanting ballerina.

For all that, the ceremony is irrecoverably corrupt. The players can know its original significance only by intuition. It has become the draw of tourists, and the subject of countless modern improvements. Yet it brought a gasp in 1953 even to the Albert Hall. This piece of primitive theatre can go straight on to our stage.

Fig. 8. *The Padstow Horse dancing, with his 'Mayer'*

We can include only two further details here. First, at a certain line in the song the Horse must sink to the ground and lie ' "quiet like, dead like" ' [3]. At another he must bounce into the air revivified.

Second, his black costume is shiny with tar. In his dancing he occasionally pursues a woman, catches her and throws his skirts over her. She is thus marked with the mark of the Horse; and this is lucky for her. It is considered to be more lucky for married women than for unmarried women.

How far, before we go on, are we in a position to try to say what all this 'means'? We can make a beginning. Speaking far too briefly we might say that in both the cases above we have been dealing with an 'imitative magic' ceremony [24]. It is designed to foreshadow good luck and fertility in the coming year. But notice that even here in these primitive rituals the law of the essence of theatre obtains. It is not what is done that matters—what is done is merely a faded symbol (nowadays at least); and it is not how it is done that matters—for all that is left of the manner is a rough, preferably good-humoured teasing; but it is the effect that is still made on people by the way the Wild Men or the Horse do this strange thing that makes it ultimately significant. That effect is of the eerie and the untellable, and in the eyes of the elders and children watching from a village window, one has no difficulty in seeing the impression made still by the method of performing an act of theatre. *See* Plate 1.

So far then we have two elementary ceremonies. One can be claimed as theatre only with some hesitation, perhaps reckoning it as a sort of proto-theatre; while in the other we may feel justified in seeing the beginnings of a deliberate art, a performing art, having its own field and its own laws—something we may trace, without at any point having to take too abrupt a step, into our theatre performance today. But some steps we shall clearly have to take, for the Padstow ceremony lacks the means for certain developments in expression.

It is not easy to say for what reason a form of theatre develops or comes to suffer change and addition. One supposes that it is because those who use it find it does not offer them sufficient scope, or that it offers scope in a style of expression that is uncongenial to some new outlook of the times. If, in our own age, the move to abolish the proscenium arch meets with realization we shall be faced with precisely such a change. Changes may be sweeping; if so we may have to define a new phase in theatre development, but some do no more than add a facility to an existing phase. What additions does the Padstow Horse make to the Bavarian ceremony? It exemplifies:

(*a*) the development of a mask into a new and self-sufficing theatrical character, a fantastic animal;

(*b*) the introduction of significant action performed to convey an idea by imitative magic or by mime (the death and birth ideas);

(*c*) a separate kind of action, not primarily mimic but rhythmic —a beginning of dance; and

(*d*) in consequence of the rhythmic dance, music.

But it goes no further; and there is even in this first phase of theatre development one source of expression of major importance to add still, the resource of words. Though on this point we ought to add that in all the above there has been nothing that has denied the use of words: mime is by no means a silent action, it is the expression of an idea by acting it, and the acting may easily contain words—and even simple dialogue. What we are now to be concerned with, however, is the employment of words to carry or to amplify the main meaning of the action—dialogue planned to tell a particular story or event; the play.

THE COSTUMED PLAYER (PART ONE)

THE BRITISH MUMMERS' PLAY

Throughout England there are various versions of the Mummers' Play. It is perhaps remarkable that it should be so widespread. It is not a local custom like the Padstow Horse but occurs from Cumberland to Lincolnshire and down to Dorset. In all the versions there is the same central theme, the conflict of a hero with an adversary, his defeat and death, his cure and return to life. But the surviving versions show almost every type of corruption and patching-up. It will be especially significant to a student to find for instance that in some versions it is not the hero who is vanquished but the adversary, while the hero is left in triumph. What are we in such a case to make of the end, when the players are involved in an odd finale—taking the care to cure and resurrect the Powers of Evil! Or when, as is likely to happen, they drop the concluding incident altogether as a defect, and thus deprive the whole action of its magic essence!

Again, a corruption in Hanoverian times has made the hero in some versions, *King* George. We go back only to find that earlier again he is *Saint* George. But is this, then, a Christian rite? Surely—no. Presumably a more primitive, pre-Christian hero lies still deeper, hidden by the politic imposition of Saint George.

Sir Edmund Chambers [16] and R. J. E. Tiddy [73] have left searching studies of many features of this remarkable survival that we cannot touch here, and The English Folk Dance and Song Society have made a coloured sound-film of a version that comes from the villages of Symondsbury and Eype in Dorset, which has some unusual additions. But we must confine ourselves here to the origin of theatre.

We may picture men in a primitive community before the days of recorded history, reaching an early stage in civilization when they have come to a ceremony like that of the Bavarian mountains. Possibly in its original, this ceremony would show certain features that are very much graver (even more terrible) than any in this millennia-old survival. But these are not our concern; they would not cause us to change our minds and say, 'This is theatre'.

Now add a particular action with a mask, and the theatre begins. And this small change is all the difference between the two ceremonies of Bavaria and Cornwall. Then let us take another step and, forgetting the Wild Men and the Horse for the moment, let

45

us suppose that the persons who are attending upon the central mask begin to encourage it with cries. Here is a positive example of such a thing: certain girls who follow the Padstow Horse cry out, when he breaks off to chase a woman, the words ' 'Oss 'Oss! We, 'Oss!' It is a curious elliptic expression. Some have presumed it to mean, 'Horse, Horse, go not to her but to us!' Or, with the south-country reversal of cases, '. . . not to she, but to we—to we, Horse!' [3]. If this be true it is a deep injunction that only needs elaboration to turn it into a choral prayer. If such cries now become part of the ceremony then we have but to add responding cries from the central mask, or from an opposite group of participants, and we arrive at a vocal exchange with significant words; and once given vocal exchange we have the possibility of dialogue—of invocation and response.

What other use will primitive man make of the voice in his rituals? One nearly inevitable use will be for a leading participant to use it to proclaim his nature—possibly at first by chanted sounds, but soon by a verbal statement beginning 'I am . . .' And what followed had to be originally a great announcement, for the speaker was at that moment the Great Power. It is then not surprising that in primitive ritual (and for a long way into, and beyond, early accepted drama itself) a recurrent feature of opening speeches is what we call *The Vaunt*. For example:

A typical opening line of the Hero in the Mummers' Play is 'Here am I, St. George, an Englishman so stout . . .' etc.

And a typical opening line by a character in *The Castle of Perseverance* is 'I am Mankind's fair Flesh, flourished in flowers . . .' etc.

Again, frequently in the Cornish Cycle the idea of the vaunting of a character at the opening of his part is enshrined in the most apt stage-direction, *Hic pompabit Salamon*—Here Soloman shall 'pomp'.

Finally, in Japanese Noh plays we find still such opening lines as 'I am Hitomaru. I live in the valley of Kamagaye . . .' etc.

So then, pursuing our thought we see this primitive group developing its technique to allow individual, pre-arranged announcements by certain players of themselves or the roles they play. Let two players now give their vaunts in opposition to each other and the way is prepared for the next element of the drama, *The Strife*. And that is exactly what the Mummers' Play is, a strife between two vaunted heroes before a group of supporting characters—agon and antagonist before a chorus.

Recapitulating now this picture of primitive men embarking on the first steps of the development of theatre, we see them begin by passing out of the Bavarian ritual and developing one of the masks to special and particular significance. We next hear their voices. We are now ready to picture the group taking a further step, and this is the step taken in the Mummers' Play.

THE OCCASION

The performances are seasonal; they thus partake of that element of the Special Occasion. The season is generally around Christmas, more especially on Boxing Day, on Twelfth Night, or on Plough Monday. The ceremony is thus concerned with the turn of the sun towards the ascendant again, and the inspiring and immense task of resuming work for a new year after the solstice.

Here then is the first of four significant elements. The second is the costume.

THE COSTUME

The men taking part in a Mummers' Play today occasionally wear strange versions of modern or period or nondescript clothes, but this is not ritual. The true Mummer dons 'papers' (Fig. 9).

A set of 'papers' is a strange thing to look at. A genuine example from Marshfield, Gloucestershire, is to be seen at Blaise Castle Museum outside Bristol. It consists of a basis of an overall or old coat, covered with sewn-on strips of newspaper, or ribbons. The headdress is similarly bedecked, and so profusely that the strips hang down and entirely hide the face and head of the wearer. The whole man is transformed into a walking, rustling, white anonymity of fluttering. Only his farm boots betray him.

The effect of this disguised figure is still closely similar to the effect of the Bavarian Wild Men. More than this, it is almost exactly the same effect as certain African medicine figures (as Figs. 9 and 10 will demonstrate).

Concerning this effect, so unexpected a writer as Kenneth Grahame has left us a brief sketch [27]:

'Twelfth-night had come and gone, and life next morning seemed a trifle flat and purposeless. But yester-eve, and the

Fig. 9. A Mummer in his papers

mummers were here! They had come striding into the old kitchen, powdering the red brick floor with snow from their barbaric bedizenments, and stamping and crossing and declaiming till all was whirl and riot and shout. Harold was frankly afraid; unabashed, he buried himself in the cook's ample bosom. Edward feigned a manly superiority to illusion, and greeted these awful apparitions familiarly, as Dick and Harry and Joe. As for me, I was too big to run, too rapt to resist the magic and surprise. Whence came these outlanders, breaking in on us with song and ordered masque and a terrible clashing of wooden swords? And, after these, what strange visitants might we not look for any quiet night . . .?

'This morning, house-bound . . . Edward, being violently stage-struck on his first introduction to the real Drama, was striding up and down the floor proclaiming, "Here be I, King Gearge the Third," in a strong Berkshire accent . . .'

Here is a very good entrance indeed into primitive theatre—an authentic impression of the solemn mystery of it, retained by an unquestioning small boy. The task of the actor is to retain this

Fig. 10. *A Medicine-man in his costume*

same ascendancy throughout all the turns and enshroudings that such a mind takes as it goes on to maturity. For this he will clearly need equipment at every phase of the story. The development of that equipment to match the convolutions of the mind is the history of the theatre.

Thus far the player depends only on his own self, his mystic costume and his grave outlandish dialogue—and by this we are reminded that the same quotation also leads us to the third element significant to us in the Mummers' ritual, the thing we are especially concerned with at this juncture—their play. It gives us a microscopic glimpse of the action, and actually quotes a vital line; what can be added concerning the emergence of these early words in the act of theatre?

THE WORDS

One somewhat remarkable observation rises at once. For some reason that is difficult at first to define, these early words are not introduced fundamentally for the sake of the meaning they might impart. One might have supposed that words came into the theatre to make clear something which without them would not be clear, but this is not so. On reflection one sees a very good theatrical reason for this apparent contradiction. Theatre is a place of action, of the thing *done*, in the Greek sense of 'drama'. If the thing done is so done that its meaning is not comprehensible without explanatory words, then it is ill done; it is bad drama and poor theatre.

A dramatic action is not a dramatic action if you have to say what it means as you perform it. All good theatre should be comprehensible (though not perhaps as deeply moving) to a deaf man, so far as the action represented goes. The Mummers' Play affords an illustration of how it can be, as I shall soon show.

The purpose of the first use of words in theatre seems rather to have been to add to the means of moving an audience. This opinion is based on two things that otherwise would be inexplicable in the Mummers' Play. The first is that the speeches themselves are often unaccountably obscure. The second is that in no version surviving today are the speeches delivered in a normal style of speaking. They are 'sing-song', or chanted; they are spoken in a deliberate convention.

It is necessary to beware of being misguided by two over-rationalized explanations here. The first would say that the reason why the speeches are obscure as we now have them is because they have suffered corruption in the process of handing down from mouth to mouth over the generations. The second would say regarding their delivery that it is simply crude; and is crude merely because it is in the mouths of uninstructed speakers who don't know enough about elocution to give a better rendering.

The first explanation would presuppose that formerly, in their primitive state, the speeches were *not* obscure, but were as clear as normal speeches today. The second explanation is seen straightway to be coloured with a certain, not uncommon, preconception; namely that all vocal delivery in the theatre is and always was intended to imitate the delivery of everyday speech—that is to say, to be naturalistic.

It is not impossible that the bases on which these two explanations rest are both fallacies. One reflection suggesting that the first explanation rests on a fallacy is that no reason can be advanced why words in any great mystery *should* be clear in their meaning. To be clear is to be certain, and thus to be limited. Certainty and mysticism cannot live together.

If the leading Mummer were to begin his Vaunt with 'I am the Spirit of Living', the whole ceremony collapses in emotional meaning like a house falling down beneath a bomb. Such a remark cannot be accepted as a fiction. It is, for better or for worse, an attempt to state the truth directly, and as such leads us into the risk of every error of which words are capable; even then in the end it cannot succeed because no one can state the Truth.

But if the player says 'I am Saint George', that is entirely acceptable. It is untrue, but we do not question it. We know, with him, that he means not that but a mystery, whether our knowledge of that fact is conscious or unconscious.

If then 'I am Saint George' is acceptable, there is no reason why 'I am King George' (or King William), or 'I am Lord George' (or as in one instance 'I am Lloyd George') should not be equally acceptable! Or indeed (with qualifications) whatever you will. The meaning is *not* of first importance.

Thus it is true, first, that a ceremony into whose words corruptions have crept is not in any way invalidated as a ceremony, but can live despite them. And second, that this being so it is highly unlikely that even the original ceremony itself was logically *clear*— either in ultimate import or in the immediate words spoken.

Here, then, is a tentative and perhaps revolutionary theory. We cannot, of course, accept it without rigorous testing. The remainder of all the theatrical ceremonies alluded to in this book are available for such a testing. But our conclusion upon examining the essential and inevitable entrance of words into drama is the apparent paradox that, in theatre, understanding the meaning of the words does not greatly matter. What does matter is that they supply yet another channel through which that deeper, or secondary, impression of the performance can be conveyed.

The words accompanying a spell are rarely comprehensible, and early theatrical speech resembled incantations accompanying a rite. The achievement of magic is not explicable; you may analyse the mechanism, but not by that acquire command of it.

THE ACTIONS

For the fourth and last point which we can profitably discuss here about the Mummers' Play as an example of developing theatrical art, we leave the new element of words and turn back to the basic, original element, action. What may we learn from the Mummers' Play to help us in forming our idea of the way in which the *act* of theatre developed?

There are three points about the actions here; (*a*) the killing itself, (*b*) the processional element again, and lastly (*c*) a new technical matter especially important for our understanding of the spatial relation between a performance and the audience who watch it.

(*a*) *The Killing*

The centre of the Mummers' Play is an action—the spectacle of the fall of the hero as he dies before the adversary. We have had something of the idea of this ritual death in the dying of the Padstow Horse during his dance. Now the Mummers' Play takes a step further and underlines the mimetic action by making it the culmination of a sword fight.

Here we are offered a transcendent example of the real strength of the theatric art, for the Mummers' Play presents the death almost entirely by means of action alone. The words have virtually no part in it and make but a trifling reference, or none at all, to it. It remains a thing *done*, not said.

This is a demonstration of the true strength of theatre because thereby we can see theatre offering us a medium for evoking emotion that is distinct to it alone. Expressed in any other medium this death is not so seizing: expressed in theatrical action it can grip the spectator with instant, inexplicable clutch.

To draw the action, or to describe it in words, could not convey just the same thing that the falling and lying still of the performer conveys. And this is not because he is a 'great actor'; nor because of any deep message in his lines. It is simply in the nature of theatre.

Proof of this can be found in the version of the play from Symondsbury (recorded in the film), where a hobby horse is, somewhat unusually, included. Beside the film, there is also published the script of the performance [36]. To compare these two in respect of one particular passage is highly instructive; and to put that passage in its context, here is a brief synopsis of the whole performance.

The version is unusual in having four parts. The first is orthodox in general, though with unusual details. It consists of a Presentation, the Vaunts, then instead of one Strife we have a succession of four Strifes; first, a separate one between St.

Patrick (St. George's ally) and 'Captain Bluster'; next, one between St. George himself and 'Gracious King'; next, between St. George and—significantly—'Colonel Spring'. In this last Strife Colonel Spring, very interestingly, falls only to revive immediately of his own accord and then, after a second Strife, is made to fall again. Next, the traditional 'Doctor' enters for the Cure, and in this case he revives all three of the dead men.

The second part of this version is entirely unorthodox and is perhaps an importation from another ceremony. Here St. George does not appear at all, but we see instead two country folk, Jan and Bet his wife (both are played by men, and Jan is played by the same actor who, earlier, introduced the performance in the guise of Father Christmas). A dispute arises between man and wife, swelling to a quarrel and a fight in which the woman (or man-woman) is killed. St. Patrick enters and calls in the Doctor, who is here named Mr. Martin Dennis, and the dead woman is revived with by-play strongly suggestive of fertility ritual.

The third part brings in Jan and Bet again, and also a very special and curious addition—a 'Hobby Horse' (called Tommy the pony). The woman mounts on his back and rides him. Jan attempts to mount and is thrown. He rises enraged . . . And now for the sixth time in this strange conglomeration, the rite of mystic death is performed, but performed with an effect in the action itself that brings us to the essence of theatre.

In the published script of the play there is no more indication of the emotion of this incident than a curt stage-direction and a reference in the next line of dialogue:

> (*Tommy throws Jan off and kicks him. Jan gets up and knocks Tommy down*)

BET: You naughty old rogue. You have killed my pony you have, you old rogue.

There is nothing whatever in this that is not present in the performance, and there is nothing whatever (in the material sense) that is added to this during the performance, yet the lines as written are crude, bare, almost contemptible; while out on the wintry roadway,* with the echoes of the chanting players' voices ringing in the onlookers' ears; with the haunting strangeness;

---

* The Film was unfortunately taken, for photographic reasons, in summer, not in the real winter.

with the effect of that raptness too great 'to resist the magic and surprise' that held the child in Kenneth Grahame; and with, perhaps, the relaxed effect following on the low comedy of Bet's revival—in the cold afternoon with all this bustle, to see, suddenly and unexpectedly, Jan lash out with his club at the Hobby-horse's head, to hear the clip of the blow, to 'hear' the voices instantly cease, and to see the foolish, gay, cavorting, innocently-malicious, fantastic creature quite sharply stop, fall and lie still in the frosty mud, brings an emotion mysteriously near to tears.

No one can see in the lines of the script alone what could do this thing to an audience. No one could draw the episode to be so moving. But the theatre can take these lines and—merely in terms of action—wrest this thing out of them, with nothing added save its own quality. This is the difference between written drama and theatre in action. The lines of Bet and Jan may be forgotten in an hour, but the spectacle of Tommy inert on the frozen road may be ineffaceable for a lifetime, through the act of theatre.

The rite now continues. The horse is revived and unaccountably takes part next in a 'smelling-out' ceremony among the audience, which may be comic today but which springs from who knows what grim original? And finally Jan himself is smelled-out as 'the biggest rogue that is here' and kicked by Tommy 'through the door'.

Part Four takes a completely unexpected lyrical note. The Warriors of the first part all march in procession round Jan and Bet with a song called 'The Singing of the Travels', outlining incidents in a farmer's life of travail. All ends with a traditional request to the Lady of the House to

> . . . *tie a bow of ribbon now*
> *On this our Christmas Holly Bough.*

(b) The Processional Element

So much for the action of the Mummers' Play. We next come to a development of the processional element.

To begin, both the line about Tommy kicking Jan out *through the door* and the final invocation to the Lady of the House, not to mention Kenneth Grahame's reminiscence, show that such a performance was once at any rate a wandering one and went from house to house. The action implied is clear; a march to a house, entry into that house, the presentation of the play before the assembled household, a final address to the Master or Lady of the house, a general exeunt, and a march to a fresh house to perform again—and so on. One of the most ancient and characteristic exclamations of a player springs from the occasion of these visits to crowded halls; it is the cry that opens so many speeches right down to the days of the Tudor Interludes—the cry:

> *Room, a room, brave gallants all,*
> *Pray give me room to rhyme . . .*

Thus they ask the crowd assembled in the houseplace for this ritual occasion, to step back for a while to permit the bringers of the play to come in.

At Marshfield in Gloucestershire, however, there is an example of a variation of this proceeding which may very likely be the basis from which the system of English medieval pageant cars arose.

Marshfield is a small but comparatively elongated town, tending to spread out along either side of a straggling High Street, lined with quiet two-storey buildings mostly in local stone, and with a few side lanes at intervals, turning off towards the surrounding country. The Church and the small triangular market place are at one end of this High Street.

In order to give their annual performance on Boxing-Day morning, the dressed Mummers, in a procession of seven headed by the Town Crier, march into the Market Place from an adjoining street. There they give their first performance which lasts some fifteen or twenty minutes (*see* Fig. 11, p. 58).

Then they reform their procession and, again led by the Town Crier, march away along the High Street to a corner farther down and give the second performance. Then they form up and proceed again in the same way to a third station still farther along the High Street. And next to a fourth point near the far end.

Thus the performance is given at either end of the main street of the town and at two stations in between.

They then make a detour on their return to give their final performance (or performances) in the garden before one (or it may have been more) of the local gentry's houses.

Let us for a moment break off to consider the great stream of the development of theatrical presentation. It would appear on the evidence we have that the whole occasion surviving today at Marshfield makes a not unrepresentative picture of an occasion in the primitive days of the pagan theatre long ago. How far we are right in making this deduction we cannot, with our present knowledge, say; but the inference drawn in this book is that, since the performance of the Mummers' Play shows a strife, a death of the hero, and a revival by magic means (even if it is today only the magic of a comic doctor—indeed maybe especially because of this) it follows it is a pagan ceremony. Possibly the chief evidence for this is that the means of revival is magic (or nowadays comic; that is, it is maintained now for a reason that is no longer understood and has to be cloaked as 'nonsense'). If it is a magic ceremony, it is pre-Christian. If it is pre-Christian, it is at least pre-10th-century A.D. in origin.

This reasoning may be fallacious, but we cannot stand still and wait to be assured; we must try to read the evidence we have with our present knowledge. With this proviso, then, we can say the following:

Provided 'primitive' man in Britain did in fact present his theatrical ceremonies in the way described above, it is reasonable to believe that with the introduction of Christianity and the consequent attempt gradually to impose the vast Bible story upon the compact aboriginal myth, the theatrical performance changed in content (giving us the Mystery Plays, as we shall see), but that the form the show took was maintained more or less unaltered.

This now would mean that a primitive community (such as Marshfield once was, but a little larger and living in a somewhat more extensive town with more streets) on suffering the impact of the new Christian belief, and having to stage its 'propaganda' with new resources for the players, might develop performances on raised platforms; but such a development would take place *in the tradition of the processional show*—such as we have outlined above from Marshfield.

We have only now to credit the organizers with the sense to put those raised stages on wheels, and we have the origin of the English pageant-waggon system of theatre that we connect with the York, the Towneley and the Chester Mystery Cycles of plays.

The only real variation, beside the use of a raised stage to help more people to see the action better, is the achievement of a much longer play, by making a number of groups of players perform successively at each of the appointed stations in the street or town.

Thus (again, I stress, on the evidence of our present knowledge) the English pageant-waggon show may have had its technical ancestor in the processional repetitions of the Mummers' Play at successive street corners—merely adding a succession of repeated performances, a raised stage on wheels to play each scene upon, and drawing each waggon from station to station for its repetition, exactly as the Mummers move down the High Street at Marshfield for the repetition of their solitary scene.

The processional element in the, apparently stationary, Mummers' Play is noticeably common, once one looks for it. Thus at Symondsbury the players still march in full costume and stirring procession, to the tune of a very haunting traditional air, when they set off to perform their ritual.

All this may grow in time to be a pretty long ritual to take into a farmhouse. We are shortly to see performances on a greater scale still, something certainly exceeding the bounds of four square walls, performances which institute in fact another phase of theatre development; but for all that, these new great shows will still have the origins of their technique in the primitive phase of the Mummers. Especially can we see how true this is when with the performance at Marshfield we notice one last particular element in the development of the primitive players' resources during this first phase of their story.

(c) The Circle

This new point is one that is more apt for description by picture than by words. It relates to the spatial relation of the spectators with regard to the performance. It is the use of the shape of the circle (see Fig. 11.) The circle is the natural shape that an audience takes up when it assembles round an open space to watch the action of a group of players. It is the gathering-round of a crowd to look at an incident; nothing more formal or more regular than that. At present all we are concerned with is to note that a convenient area to perform any group-action is one that measures much the same one way as another—that is, it is roughly

Fig. 11. The Marshfield Mummers' performance

'circular'; and that, to see the action in such an area, the spectators will gather anywhere they choose around this area to watch; which means—since they do not want to be unsighted by other spectators in front—in a more or less even 'ring' round the area. And once that ring is complete, in a thickening of that ring, with more layers of onlookers as more spectators arrive.

Just as the lines of the Mummers' Play gave evidence of the indoor technique in the call for 'Room, room!', so other versions give evidence of the circular technique out of doors; thus the 'paceakers'' play (an Easter variant) from Heptonstall, Yorkshire, begins with the now-corrupt speech [73]:

> *Ring a ring I enter the or, to see this merry act begin.*
> *I'll act it right and act it safe, and act it on a public state:*
> *And if you can't believe this words I say,*
> *Step in St. George and clear my way.*

Before considering this circle further it is worth while to break off to inquire why its understanding is so important.

It is always important to see the shape of a performance. One thing of the utmost desirability in any record of an unfamiliar style of theatrical occasion is that the record should include sufficient information for us to visualize the whole lay-out—not the actor alone. Our knowledge is hindered when observers report details of an action or ritual, but neglect to help us to form a picture of the immediate surroundings.

Our requirements are very simple. The three items which it is of greatest importance for us to have described are:

(a) the area in which the action takes place;
(b) the way the spectators are situated with regard to that area;
(c) the way, or ways, by which the players enter and leave that area.

Any study of what the players do in the performance itself however detailed and sympathetic, is weakened if we have not those three details first; and it would bring a new illumination to our understanding of theatrical procedure (especially when in primitive or unfamiliar conditions) if we could prevail upon all observers to take these three points as a formula to head every description.

Many accounts of theatrical performances are invalidated for us because they do not include the means for readers to put the action into any sort of setting. There is in this perhaps an indication of how little we have realized, in the past, the need to see a performance not as an isolated thing, but as an action presented before an audience and in specific surroundings. We tend, when we describe a show, to isolate the centre from the rest with all its vital atmosphere. This may be a consequence of our present picture-frame convention in the theatre of today, where the aim seems to be to cut off the show as independently as possible from any consciousness of the outside world. Such an isolation simply could not take place in any of the early phases of theatre development. All early theatre shows were essentially seen and experienced in the conditions of normal reality—of light and weather and landscape—on the familiar earth, under the every-day sky; or at night in the homely hall of a normal country house, by the usual candle- or torchlight.

Right through all the first five phases of theatre development, the physical surroundings in which the show was given were fully visible and were an inextinguishable part of the spectator's impression of the show. It is essential to realize the fact that, until the phase of 'Stage Illusion', they were visually inseparable from the show.

At Marshfield, the description of the above three essentials is simple.

The area of the action is a street corner or the ground of the open market place.

The spectators dispose themselves in regard to this area simply by coming and taking up positions at will round the sides of it.

The entrance to the area for the players is by a side street between the surrounding houses, and through the 'ring' of spectators at that point.

The entrance once made, the players separate and spread over the area of the place to form a 60-ft. circle of seven men. There in solitary formality they stand—stations, as it were, of the drama. Each actor can, in his place, declaim a speech when required; or any one of them can leave his station and move round the ring at need, or march into the centre to meet another player or players to take part in some concerted action. 'Come in, Bold Prince!' is not exclusively an invitation to the character to enter through a door; but it can be used simply as the cue for that particular player to leave his station at the edge of the circle and *come in* to the centre to take part in some action, or merely to take up the speaking in his turn.

It is sufficient for our purpose at this point to leave the description of the circular arrangement of the Mummers' Play with this comment; here is a large and simple scheme, it is important to notice because it already embodies the basis of one of the most developed theatrical techniques that we shall find in the next phase, a technique which is to run parallel with, and perhaps be more important than, the wheeled pageant system of the medieval Mysteries—that is, the performance in a Round.

SUMMARY

The Mummers' Play, then, is (like our first ceremony) an action; and (like our second ceremony) an action of death and resurrection. But to the action there now are added traditional words. These words have no high poetic meaning, indeed much of what survives today is gibberish. But this makes no difference. Something has been added to the act of theatre, and the opportunity is already created for the introduction of the poet as a specialist in words. Of this we shall say more later.

Concerning these early words, it is curious to learn how many major traditional theatre manifestations of the world do go on without the majority of the audience, or congregation, understanding a word that is said in them. Thus, few but specialists can follow the dialogue of a Noh play in Japan. The greater part of the Tibetan festival dramas is in a court language now out of use In the Burmese theatre, till some years ago, only courtiers could understand the language of the plays. But we have seen with our approach to the subject in this chapter how much more there is in theatre than depends on the meaning of the words. Even did we doubt the fact, we need only visit a performance in a foreign tongue by a theatrical company that is accomplished at its job, and we shall feel how, even today, this primitive feature of the theatre craft is still at work, and how much of the occasion can still come over to us when the dialogue itself is incomprehensible—and especially is this true when the theme of the play is familiar, as it was in all early theatre.

In addition to these considerations about this new element in the story of developing theatre, the Mummers' Play has given us reason to consider four other items:

First, the element of Special Occasion arising from the time of year of performance, and the significance of the season;

Second, further details about the development of primitive theatrical costume;

Third, the Action considered in the light of the subject for a play;

And fourth, the Action on the one hand presented as a procession (or by repetition at various places in the intervals of a procession), and on the other the Action presented as a stationary performance within a circle.

In every example of theatre so far described the whole dramatic technicology has been confined to one single thing—the Costumed Player.

The Costumed Player (Part Two)

THE ABBOTS BROMLEY HORN DANCE

KATHAKALI

    THE SETTING

    THE COSTUMES

    THE ACTIONS

    THE PERFORMANCE

BALI

    THE BARONG PLAY

THE NORWICH DRAGON

THE MONS LUMEÇON

THE COMIC HUMAN INTERLUDE

The Costumed Player (Part Two)

I have used the term 'Costumed Player' to cover the player and what he wears or carries; that is, to include his mask or make-up, his costume, his 'hand properties' and his instruments of musical accompaniment.

The contention of this book is that no matter to what part of the world we turn, whether we look into the deep past, at primitive civilizations existing in the world today, or at ceremonies surviving from primitive times into advanced civilizations, theatre begins with these elements (or variants of them), and with no other elements. These are the elements of the first, or primitive, phase of theatre all over the world and now as in the past.

We should, however, in order to widen our understanding of this first phase, consider something of some of the variants on these elements. I propose to mention four:

First, an English variant, concentrating on a particular development of dance and music;

Second, an Indian variant developing make-up and costume in an outstanding way.

Third, a Balinese variant, combining almost all developments possible in this phase;

And fourth, a Flemish variant developing the theme of the 'fabulous animal' with a somewhat unexpected result.

There are two ways of developing theatre as a more effectual, or more suitable, means of expression. The one way is to introduce completely new methods into your technique in order to cope with new problems that your expanding times force upon you; the other way comes about when you live in a civilization which does not greatly change (for example, some of the civilizations of the 'timeless' East). Then your progress may take the line not of innovations, but of almost infinitely involved developments and refinements of existing things.

In the next phase we shall be concerned with certain of these innovations in theatre; but before we leave the present phase we pause to consider these four additional examples offering special developments on things we have already seen. Two of them still belong to 'primitive' theatre without question, but the other two achieve heights of sophistication which have become a source of marvel to the greatest theatre specialists of the world, and remain so to this day.

THE ABBOTS BROMLEY HORN DANCE

We begin with an example of this 'Costumed Player' phase where the variation is not in the direction that was taken by the Mummers' Play with the stress on words, but in that of dance and its musical accompaniment, the show remaining verbally dumb.

Going back to primitive man, just before the stage that we have imagined might correspond to the Padstow Horse, let us ask what could come of it if the players were not to take the direction of high development of a particular mask? If, for example, the horned men merely stuck to the processional element in their rite and eliminated practically everything else except the rhythm of movement in their procession? Perhaps the answer might seem that, theatrically, nothing could come of it; but, in fact, procession linked with rhythm can be a pregnant union. We have seen at Padstow how rhythmic movement in a ceremony tends to draw to its assistance rhythmic sound, that is to say, musical accompaniment. It is by developing just this line that another no less renowned British 'survival' first took its shape—in the Abbots Bromley Horn Dance.

Here is a ceremony that is close enough to the Bavarian Mountain rite for the performers each to bear a pair of antlers; not now as a headdress however, but (rather curiously) as a sort of standard, carried on a short pole in the dancer's hands. The rest of the costume is not primitive, but a later accretion, nondescript Tudor in character. The ceremony has settled down to a definite shape nowadays but there are remnants of earlier stages, which may

66

seem merely whimsical intrusions, such as a man-woman and a rudimentary hobby horse. But what has become, and remained up to our own time, the chief feature of the ceremony is a very strange, very rhythmic, slowish step dance, which the horn-bearing men perform to the accompaniment of an interminable, haunting, minor air on the fiddle. The effect is almost hypnotic. No power, it seems, could ever arise to check or bring a halt to this dance as it pursues its mazy motion through the streets, into gardens, occasionally setting to opposites in two lines, occasionally promenading to bring luck to all that live about.

This ritual can confidently be classed as theatre or at least as an incontestable example of performing art, because of this very effect which it has the power to produce in the spectator. So peculiarly belonging to theatre is this effect that no other medium can convey it save the actual performance itself. Here once again, then, is theatre in its own right.

KATHAKALI

It is profitable to inquire, once we have seen how far the dance-and-music side of Costumed-player theatre can develop, whether any other side might be similarly worked on by primitive man in his search to widen the means at his disposal.

The truth is that almost any element can be so enhanced. For instance, one form of theatre surviving today has reached quite exceptional and significant intricacy by exploiting make-up and movement. This is the Kathakali 'danced drama' of Southern India [33].

Kathakali shows a kind of theatre more advanced than any we have discussed so far, and our task of assessing the character of the great theatre forms of the world now begins. It is a task that can unfortunately hope for no sort of completion in so small a book as this, but limited as we are, in knowledge as well as space, to a mere selection of world theatre forms for discussion, Kathakali must have a place.

It is a very noticeable feature of modern Western knowledge of the theatre forms of the world, that the theatre of India is among the most sparsely documented. It is hard to find either informative pictures or informative descriptions of theatre in

India. I owe to a chance conversation with Professor Arthur Waley some twenty years ago, the suggestion that a study of Kathakali might do much to fill this gap in our knowledge.

Kathakali is, *par excellence*, an example of Costumed-Player theatre. It has developed without ever encountering the need to adventure into the problems of accommodating large audiences, or of erecting raised stages, or of designing elaborate backgrounds, or of evolving scenic machines, or of building playhouses, or of recognizing (let alone having to solve) such a problem as the nature of 'stage illusion'. It has remained almost purely costumed-player theatre. But it has raised the arts of costume and make-up and the language of movement to levels that have not been passed, and rarely equalled, even in the latest phases of the theatre in modern times.

THE SETTING

In Kathakali the performance takes place quite simply in a temple courtyard or a garden, mostly in the open air and at night. The acting-area is specially treated earth with a stretch of matting. In front, between acting-area and spectator, is an oil lamp of a characteristic shape with an open blaze from a group of wicks, raised upon a stand to about waist high. The actors enter the area either by passing through the audience or, more commonly, from the back of the acting-area but by a special means unlike anything we have met so far in our study. It consists simply of a length of cloth some twelve feet long and eight feet wide, suspended at either side to form a curtain—not however suspended from any rod or post but held up by two assistants. Behind it an actor takes his place before his entrance, and at cue it is let fall and he is revealed. At the end of a scene it is raised again as a concealment and dropped once more for the beginning of the next passage (*cf.* Fig. 12, p. 73).

To this front curtain we shall have to return when we have described the actors and their movement which are the real concern of our story in this chapter.

THE COSTUMES

The make-up and dress of the Kathakali theatre are among the most highly conventionalized in the world. A Kathakali player belongs with the great theatrical figures of the Japanese Noh theatre, the Chinese classical 'opera', the Javanese *topeng*, the Tibetan temple dances and the Western ballet—and at the same time he still retains something in common with the primitive witch-doctor in his full panoply.

A modern student of stage-costume is always brought up to believe that the essential of a good dance dress is that it should be light, easy to move in, and should not obscure the lines of the human figure. It is remarkable that many of the greatest traditional dance theatres of this world have evolved costumes which seem completely opposed to these ideas. Kathakali costume is an outstanding example. The clothed player is a voluminous figure (Plate 2*a*), whose garments are so elaborate as to affect even the pose of his legs and feet, giving him a straddle and a stance on the outside edge of the foot. The headdresses are of wood and, for some characters, include a vast decorated solid wooden halo (or even a trio of haloes) behind them, that offers some burden for the neck to bear; and the body garments, with their long sleeves, their many skirts, their scarves, and added hanging pieces and ropes of ornaments (all tied upon the player with eighty knots) make him so hot that, since the convention of the style demands that an actor always face the audience, the garments are left open behind the body and it is said that an assistant can take advantage of this to fan the player's back in pauses during the action.

The make-up is even more highly organized. Since the actors do not speak and the whole of the 'dialogue' as well as the narration is spoken by a separate reciter, the face can be nearly immobilized. This allows, beyond some vivid colouring and patterning of the features, the development of a particular convention not to be found in any other theatre we shall study—namely, the building up in patiently accumulated layers on the face of a sort of exquisitely sculptured rim round jaw and chin in the manner of a decorative beard. The material of the modelling is a dead-white rice-flour paste, and its application requires some hour's progressive work by a master specialist (the highest-paid member of the troupe), while the actor lies supine on the ground, and similarly builds up his mind, layer by layer, into his part, in a relaxation that withdraws him farther and farther from the outside world. The final act of his preparation is to assume his huge double ear-rings and great headdress, having first sprinkled it with ritual drops of water.

It is of some significance to notice how, in most great theatres of the East, the assumption of costume is looked upon by the player as a ritual act even today; and it is accompanied by some moments of meditation or a gesture of prayer, or an act of remembrance to the player's teacher. Thus, even in the most sophisticated and highly advanced systems of theatre yet evolved, the idea of assuming the costume still retains the original sense of a ritual purpose.

THE ACTIONS

Surprising and near fabulous as are the dress and make-up of a Kathakali actor, they might almost be called trifling and secondary matters compared with his attitude to his system of movement. We must remember that the Kathakali player (save for certain particular inarticulate sounds allowed to demon characters) is vocally quite silent. His whole story, then, has to be told in action. What (in the terms of our opening proposition) he has to address to the audience must be addressed, despite his immobilized face and his exceedingly hampered limbs, entirely through movement. Hence the name of his style of theatre—Kathakali or Attakatha; story play, or danced play. But the end-product is so far beyond the idea we have in the Western World when we use the word 'mime' in the sense of dumbshow, that a western actor can but pause and say, 'I did not realize that it was *possible* to go so far!' So advanced is this technique of Kathakali movement that, rather than attempt to describe it, I prefer to give some picture of a fragment of it by roundabout means.

The Shell Film Unit made in 1948 a film called *Lord Shiva Danced*, in which the members of Ram Gopal's company gave brief examples, under somewhat limiting conditions, of four great schools of Indian dance, Baratha natyam, Manipuri, Kathak and Kathakali. The first three were represented with short characteristic dances by members of the company in costume. But the problem of representing Kathakali stood out.

It was solved in a significant way. Instead of a highly elaborate set, with awe-inspiringly dressed players behind a flaming oil lamp, there appeared one old man, grey-haired, bare-headed, bare-armed, and seen only in head-and-shoulders. He was lit by studio lights against a background of darkness.

This old man then told a story, with impassive face and frozen mouth, but with rapt memorable eyes, and his two naked arms and hands. The story was no largely-blocked-out legend of gods and heroes, suitable for gesture. It was infinitely fragile. It simply consisted of his looking at his hands as a lotus flower and noticing, with his eyes, a bee flying above it, and creating with one hand the flying and alighting and sipping of the bee; and then noticing with his eyes another bee flying above it, and creating with his other hand the flying of the other bee, and the sporting for a moment of the two around each other, and so their breaking off, parting and flying away. The old man was Chandupanikar, Ram Gopal's *guru*, or dance teacher.

So much was there, even for the uninstructed watcher. What more subtle language of *hastas*, or hand gestures, was employed or might be employed in such a slight passage is not for us to seek to know; unless we abandon our purpose here of tracing the seven ages of the theatre. For on one aspect of one example of the first age alone we could well expend a period of research as long as art is long before ever we sought to record it.

In Kathakali then, still without going beyond himself and what he wears or carries, a player may reach a technical virtuosity of expression that would seem to bear comparison with the craft of an Irving or a Bernhardt—and as for artistry, that of course is always a matter of the individual and not of the technique.

THE PERFORMANCE

To such a height as this, costumed-player work can reach, but in what has been described there is already to be discerned a sign of other things to come. The careful reader may have noticed it in the mention of the Kathakali curtain. Here is an effect *added* to the costumed player, that is to say the first hint of *secondary technical resources* coming into the development of theatrical presentation. Some valuable information on this subject is in A. Meerwarth's article written originally in English and translated into French for publication in the *Journal Asiatique* [43]. It gives a first-hand account of the preparations for a specially invited Kathakali performance in a garden in Central Travancore in January 1916, and we offer this re-translation of part of the account.

'They spent the day building the "scene". This was a simple *pandal*, such as is used for all kinds of outdoor performances and ceremonies. It consists of four poles of bamboo, planted in the earth at the four corners of a square with sides of about seven feet. These poles are nearly ten feet high and their tops are joined to one another by four other transverse bamboo poles, corresponding to the sides of the square, and by two diagonal poles. This roof skeleton is covered with coco-tree leaves. The floor of this "scene"—the *ranga* as it is called—is first washed with a mixture of cow-dung and urine, which the Hindus commonly use as a purifier; afterwards they strew it with sand and grass, and the back part is covered with matting. Some strips of green banana-tree bark are hung at the back of the *pandal* to serve as a backcloth. From similar bark they cut ornaments in the shape of flowers, chiefly the lotus, with which they surround the bamboo poles in the fashion of spirals rising from base to top. The clear green colour of the bark has a very pleasing effect on the yellowish white of the bamboo. Other elements of similar bark are also cut in the form of leaves and planted in the earth round the bamboo poles; others are bound round their tops, which thus resemble the capitals of columns. Similar arrangements of leaves decorate the centre of the poles, and *palmettes* cut in the same green banana bark are attached to the cross-pole forming the front. . . . The curtain, which plays a fairly active part in the presentation . . . is not fixed, but held by two boys who lift or lower it as the action requires. . . .

'About ten o'clock in the evening . . . the performance began. The great copper lamp, filled with scented coconut oil, in which six wicks are placed, is lighted: it mixes its light with the brilliant rays of the tropical moon. The curtain is lifted up to shut the scene from the eyes of the audience, in such a way as to leave uncovered only the upper third of the *pandal*. Behind, on the "scene", the *pattukaran* accompanied by the musicians sings the . . . prayer to call a blessing upon the actors and audience. Beside the persons just mentioned the two opening players are on the "scene".

'The prayer over, the *pattukaran* and the musicians go behind the backcloth (?), to remain there through the performance. . . .

'The curtain is lowered, and the chief hero of the piece, Vishnu-Krishna, appears in the scene, holding to his breast his consort Lakshmi, a tableau familiar to millions of Hindus. Then the curtain rises up once more to be lowered afresh some seconds

Fig. 12. A Kathakali performance

later and the god, coming alive, begins to dance slowly to the words of the *pattukaran*, accompanied by the musicians . . .'

The arrangement here described can be translated into a sketch-diagram as in Fig. 12. This sketch and the sketch in Fig. 11 (showing the Marshfield Mummers) put together, will illustrate the first steps in the organizing of a ritual act into a form suitable for a theatre spectacle. One shows the performance arranged in a circular place with entrances made through the ring of audience; the other the introduction into the place of a small tent or awning, or 'house'. Besides entrances through the audience, actors can now use this awning as a sort of focus for their action, and 'enter' (or be discovered) by the means of dropping a curtain.

But for all this, there is one reflection about Kathakali theatre that cannot be avoided. For some reason (not, perhaps, easy to decide) Kathakali has not become widely known. It has not drawn an audience from beyond the sea; it has not offered a meeting-ground for East and West. It is just possible that it may suffer a limitation in the fact of its ancient stability. The very closeness of weave of its minute and penetrating technique, to-gether with its essential reservation to ancient subjects removed from daily life, may give it an involute quality. Something of this sort has threatened the Chinese Classical Theatre and the Japanese Noh performance. There would appear to be a lack of that restless western element that has produced our characteristic dictum —'Variety is the spice of life'. I do not know how far this supposition is true. There is, however, a theatre of the East that, while it has remained also in the pure costumed-player phase, and has similarly evolved an intense concentration in its technique, has yet, in contrast, made a very wide appeal to the outside world; and this is the theatre of Bali.

BALI

The theatre of Bali is in many ways not unlike other theatres of the Far East—for example, that of Cambodia, or of Burma, or of Thailand, or the *topeng* and *wayang wong* of Java. All these present similar legends and characters, all have highly developed dance, all have remarkable costumes, several have superb masks; and there is perhaps no reason beyond Fortune for the singling out of Bali. But Bali has been immensely fortunate; in climate, in the manners of its people, in the beauty of its landscape, in its hospitality, in its perfect holiday atmosphere. Added to these attractions, its forms of theatre are unusually rich, and have been preserved (despite their wide popularity) with some authenticity of character. They illustrate effective uses of almost all the possibilities of costumed-player theatre, and at the same time have had the fortune to stay free from any of the developments that mark the later ages of theatre.

If any aspect of the costumed-player techniques has been exploited in Bali farther than perhaps other theatres have gone, it is that remarkable aspect of movement which was anticipated in a primitive form by the Abbots Bromley horn dancers—that is to say, the hypnotic effect of rhythmic dancing. This in Bali has evolved to a custom of trance dancing that has become famous throughout the world.

Unlike Kathakali, the Balinese dance drama is well described and illustrated in western reference books. It is sufficient, therefore, to confine the present notes to what follows.

Balinese performances are varied and so one description can at best be no more than typical. Many dances have their own form of presentation, but as an example of pure costumed-player

Fig. 13. A typical Balinese playing-place

theatre, exhibiting all the elements of the style, the Balinese *Barong* play is outstanding. Before going into details, a word about the general nature of Balinese presentation.

Two remarks are of great help here. First: 'In Bali, any place that is surrounded by a close-packed mass of humanity is a stage. The dances are designed to be seen from all sides so that the background is always that of the people' [29]. It is perhaps worth remarking that the word 'stage' here is used to mean the 'acting area', and is not intended to suggest a raised platform; there is no such thing as a raised stage, either in Bali or in the First Phase of the theatre. The second remark [29] confirms this: '. . . the stage, which is generally no more than a hollow square of which the orchestra forms one side and the audience the other three' (Fig. 13).

The *place* for the performance, then, is a stretch of ground; it may be anywhere suitable, outside a temple, in a courtyard, in a village street, on the bare earth [79]. The *audience disposition* is an informal grouping round the sides of the space. The *entrances* of the players are through the audience or from any convenient building. The surroundings are those of tropical sun, or on occasion moonlight and lamps. The players are gaily costumed in traditional dress assumed in a ritual atmosphere. Only a few characters are masked. 'There is no such thing in Bali as a performance for which admission is charged' [29]; and except for certain shows specially arranged for tourists, the Balinese theatre would appear to be entirely non-commercial. An interesting question thus arises—Is it then non-professional? The origin of the professional theatre is going to puzzle us again in our story. But, in Bali, any 'money paid to a society is almost never distributed among the members, but is instead put into the treasury to buy new costumes or instruments, or to pay a celebrated teacher for further instruction' [29]. The orchestra may be elaborate. The dancing may be subtle to a degree. There is free use of improvisation on occasion. The stories are the stories of the Hindu epics. It is interesting to note (in view of our earlier deduction that when words are spoken in the primitive theatre it is not their meaning that is of first importance) that 'Princes and such high characters speak in Kawi, the classical language of Java and Bali, which is unintelligible to all but a few highly educated people; the clowns discuss the prince and princely sayings in the vernacular' [29].

THE BARONG PLAY

Leaving aside the many other forms of the dance we turn to the Barong as an outstanding example of the fabulous animal in primitive theatre technique. To visualize the Barong one has to think of a sort of oriental dragon. Speaking generally his back is at the level of a man's head (Fig. 14). His flanks are made of very rich swags of hair or cut strips of material. On his back are plates of cut leather. He has a splendid arched tail. But his most remarkable feature is his vast, elaborate carved mask, with its lavish leather surroundings, all worn in front of the wearer's breast, so giving a characteristic hunched-shoulder quality. He has human legs showing below this completely inhuman and fantastic upper part. Most Barongs are four-legged, and are animated like a pantomime animal by two men whose bodies are concealed inside the Barong and whose legs—in horizontally-striped trousers—and bare feet appear below.

The details of a Barong's appearance differ in different parts of Bali at least as widely as the dress of St. George in the various versions of his play in their different localities.

In the same way, the framework of the play or act in which the Barong appears differs in different parts, as the St. George's play does. But as in the St. George's play, there is a general unity of

Fig. 14. A Balinese Barong

underlying theme. The Barong play is also a death-and-resurrection play; whatever its variations in detail, it generally retains:

—a fight between the Barong-dragon and an evil witch-figure called Rangda;

—the temporary defeat of the Barong;

—an attack upon the Rangda by ordinary villagers with daggers;

—the magical turning of the daggers upon the villagers by their own hands, and their trance-orgy of self-stabbing;

—the revival of the villagers by the benevolent, circulating Barong, with magic in its beard . . .

Then 'the Balinese are fearful of displeasing the evil spirits, so the play never reaches its logical conclusion, the destruction of Rangda. She merely disappears . . .'[29]. Ought one to say—'how idle an end'? Or—'how true'?

Perhaps there are deeper thoughts here. In Kathakali it is sacrilege not to finish a play. In Bali it is 'sacrilege' (or at least *tabu*) to finish it. The thought cannot be forbidden that in England it is '*tabu*' to speak the last line of a play at rehearsals. . . . These ideas, like so many antithetical things, are identical in source; fundamentally they indicate the 'sacredness' of the actual performance.

Returning to the Barong play; we have seen a version of the enactment of a Strife and of a Death at Padstow, in the Mummers' Play, in Kathakali, and now in the Barong Play. In all a Fatal power fought against a Resurgent power. It would be perhaps too particularizing to stamp these powers simply as Evil and Good. And in all, the Life power or its representative perished first

Fig. 15. The Norwich dragon

before the power of Death. In Bali, the Life power is the Barong, a mask, so developed as to have grown into one of the great theatrical animals.

When a Balinese dancer assumes one of the many traditional costumes for a performance, she will frequently stick a fresh flower in her hair. (Or even into *his* hair, if he is a man.) This is of course a very common adornment for a dancing woman, though maybe less common for a dancing man—but still, not all that uncommon even for him. But in Bali they go a step further, and do something that, in my experience, is very uncommon; they stick a fresh flower in the headdress of a mask.

It is strange how much one associates the freshness of a flower with the living body only, and overlooks its possibilities of fragrance for a 'dead' mask. But in Bali, how living this small touch makes the delicately fashioned masks, with all their grotesquerie and filigree leather extravagance that one might have supposed made them decorative enough! But no; the Balinese adds a flower in the hair of a mask—and very nearly endows it back again with the touch of humanity! (*c.f.* Plate 3.)

The Barong of Bali and the Padstow Horse, however they differ, have one thing in common. Both are additions to, or extensions of, a mask. It does seem, therefore, that the mask is an object that, though originally designed (we presume) to 'remove' a man's face and endow him, as a man, with other than human characteristics, can yet of itself assume theatrical personality and, to all intents and purposes, supplant the man. It can become a complete theatrical creature on its own, with the man only as animator. How much, in essence, is not all theatrical characterization this?

Both the Padstow Horse and the Balinese Barong are almost amorphous creatures; they have little shape of themselves, until they are assumed by human beings and brought to life in a performance.

But at least one example exists of a fabulous animal that has become an object in its own right, and has as much shape as any mythical beast can acquire, and maintains that shape with the fascination of a carving, even when it is discarded in a museum. It is a shape so strikingly in a medieval image that it conjures up St. Michael and the fallen angels of a country church window.

The Norwich Dragon and The Mons Lumeçon

The animal is to be seen at the Castle Museum at Norwich. There is no question whatever but that it is a dragon (*see* Fig. 15).

It has a barrel body, flexible neck, a vivid carved head with moving jaw, wings, and a tail of an unexpected nature. It is occasionally carried in a procession on rare civic special functions in Norwich.

Here is an entirely different world of craftsmanship from the filigree leather and flowers of Bali, yet it is of the same world of magic—a world an English or German craftsman knew as well as a Balinese, or a Chinese, or a Cambodian.

But as far as a conception of a dragon for theatre goes, it is not unique. Its great interest for this history is that there is another processional dragon of an almost identical design, similarly associated with ceremonies. And the other dragon is at Mons in Belgium.

A travel leaflet, or a local picture postcard, will witness to the ceremony at Mons, and show a group of figures in the town square. Here the animal bears the name of *lumeçon* and is associated with an elaborate ceremony. I have not been able to find any information about the ceremony with which the dragon at Norwich was originally associated; he remains something of a mystery. How far can we solve his mystery by studying a parallel performance in another country?

This is one of the big questions of theatre research. At present

Fig. 16. *Detail of drawing of the* lumeçon *at Mons*

the answer must be (as so often): We do not know. But the following two scraps of information are worth reflection:

In *The Times* [74] a photograph of the *lumeçon* ceremony appeared in an article on travel to Belgium. A reference is made incidentally to the staggering ceremony at Binche (where the headdresses are among the highest in the theatrical world), *The Times* calls it 'the greatest alfresco fancy-dress ball outside Spain'. Then we read that 'On Shrove Tuesday the Montois go to Binche, but on Trinity Sunday the Binchois go to Mons. There is no suggestion of rivalry in the two fêtes for they are quite different in origin and character . . .' Now what do the Binchois see when they arrive? What happens at Mons? The article goes on to say that at Mons:

'Sir Gilles de Chin himself appears in his traditional fight with the *Lumeçon* or dragon. The combat takes place in the Grande Place, whence Sir Gilles, on horseback, with his suite, the *pompiers* in glittering casques of copper, the drummers and trumpeters, repairs after the morning procession.

'This procession is the oldest of such survivals in the country, having its origin in homage to St. Waudru, who in 750 founded a monastery here . . .'

Thereafter the writer begins to lose touch with the ceremony we are so interested to hear about.

But if we turn to our second scrap of information we may fill in some gaps. Among the material of the Douce Collection of the Bodleian Library at Oxford, there is a very simple pencil sketch dated 1833 which shows the whole of the Mons ceremony. It is inscribed:

'This unfinished sketch of the annual Kermis at Mons was made by M. Delmotte, formerly librarian of that city. It was presented to me in Sept: 1833 by my worthy friend Mr Hill. Some say it alludes to the combat of S: George and the dragon. Others suppose it relates to a battle with a dragon by a chevalier Warre (or some such name) assisted by his dog "Chien-chien".'

The fabulous animal represented in this sketch is shown separated from the rest of the picture, in Fig. 16. It is a perfect international equivalent of the Norwich dragon as comparison of the pictures will show. Thus from Bali we may turn to Belgium and to Britain and still see parallels in the craftsmanship of early theatrical technique.

THE COMIC HUMAN INTERLUDE

But all these theatres have dealt with gods and heroes.

Some human element was admittedly introduced by the dagger-dancers in the Balinese Barong play, but though these were ordinary villagers their effect in the play was not so much an individual effect as a kind of impersonal mass chorus. Moreover the trance element in their dancing took away from their personal character and increased rather their impersonal character.

Therefore the general conclusion is that, strangely enough, it is only the curious, corrupt survival of the British Mummers' Play at Symondsbury that affords a solitary instance of ordinary, everyday people entering the scene in their own right. And this was in a comic interlude.

One has to ask: How much should great theatre operate in terms of human people and human problems?

In one sense the problems of gods are human problems told in a particular form: all the same, the theatre in its first phase, though it explores many techniques, does not in general introduce the human figure among its great masks. Mankind will make his entrance in the second phase. Indeed it is not impossible that the introduction of human characters among the divine and demonic, and the movement forward of the theatre into a new phase, were closely interdependent the one upon the other.

It was hinted above that the door through which the ordinary human figure on its own account entered the sacred province of the great masks of the theatre was in fact the comic interlude. There is some reason to believe that this is a hint of the truth.

The reason is that a time comes, especially when the play of gods and heroes develops to gigantic proportions, when the spectator must feel the need for relief from the high concerns of great immortal themes; and a pathetic consciousness begins to form of little man confronted by these things—seeming by contrast comic in his limitations, yet peculiarly valiant in his one invincible power to take knocks; the Eternal Butt. His only defensive resource is a jest or a scurrility, his only weapon of offence to raise up against it all is the phallus, or a need 'to be undone and seduced when life becomes too much of an obstacle to step over with ease and dispassion'. It would seem that such ideas prompted the earliest 'Interludes'.

The next phase of theatre shows the expansion of the act of ritual into a huge festival, with the play taking on the full character of deliberate drama. Together with this there is some decline in the barbaric splendour of costume, there is a rise of comic relief, a new problem in the accommodating of vast audiences, and finally the regular addition to the player's primary resources of *secondary aids* to his performance—aids created by impressing outside objects to his use. Chief among these at first are the Circle, and the central Awning, both of which we have already foreshadowed in this chapter.

And behind all this there lies a curious germination of the Interlude, later to spring to a significant flower.

SECOND PHASE

The Great Religious Festivals

GROWTH IN THE THEATRE
    ADAM DE LE HALE
    THE CAUSE OF THE GROWTH

THE TIBETAN FESTIVAL DRAMA

THE MEXICAN FLYING FESTIVALS

THE MEDIEVAL ROUNDS

OTHER SYSTEMS OF MEDIEVAL PRESENTATION
    LUCERNE
    MONS AND VALENCIENNES
    PAGEANT WAGGONS

PROFESSIONALISM

EARLY NOH

CAMBODIA AND THAILAND

GREEK FESTIVAL THEATRE PROBLEMS

SECOND PHASE

The Great Religious Festivals

GROWTH IN THE THEATRE

Phase one of the development of the theatre, though it was concerned with the simplest systems of presentation, included examples of techniques of high complexity. It is necessary now to forget these complex techniques and return to the field of primitive presentations again, in order to see how certain forms of theatre on the other hand did *not* develop by perfecting their technique within one simple system, but by advancing to a different system which was more complicated and required wider resources, and which was in fact called into being by a new demand that the progress of civilization made upon the players.

The First Phase of the development of the theatre is over, and it is passing out of the atmosphere of prehistoric times into the era of early history. Suppose, now, that primitive man has already reached the system of theatre such as we saw in the Mummers' Play but that his growing civilization now imposes upon him the need for a great reformation in the conception of the *size* of his show; a need for expansion both spiritually and physically—in content, in length of performance, in scope of action, in size of audience. (The possible motive force for such a change will be discussed below.)

An example of a community which has reached such a stage as this, and remained at that stage despite the vicissitudes of the world outside, is to be found in Tibet. It offers a useful study on which to base a picture of this next development in theatre. No records exist with first-hand accounts of such an early stage, and in their default a survival such as that in Tibet becomes our only evidence.

It does not, unfortunately, afford us a completely unbroken transition from the theatre of primitive ritual that we have pictured in the last chapter. There is a gap. We still have to find a ceremony half-way between what I may call the advanced primitive rite and the great festival drama. Yet the great festival drama could not have sprung into existence on one single occasion fully formed.

ADAM DE LE HALE

There is perhaps one tentative suggestion for a link, and it does illustrate the humanizing—even satirizing—of the primitive rite though it lacks any touch of the religious reformation that overspread the rite. It is a short French play of the unusually early date of about 1276. An immediate curiosity about it is that we know the author; few individual, early-medieval playwright-poets can be specified in this way. Adam de le Hale, also called Adam le Bossu, lived in Arras. He was a poet and student of the troubadour style.

He once went from Arras to Paris to take up further studies, and before he went he did what seems an unprecedented thing; he wrote a play about a man called Adam living in Arras and about to go to Paris to resume his studies on a certain date, and actually set the play in reality—at the pub of the town he was to set out from.

The cast includes, besides fictitious characters, members of his town mentioned by name, and in the play there are exchanges between real, named people in the audience and real, named people on the stage. But it also includes another group of entirely non-human characters, several 'fairies' under the lead of Morgane, who come to attend an ancient spring ritual in the town (whence the mysterious name of the play—*Le Jeu de la Feuillée*, the Play of the Leafed One). The play ends with an allegory satirizing (as it seems) both humans and non-humans.

It is difficult to say whether this play belongs to costumed-player theatre, or is an elementary example of a new phase. As has been shown, it hints at a spring-festival occasion. In its setting it still displays a simple idea, but one that to us is now unfamiliar; it resists any impulse to invent a special 'scene', and is content to take place in *reality*, at the occasion of the performance, and it uses for the background of its action the real inn before which it would be actually played—an inn from an upper window of which, one character is mentioned in the script as pouring a pitcher of wine upon the head of another in the play below. Beyond this is the overtone suggested of the well-known streets around leading to this inn. Down these the fairies are to come. Its setting, then, is the real world, not a fiction.

Whether Adam de le Hale was merely one of a number of ingenious minds awake, as early as the 13th century, to the possibility of a new form in drama, of whom all have been forgotten but him; or whether he was an unparalleled innovator, far in advance of his time, we do not know. But however that may be, he does appear to have side-stepped the great expansion in size that the theatre-show was about to suffer under the coming new religious pressure, and we do not find his like until, two centuries later, we come upon the bright, satirical and philosophical minds that created the entertainments for lords and their people which we call the Interludes, and which were to institute a further revolution in theatre history.

Thus Adam de le Hale offers a mystery, an original playwright before his time. But he is not known ever to have turned his 'troubadour's' hand to the creation of the type of new, cosmic, religious show, that was then to revolutionize theatre, and so composed a great festival script, such as we are now to see. But whether he offers a link or not, the Tibetan festival play does illustrate the next move and the players' immediate problem of the expanding show.

The richness of the theatre in Tibet—that reserved country where so many lines of tradition have pursued an individual course little touched by influences from outside, save only the influence of Buddhism—is not as widely known as it deserves. Admittedly, a few readers of travels will at once picture a grotesque figure with a huge and aweful wooden mask, who is generally called a 'Tibetan Devil-dancer' and who is said to take part, with a rout of similar figures, in certain ceremonies in remote lama monasteries. But even his ceremony, had one space here to describe it, would prove a little more significant than that.

The indigenous peasant-dance, however, of men with whirling girdles of yaks' tails and entirely distinctive, flat, kite-shaped leather masks, bearing trefoil decoration, is nearly unknown here; and the third manifestation of Tibetan theatre, the great mystery-play Festival itself, is only a degree more familiar. It is this latter, nevertheless, that offers us the material for opening a Second Phase of theatre development.

The Tibetan festival play illustrates the players' solution to their great problem of the expanding show. This expansion is an expansion of audience as well as of performance; and it thus raises two technical problems—How are the players to accommodate this greater audience? And how are they to arrange themselves and their show so as to be best seen by that greater audience? These are two fundamental problems that apply all over the world and henceforward will colour almost all theatre development.

One way to cope with a big audience is simply to develop the processional theatre method to much greater proportions, but that seriously restricts the nature of the show. If your show gets to be elaborate and long, and your audience begins to run into many thousands, you may well have to revolutionize your whole system of theatrical presentation.

THE CAUSE OF THE GROWTH

In what follows, the main difference from the primitive rite is primarily this remarkable matter of size. The new Festival is far longer than anything we have seen so far; indeed it may run into several days of performance. It generally entails the use of far more performers. And it commands (and has to accommodate) an audience now possibly running into thousands.

What was the motive in primitive man's development which brought about this great advance in size?

It may possibly have coincided with some development and expansion in religious belief. Certainly the festival dramas of Tibet repeatedly portray the struggle of Buddhism to destroy and supplant the earlier Bon worship. And in the Western World, the great Festival phase coincides with the spread of organized Christianity in the Middle Ages.

We need still to establish whether the surprising early flowering of this particular phase of theatre which took place in Classical Greece and went so far was coincident with any deep reformation of religion. There is, however, no doubt that it was a religious festival; and also that the expansion of the nature-rite of Dionysus

Fig. 17. An African ceremony before a hut

into 'tragic drama' took place at a time when Pisistratus was 'raising Athens from a small country-town to a city of international importance' [37].

One other thought may be added at this point, concerning the possible reasons for the expansion of the theatre performance. In a conversation between Mr. John Ekwere, a Nigerian student of the theatre, and the present writer, the surroundings of a simple drum and dance festival were discussed; they proved to be what we have come to expect—an open space in a Nigerian village to which the players come, and round which some few hundred spectators gather, to watch, somewhat as in Fig. 17. But if (as Mr. Ekwere added) a drummer was particularly famous, word would go out to several villages and a mass meeting might result, involving a larger space and the accommodation of an audience now running into the thousands. How was the accommodation arranged? Simply by raising up those more distant spectators who stand on the outskirts of the crowd, on mounds of earth flanking the main assembly space. Already this is within distant sight of the constructed amphitheatre. And it is in this case the fame of the player that has caused the increase in size of the audience-group.

THE TIBETAN FESTIVAL DRAMA

The Tibetan festival drama takes place in a formation very reminiscent of the circle of the Marshfield Mummers but of greatly increased dimensions. It also incorporates a new 'secondary resource', which is in the nature of an expansion of the simple *pandal* of Kathakali theatre—that is to say, a canopy; but now in the centre of the place.

The site of the performance (which is presented in August-September) is a vast plain in the Tibetan mountains. One such, described and illustrated by Marion Duncan [21], is at Batang near the Yangtze River, within roughly equal distance from the boundaries of Assam and China (*see* Plate 2*b*).

Around the circumference of the area the spectators gather, before the performance begins. The rich people gather sufficiently in advance to set up tents and stock them for comfortable living, for these are to be their homes, from which they watch, during the probable five days the festival lasts. The poorer people travel in from their houses to the festival each day, take up what positions they can round the circle standing or sitting without any awning, and return home each night.

The size of the acting-area is not, apparently, stated by any eye-witness. It would appear from photographs to be between 100 ft. and 200 ft. long and somewhat less across.

In Batang, near one end of the festival ground stands a substantial two-storey building where a representative of the monastery stays during the festival, and in which the considerable wardrobe of costumes is kept, and where the players dress.

Down the middle of the open area is erected the great canopy which serves as a sort of scenic centre for the action (Fig. 18). It consists of two richly patterned awning-cloths, put end to end so as to form a long tent roof, and held up on three tall king-poles, one at either end and one in the middle between the two cloths. The poles are supported, and the cloths held out, by long guy ropes made off on tent pegs in the ground.

The two halves of this covered space have slightly different theatrical functions. The half to the east is so placed that it takes

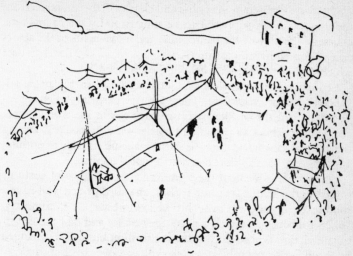

Fig. 18. *A performance of a Tibetan festival play*

in as its centre a small growing tree, which forms the focal point of several of the dances, and which is preserved there for this purpose. Otherwise this half is empty.

The half to the west is differently specialized. In it, to begin, is stationed, upon a roofed chair at the far western end, a figure of the holy man, Druhtoh Thangthang, who was invited from India by the Tibetans to institute a new age in their country. He now presides over the festival, and before his figure are laid offerings. Next, between this figure and the centre pole are grouped certain cushions, seats and tables, used in the presentation of interior scenes in the plays.

The style of the acting is a mixture of recitation, dancing and narration. The scripts of the plays contain both actors' speeches and passages of narration for the commentator. The dancing forms the chief part of the display and is accompanied by cymbal and drum, in a complication of rhythm. The instruments cease before any chanted passage begins. Concerning these vocal passages, Duncan [21] makes the following comment which is highly significant when compared with our conclusions about the words in the Mummers' Play:

'The recitation or chanting . . . of the poetry . . . is delivered in a rapid, unintelligible tone, beginning and ending in a high-pitched cry. Phrased in the polite and classical Tibetan, taken from the play, it is not supposed to be understood. One follows the course of the play by the pantomime and movements of the actors except for short comic interludes spoken in the local dialect which, full of coarse jokes, delight the audience.'

Costumes are somewhat simpler than those in the more advanced types of Phase One. There are rich garments when appropriate, but for the smaller parts ordinary gowns are worn. Some characters such as sorcerers and spirits wear masks, but among the normal characters there is little make-up. There is nothing approaching the elaborate conventions of Kathakali.

Similar use is made of the significance of a change of costume to that in the Tudor Interludes; thus, an exiled prince 'will have a sombre cloak thrown over his yellow gown. . . .' Similarly, 'when robbers . . . attack a party they buffet and cuff the unfortunate victims whose clothes are not torn off but merely changed by throwing a grey robe and grey skull-cap over their apparel'.

The acting delivery is not naturalistic, and is given on a single note, or chanted swiftly, but it does permit of a good deal of emotional expression, and is capable of inspiring an audience to tears or to laughter.

The following comment of Duncan's [21] suggests a quite remarkable parallel with the English procedure, as will be seen when we come to consider corresponding performances of festival plays here. He says,

'The caricatures of home life given between regular scenes of the play are replete with homely wit and puns which so delight the children that their crowding close is controlled by monitors beating the ground, in front of the players, continuously with whips.'

Thus we may understand that one of the features of such early great festival shows in a circle was that part at least of the audience were free to move about at will and to approach, or remain apart from, such actions as they chose. To regulate any crowding-in, special officials were present at the performance to keep the necessary space free for the players.

When properties are employed, some are the objects themselves, some are conventional substitutes—a mixture of realism and fancy. And in connection with these conventions we come upon a passage in Duncan so significant for our picture of developing theatrecraft that it should be quoted in full. It gives an admirable account of the first steps taken in impressing to the actor's use certain 'secondary resources'. This time they are not resources whose purpose is (like the great tent roof) to supply something in the nature of a visual setting-off for the whole performance, but rather to supply the place in a given scene of some object or surrounding that is required by the action of the scene.

Here we must interject a particular comment. We have seen that in the Kathakali theatre something of this purpose has been filled in quite a different way—namely, by so intensely developing the player's range and command of mime and gesture language that he can himself, still keeping within the limits of the first or costumed-player phase of theatre, present an entirely legible and comprehensible idea of any object (and indeed of many abstractions) just by means of his *hastas* or hand (and eye) movements alone. He has no need to have recourse to an object itself, not even to a stylized symbol of that object, as an item among his secondary resources; he is so advanced that the object is 'created' fully (for his purposes) out of his primary resources alone.

But for some reason very few schools of theatre have adopted this course—perhaps because of its highly abstract and intellectualized approach. Instead the 'scenic property' came into being. The player imports an extraneous object into his action and says, in effect, Let us pretend that this is a house . . . etc.

Here is this innovation, shown at the moment of its inception as it were, from Duncan's account of the Tibetan play [21]:

'In substitution of the real article a house is a staked square enclosed by red cloth. A forest consists of green tree branches stuck into the ground, and when some of the branches are tied into the shape of a wigwam it is the hermitage of an anchorite. Branches stuck in the ground around a chair is a courtyard or a place of assembly in the open. A hill or elevation higher than the surrounding area is a chair on which the observer stands and is used principally to see a long ways off; formerly indicated by shading the eyes with the hand but now modernized by the use of a pair of spectacles or a telescope. An individual ready to ascend into the sky puts on a white scarf, mounts a chair and jumps down to run away. A boat is a wide band of brilliantly coloured cloth around a rectangular framework held up at the front and the rear by oarsmen whose legs propel the boat in spurts while they paddle with long poles. The passengers walk in between the oarsmen. A tree branch serves as a horse ridden astride by the horseman carrying a string of bells. Animals necessary in a nomadic encampment are portrayed by half-naked boys with dog and cat face-masks and they tug at their ropes like real animals. Religious exorcism is most realistic, for the exorcist, sitting on a rug in a rope-enclosed space, mutters charms, rings bells, and manipulates his hands and fingers in the prescribed motions. Genuine house furniture is transported bodily for inside scenes, the matron churning with a regular butter churn and the priest using barley flour for his offerings. Flour is kneaded on a wide board and the teakettle spouts steam above a fire placed between three stones, ready to feed the beggar princess whose approach is heralded by the lunging watchdog. The shedevil is killed by an arrow shot feebly towards her, or her headdress is sliced off with a sword.'

So then—just as with Kathakali we experienced the impression that there was an example of ritual developing into a stage that we need have no hesitation in labelling 'theatrical'—here before this Tibetan list we similarly experience the impression that with such conventions we have reached a world that can be mistaken for no other than the world of the theatre.

But the means to create the 'theatrical' element are, in the two categories, entirely dissimilar. The only point in common is that they are both ways in which developing man sought to add to the resources available to him when he presented before an audience an act of theatre.

The means of theatre are expanding.

One odd discovery offered by all the above is that although the problem of accommodating a larger audience has cropped up and been settled, yet it has been settled in a way that has so far made no proper provision for ensuring that the audience shall see that performance uninterruptedly. Thus, though the wealthier spectators in Tibet had established themselves well enough in their tents, the moving commoners are limited to no definite position, and they must therefore often come between the action and the occupants of the tents. And the tents are pitched on flat ground like the rest; no attempt is made to elevate them to a point of vantage.

So we are forced again to a strange conclusion about early theatre. Just as it did not matter whether you heard all the words of a show so also it did not matter whether you saw all the action.

Presumably in Tibet if a passage occurred in the play that particularly interested the occupants of a tent, there was nothing to stop their rising, leaving its shelter, mingling with the mob and going to have a close look (so far as the 'monitors' permitted them). This attitude of mind seems to be true of all such theatre, more so perhaps than one would first suppose—and certainly of all long-drawn-out theatre. Thus a Chinese audience before a three-night mammoth play will take tea and relax at times, and call for towels to refresh themselves with. And even in Italian Grand Opera, a box was a social centre as well as a spectators' viewpoint.

There is a further item to add to this brief sketch of the Tibetan performance, and again it introduces a step forward in theatrical technique.

Play-scripts now exist, recording (though as yet perhaps only very loosely) the words of the performance, and embodying the story. And they are composed in a specialized language of heightened quality—in fact, in poetry. These scripts exist, and are adhered to today, despite the fact that the dialogue is largely incomprehensible to the ordinary spectator.

Perhaps it is not irrelevant here to notice Bharatha Iyer's remark [33] that in Kathakali the spoken word is regarded as 'a needless burden on the actor and imperfectly equipped to discharge the function it was called upon to bear'. This view of the frailty of words is significantly in opposition to those who hold that the author's lines should be inviolate in the theatre. Apart, however, from this curious thought we are concerned here to ask what exactly were Tibetan plays like.

A small number have been translated into English, not all perhaps in a completely felicitous style, but sufficiently to suggest a very high sense of dramatic poetry in the originals. This sense of poetry is a new element. Did it come from the players themselves, or from specialists in another art existing outside the theatre? It may be claimed (from what we have seen above) that actors came to *speak* spontaneously in their rituals; but did they use poetry spontaneously, or was poetry an opportunist intrusion from without?

If we are right in supposing that this phase of great expansion in the scale of theatre sprang from the promptings of a new religious development, then we may easily come to believe that clerics who represented that new religion would seek any means to spread it; one obvious means was to impose its new legends upon the legends of the old religion such as were presented in native theatre ceremonies. Given this means of propaganda, they would gladly set to work to frame the words of their new legend in the most seizing style they knew—and hence the best poet among them would be selected and set to work.

If this be true, then this phase of development in the theatre is scarcely a natural phase, arising from the original performers' own desire to make their medium more effective, but is an induced phase, coming about by design, through outside people arrogating the theatre art to their own use not for the sake of bettering the theatre, but with the purpose of furthering different ends. It would then not be a direct development in theatre history, but an impingement from outside from which theatre suffered in its own progress.

But to return to the Tibetan scripts: the especially striking thing about them is that, in spite of their primitive nature, it is in them, and in similar scripts from other countries in this same phase of theatre development, that there is first to be seen the emergence of the human being into the drama as a principal character.

What is perhaps the greatest of the Tibetan plays, *Tchrimekundan* [78], still deals with a divinity—or a human being who became divine—in that it shows the life of Prince Gautama, that is Buddha himself. Others deal with saints such as *Nansal*. Others, however, deal with historical human beings (so recalling the Elizabethan chronicle plays). But through them all there is a human element in the handling of character that may well be taken as a pattern of the entrance into the ancient theatre-rite of the mask of the ordinary man or woman.

THE MEXICAN FLYING FESTIVALS

Once the theatre has reached the introduction of 'secondary

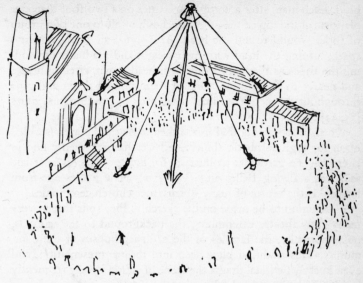

Fig. 19. The 'flying dance' of the Otomi in Mexico

resources'—resources external to the player and what he wears or carries—notable new possibilities are opened. Just as a simple mask could develop into a complete personality and come to be the central character of a ceremony like the Barong and the Padstow Horse, so the secondary object itself can be animated from a mere scenic property to become the whole mechanical and technical centre of a ritual, without which the ritual could not exist. The simple awning of the Tibetan Festival stands at one end of the scale, nothing more than a shade over part of the show; but at the other end of the scale (and keeping to much the same level of theatrical development) such a 'scenic object' can achieve its own end like a mask, and dominate the whole performance— even though its manipulation is so exacting as to inspire amazement and so dangerous as to risk the lives of the performers.

Such a development of a secondary technical resource is reached in the *voladores'* dance of ancient Mexico. It survives in several villages to this day much like a Mummers' Play; but its technique is very different (*see* Fig. 19).

Four or six men climb a seventy-foot pole planted for the purpose in the village square. It is provided with a revolving head. Each man, after a vertiginous dance on a two-foot-diameter platform at the top of the pole, attaches himself to one of a group of ropes wound round the head. At a signal all swing out into space, turning the head with their weight and gradually unwinding the ropes as they whirl outward, head down, circling nearer and nearer to the ground. One of them plays a drum and pipe throughout this act. The ritual dates back to pre-Christian times [25, 32].

We shall repeatedly find in the theatre that the player is called upon for high acrobatic ability; and we shall repeatedly find in later phases a particular enthusiasm for flying effects (even as late as Kirby's Flying Ballet and *Peter Pan*) while a 'descent from heaven' is the centre of many Renaissance church ceremonies.

A reflection to be made on the sketch in Fig. 19 is that in very many early theatre ceremonies, the background to the action is, quite normally, the façades of the ordinary houses of the community. This tradition bites deep into theatre presentation, and even in early fictional drama the scene of action is very frequently laid 'Outside So-and-so's House'.

THE MEDIEVAL ROUNDS

To recapitulate: As time goes on, the primitive players move from a masked religious rite to a rhythmic act given by a specialized mask; they add words; then at a religious revolution they expand the show, put aside 'superstitions', reduce the masks, bring in human characters, begin to add secondary resources to the players, and suffer the incursion of poetry. This stage of development has been exemplified in the Tibetan harvest festival, with its great, circular acting-place, and its tents.

A development almost exactly similar to the Tibetan took place about the 14th and 15th centuries in Western Europe. The resemblance is in fact so striking and covers so many details that a medieval Englishman or Frenchman would probably feel far more at home among the audience at Batong than a Modern; and a playgoer from Tibet could have attended certain at least of the performances of medieval Mysteries and Moralities and found their arrangement and style pretty nearly familiar to him. True, he would see in certain built-up and crowded medieval towns, some strange spectacles on carts that had little parallel in his own land, but if he turned to the open country in Lincolnshire or in Cornwall or in Touraine, he would see something quite recognizable.

He would see the sight diagrammatized in Fig. 20. It is worth comparing this with Fig. 18 in detail, and relating both with the earlier scene in Fig. 11.

In both England and France, one method of presenting the expanded performances, inspired as in Tibet by the spread of a new religion, was in a Round. The western system of Rounds is basically identical with the Tibetan system. It shows, perhaps, one additional feature in the provision of earthen mounds for certain of the spectators (reminiscent of the Nigerian drum festivals).

About this system of Rounds three pieces of evidence survive which enable a very full picture to be reconstructed; they are: an actual plan from an English manuscript play of about 1425; an eye-witness picture in a French miniature of about 1455; and certain actual earthworks built as theatres and standing to this day. The play is *The Castle of Perseverance*, the miniature is by Jean Fouquet in the *Livre d'heures* of Etienne Chevalier, and a typical earth Round survives in the village of St. Just in Penwith, Cornwall.

The essential element of a Round is the central plain, whose dimensions might be not far short of those in Tibet. In England this plain received the special name, derived from the Latin (in which language most medieval stage directions were written), of *platea* which is anglicized into *placea* and then into the straightforward 'Place'. To be 'in the Place', then, meant in medieval theatrical parlance to be in this central plain.

Around the perimeter of the Place, tents were set up, again similarly to the Tibetan. There was however an important qualification; these 'tents' were higher structures with a wooden framework (covered with hangings), and a highly-raised floor within—a floor perhaps eight feet above the ground. The occupants could then see over the heads of the people standing in the Place.

But some of the tents had another use; their value as a vantage place was exploited not only by the spectators for seeing better, but also by the players in order to be better seen, in just the same way that, in the Marshfield circle of Seven, given a greatly increased show and audience, it would clearly pay to elevate each

Fig. 20. Diagram of a moated Round, showing a 'Place' surrounded by a circular earthen hill, with five 'tenti' or scaffolds, a central tower and an entrance bridge. Spaces are kept clear among the spectators in the centre, and before each scaffold. The actors dress in a pavilion outside the Round (based on the Lincolnshire Castle of Perseverance)

player in his station round the circle so that he might be the better seen by the greater crowd of thousands.

Immediately technical problems begin to flock in. A player may now be better displayed to some of the audience so long as he remains in his own solitary station and declaims his lines from there; but if he is called upon to 'come in' into the circle to take part in action with another player on the ground, what is he to do?

Further; a tented scaffold on the inner border of a thick ring of spectators will be very well for those standing opposite and facing it, but very ill for those standing on the same side and behind it.

The very existence of these problems, and the fact that they were solved, is evidence of a pretty high degree of thought and organization in medieval theatre.

What, in fact, they did was this: If the ground were hard, they barred off the whole circle with a fence and built the scaffolds inside against this fence, allowing the spectators either to sit on certain of the scaffolds, or to stand or sit on the ground in front of the scaffolds, and so round the edge of the Place itself.

If on the other hand the ground allowed digging, they raised a huge circular mound of earth round the Place, leaving the hole from which the earth came as a circular ditch skirting all, which they filled with water. Thus they had no need to wall the place about; ditch and hill together prevented unwanted gatecrashers.

The inward side of this circular hill (recalling at once our Nigerian example) will offer an excellent grandstand, and if terraced for seats—possibly with stone as was done at St. Just—would save the erecting of any audience scaffolds. If the play demanded seven actor's scaffolds (as an imaginary, expanded version of the Marshfield play would have done), or between eight and thirteen scaffolds (as the Cornish cycles actually did), or five scaffolds (as the Lincolnshire *Castle of Perseverance* did), then these could be simply built directly on the summit of the hill, and the steps in the inner face used for access to them (*see* Fig. 20).

Otherwise, in the walled formation with no hill, access for the actors to the scaffolds from the ground of the Place would be by a simple ladder.

Given the enclosed arrangement pictured above with scaffolds on the outer circumference and audience within freely encroaching on the ground of the Place, then it is clear that when a big audience crowded inside, much of the free playing space in the centre might be overrun. To guard against this, the medieval manager did just what the Tibetan manager did—he appointed a number of 'monitors' (possibly with staves) to mingle with the audience in the Place, keep them back from the centre where important concerted action would occur, and also clear a passage through the people for those moments when a leading character left his 'home' (or *domus*), his tent (or *tentus*), or the scaffold where his seat was (his *sedes*)—all these names were used—and descended to the ground or *platea* to journey to the scaffold of another character, or to meet him in the centre.

The ancient name of such an official in England was 'styteler' or 'stightler', from the verb to 'stightle' or intervene. And it is perhaps not irrelevant to remark that in Norfolk recently an old inhabitant could remember how, at the time of the early 'cinematograph palaces' there, a brawny individual employed to keep order was known as a 'stiftler'.

Concerning the valuable central part of the Place—valuable for elaborate action to be widely seen—another similarity with the

Tibetan exists, but with a difference. Instead of the great awning of Tibet, the English might build a representation of a church, or a chapel, or a castle according to the need of the play. This was probably a skeleton structure so that spectators could see through it and so have their vision less impeded. In *The Castle of Perseverance* this central 'scenic object' was a circular castle-tower raised on four legs and accessible from below by a ladder, so that players could appear on the battlements above.

Finally one other element played a part; this time something reminiscent of a feature in Kathakali—namely, a curtain. Each of the peripheral scaffolds might have a working curtain, drawn by a cord, in front of it so that it could be closed or unclosed at will and its occupants revealed or hidden.

The audience entered through a gap in the hill and by a bridge over the ditch. The players dressed in a Pavilion outside the circle (reminiscent of the wardrobe-building beside the pageant ground at Batang), and entered either by mounting the hill and walking round the rampart, behind the spectators, and slipping through the back curtain of their scaffold, to be ready for discovery; or if the character were a stranger suggesting a connexion with the world without, he might come through the gap for the public and stride into the thronged Place down a lane cleared by the stytelers. As, for example, Death probably did (and with great effect) near the end of *The Castle of Perseverance*. (For a detailed discussion of the Rounds and a description of the performance of *The Castle, see* [66].)

The scripts of English and Cornish shows written for these Rounds vary greatly. Some are purely religious epic cycles like the three-day *Creation of the World, Passion* and *Resurrection* of Cornwall. Some are almost free-thinking, philosophical conceptions of the problems of life, like *The Castle of Perseverance*; some are 'normal' English Mystery cycles, like the Hegge Plays (also known as the *Ludus Coventriae*). Some are Saint's plays, like the *Mary Magdalene* of the Digby Group. Some are completely unexpected, popular sensation-draws, such as theatre-people have perpetrated so often since, based on pure stunts and sensationalism, like the so-called Croxton *Play of the Sacrement*, which is a quite ingeniously constructed blood-and-horror play that might well have fathered Shakespeare's *Titus Andronicus*. And lastly there are large, bland, shrewd comments on current corruption like Lindsay's *Ane Satyre of the Threi Estaits*. All these were played (and many more) in the Round system.

We know little of the player's style of delivery in such plays, and only a little more of the detailed items of presentation, such as costumes and properties. But if so much else is similar to Tibetan productions at the same phase, we may not be wrong in supposing there would be no inconsistency for a medieval manager to represent a garden, or Paradise, by a fence of four stakes with a cloth stretched round them and a plantation of branches within, in much the same way that a Tibetan manager did.

We have seen that there was a not dissimilar attitude to the significance of costume.

Finally, if the Tibetan actor chanted, danced and performed to rhythmic music, it is well to remember that in England individual speeches might have been delivered conventionally (in the Mummers' tradition); that there are many suggestions that dances might be called for in the performances; and lastly that there are repeatedly directions asking for music to be 'piped up' and for songs to be sung.

Among the plays for performance in medieval Rounds are some quite superb poetry and some startlingly subtle scenes of human psychology. A special example of the latter is the searching triangle-study between David, Bathsheba and Uriah in the Cornish Cycle—capable of as minute study as a relationship in an Ibsen or an Anouilh.

OTHER SYSTEMS OF MEDIEVAL PRESENTATION

Three other systems of presenting the great festival plays of the Middle Ages are known; but so far the evidence on which to base a picture of these is less complete than for the Rounds, and our current ideas may contain several errors.

The first (which we know best) is the grouping of a mixture of 'tents' and properties over the ground of a town square as at Lucerne in Switzerland; the second, the stringing of a number of 'scaffolds' together in one straight line and elevating them in a row on a long raised stage as at Valenciennes in France; the third (of which we know least) is the splitting of the 'scaffolds' into completely independent units, mounting each on wheels and drawing them round the streets of a town in succession, each stopping at pre-arranged stations to perform its own play or part of the cycle, then moving on to repeat it at the next station in a development of the processional method that has already been referred to above. Such a system was used at York, Chester and other towns in England, possibly in the *jeux sur chars* in Picardy, in Belgium and in the *carros* of Spain.

LUCERNE

The evidence for the Lucerne performance rests in two plans prepared by Renward Cysart for the two-day performance in 1583, and now in the Zentralbibliothek in Lucerne. No adequate study of these documents seems to be available in English, though the plans are reproduced [5, 46].

It would appear that for their Easter Play the inhabitants built in the Weinmarkt Square a number of scenic objects. Above, I called these 'tents'. They are not necessarily tents in the present-day sense of a stretched canvas covering, but in the technical sense of the word *tenti* used in medieval theâtre. Such a theatrical object could be called—indifferently, so far as our present knowledge goes—*domus* (a home), *sedes* (a seat), *locus* (a place; to be distinguished from *platea*, the specific Place itself), *pulpitum* (a pulpit—and *The Oxford English Dictionary* gives as its first definition of 'pulpit'—'a scaffold, stage, or platform for public shows, speeches, or disputations'; only second comes the meaning of a structure for a preacher in a church), or it might be called a 'house', or in France a *mansion*, or even (as in the play at Mons to be referred to) a *maisonnette*. It might, so far as we know, be anything set up in the *platea* or Place to serve as the centrepiece for the action of a certain scene, or it might equally well apply to the scaffolds of the actors set up on the perimeter of the Place in the Round system. So wide is the significance of the first idea of scenery.

Some of these scenic objects at Lucerne seem elaborate—such as the realistic Hell Mouth in the south-west corner of the square; a raised Heaven in the form of a platform, railed and draped, against the façades of the houses at the east end (Fig. 21), and approached by a ladder or ramp; and a Temple in the middle of the long south side. The latter was probably of typical skeleton construction, like the tower in *The Castle of Perseverance*, being merely a dome on four legs sheltering an altar, and was certainly

Fig. 21. The Mystery performance at Lucerne; the North side of the square is at the bottom-left

associated with a fenced-off enclosure or forecourt approached through an arch, much as the Tibetan gardens.

Others of these scenic objects were more simple—a column supporting the golden calf, near the centre; a table; a tree for Judas; a plain rostrum with a flight of steps for Abraham. Paradise was a fenced enclosure on the ground in front of Heaven, containing a tree, etc. And so forth. On the first day a representation of the River Jordan ran through the square. On the second, this and several other objects were removed, and the three Crosses set up a little in front of Heaven. The audience appear to have been accommodated in a main grandstand built at the west end of the square, and also in smaller stands lining the two sides, and no doubt many occupied the windows of the houses (some of them five-storeyed) that surrounded the square.

In summary, it would seem then that instead of formal raised scaffolds round the Place as in England, this Swiss system of presentation tended rather to use built objects set up about the floor of the Place, more or less indiscriminately. Instead of a plain Place with most scaffolds round the edge and perhaps one in the centre, they preferred a fairly full Place with scenic objects dotted about in some profusion here and there.

OTHER SYSTEMS OF MEDIEVAL PRESENTATION

MONS AND VALENCIENNES

The Valenciennes performance of 1547 is documented for us by one principal, and twenty-six subsidiary, miniatures painted by Hubert Cailleau (who performed some small parts in the play), now in MS Français 12536 at the Bibliothèque Nationale, Paris; and another version, slightly different, exists in the library of Baron James de Rothschild, Paris.

It is perhaps true that the great performance at Mons in 1501, on which Gustav Cohen has published such a valuable treatise [18], was performed similarly.

In this system, a scaffold stage of very considerable dimensions (at any rate as to length) was set up. Along the back were, at Valenciennes, six (or seven) main 'houses' all apparently elaborately built (Fig. 22); they were A Hall, The Temple, The Palace, The Sea, Limbo and Hell. The sea was of course along the floor of the stage. Above the first Hall is shown a great circular Paradise, but (in an otherwise so realistic drawing) curiously ill-supported. In addition to these main 'houses' there are four minor houses or localities indicated by doors or turrets in a back wall running behind the main houses; in this way Nazareth, Jerusalem, a House of the Bishops, and the Golden Gate are all shown sandwiched between the greater units. In front of the Nazareth door is a little wattle enclosure with a gate. A total of some twelve *loca*.

At Mons, on the other hand, the story is almost unbelievable. One item of expense recorded by Cohen is a payment to (*see* p. 536 in his edition):

'sr Jehan Portier, prebstre, pour au command de messrs Eschevins et commis, avoir fait IIII^{xx} XVIII briefvés de grosse lettre des Lieux sur le Hourt . . .'

—and in case we should have any doubt just what these *briefvés* were for, we are also given an item (p. 565):

'Pour espingles, cedit jour, sur le Hourt, pour atachier pluiseurs briefvets . . .'

Thus we may, as I see it, understand that Portier was paid for having written no less than ninety-eight legends in large letters for the 'houses' on the stage, and that these were in fact legends (or location boards) to label the scenes, because we know also that they incurred the purchasing of *pins* in order to attach them.

Fig. 22. The Valenciennes stage

In his study of the play, Cohen is able to list sixty-seven different 'scenes' for the action, and even then he cannot have reached the full count, for some (not easy to recognize unless we approach the study of the script through some such introduction as *The Castle of Perseverance* affords us) he has not included at all in his list. As a single example we can quote how (*op. cit.* p. 19) Sathan sends Humain Lignaige to Orgeoul—which is exactly the same as if the Devil sent Mankind to Pride's house—and we then read the stage direction:

'ORGOEUL, estant en son lieu, accompaignie d'Ire comme de sa femme . . .'

which we read as:

'PRIDE, being in his *sedes* or 'house', accompanied by Wrath as his wife . . .'

This certainly seems to imply that at the Mons production Pride had a separate *lieu* (another word to add to our list, corresponding with *loca*) or 'seat', just as Covetyse had his separate scaffold in *The Castle of Perseverance*. But no such place for Pride is included in Cohen's list of 67 'décors'. Thus (supposing some others to be similarly implied in the script, in such a concealed way) we can, perhaps to our surprise, realize that the *Passion* of Mons may well have run to ninety-eight separate representations of 'scenes'. But we must remember that the performance lasted for eight days, and the legend on any particular 'house' might have been changed overnight to turn it into another scene for the morrow. As was possibly also done at Valenciennes.

Cohen's view is that the system of presentation at Mons was to build a long stage, probably similar to that at Valenciennes, against the façades of a number of houses on the east side of the *Grand Markiet* or main square of the town, on which were aligned these 'scenes', and to build a great grandstand for particular spectators against the façades of the houses on the west side to face it. The ordinary crowd stood on the ground between. The stage was called a *hourt* (cognate, maybe, with our word 'hoarding' and thus very closely related in meaning to 'scaffold'). But the grandstand for spectators was also (rather confusingly) called a *hourt* (or a *hault hourt*) though it had *ghalleries*, and in this way lands us into the same equivoce as the English system does, for with us 'scaffold' may mean either a 'stage' for actors, or a 'grandstand' for spectators.

The space of ground between the two scaffolds at Mons, that is between the stage and the grandstand, was called the *Parcque*. This word, then, would appear to be equivalent to the Latin *platea* and to our Place. And surely enough we find some of the actions directed to take place on *le Hourt*, and some *par le Parcq*, just as in England we sometimes find an actor directed to 'descend' from his scaffold and proceed with his scene 'in the Place'.

PAGEANT WAGGONS

Before we mention the third and last system, there is need for a short observation.

There are many points in the history of the theatre where information is lacking. Sometimes these gaps can be filled indirectly and by inference. One indirect way is to work by parallels with surviving ceremonies, taking it as a principle that a ceremony which shows ancient features today is *to some extent* parallel with a ceremony of ancient times. There are hazards in this method. So far in this book such hazards have had to be faced, and the reader has always been informed when the descriptions he has read were of survivals.

In the medieval period in Britain, however, there is sufficient evidence of actual methods of performance in Rounds for the above picture to be drawn up. What is curious about the position is that the popular (even to some extent the scholarly) idea of medieval shows takes very little account of these Rounds. Instead it turns to another system of presentation altogether, the wheeled pageant-waggon system, and suggests that this is the typical system. But as soon as the questions are asked: How did the pageant work? What was a pageant like?—it becomes clear that there are many gaps in the evidence at present. To answer is surprisingly difficult, and the fact has to be faced that, so far, no one has discovered how an English pageant show was managed in practice.

Much can be written about what seems likely, or might be possible; but all attempts up to now provoke doubt over this or that essential detail. And the fairest statement to make is: We know the pageant system was used for the York, Chester and Towneley cycles and possibly others, but how it was used we do not know.

This further observation is also relevant. A pageant is a stage-floor on wheels; what was there upon that floor? Was there (*a*) an elaborate built setting (such as the Ark or the Stable at Bethlehem) suitable for the performance of one scene only in a Mystery-cycle? Or was it (*b*) completely empty, save perhaps for a chair? Or was there (*c*) an organized background of some kind, of a more or less permanent nature, suitable for players' entrances and exits and offering a setting, with modifications, for any kind of scene?

If it was (*a*), then it was no use for any scene save the one for which it was equipped. If (*b*), then it was neither effective for an elaborate kind of scene such as a Guild presumably spent much money in maintaining, nor was it of any use for a general company of professional players—who have special needs of their stage as we shall show in the next chapter but one. And if (*c*), it might be admirable for general players, but would seem ill-fitted for specific presentation of one scene only in an elaborate and varied cycle of plays sponsored by Craft Guilds partly to exploit their crafts.

The conclusion would seem to be that the pageant-waggon, at any rate as used in the English Mystery cycles, was not a general stage suitable for any play, but a specific setting for one scene only, elaborately built and painted and mounted on wheels. If so, then what we have to visualize is something like the pageant cars shown in Van Alsloot's painting of *The Triumph of Isabella* in 1615 (Fig. 23).

Fig. 23. The possible appearance of a pageant waggon

Such a pageant is a specific mounted scene, not a general stage.

PROFESSIONALISM

A notable thing about this great festival form of theatre is that there are to be found many indications that while a presentation was being prepared, the organizers might send to a neighbouring town to seek the help of some individual who had been successful in an earlier presentation. Especially was this so of individuals successful in the technical departments or in the training of players.

Such invited persons might be paid for their services. One can hardly doubt that some of them would become specialists. If so the possibility of *professionalism* in theatre is now open.

The coming into being of professional theatre-men is a matter of importance, for with it the establishment of a tradition in technique becomes possible, where specialized developments in method are deliberately sought by men growing skilled in a craft.

The above men were specialist technicians; what now about the origin of the professional actor himself?

Clearly, little specialized skill of a professional nature can be acquired by players who live in a given town, work at their normal jobs during most of the year, and only gain practical experience of playing for the day or two of the annual festival. Thus, it is interesting to ask: When did the professional player come into the theatre?—by which is meant the man who earned his living as an actor and performed frequently enough to make acting his whole-time occupation, and for whom proficiency in technique would become a conscious goal.

It would seem that the professional player (as opposed to the professional technician, whether trainer, or arranger of the performance or the effects) might have come into being not among the performers of the great festival plays themselves, but among the more ancient entertainers, bards and minstrels, who are likely to have specialized to a professional degree at a very early date. Some of these men may well have reached a social position of some distinction, and even been able to employ one or two assistants for their acts. It is to such men we seem most justified in turning to discover the basis of the professional player's art. It is in such men that we seem likeliest to see the long development of experience in the handling of an audience.

There is a very urgent need to bring in, somewhere about this point in a history of the theatre, the professional actor. Too many historians in the past have ignored him. They have concentrated on the amateur character of the Mystery presentations, and have almost glorified the non-professional element. But in the background of all this there are the shadowy figures, already in existence, of the men who sought their living by playing to the public—the men and women, who first relinquished the normal pursuits of citizens or country-folk and became dedicated entertainers. Men and women of the class from which the Commedia dell' Arte was later to spring, and who were called in my grandmother's day by the strange titles of 'pros' or 'theäts'. Men and women who were, in the Elizabethan period, to suffer the stigma of being classified with Rogues and Vagabonds.

The inclusion of 'women' above is intentional. Though it is common knowledge that women's parts in the Elizabethan public playhouse were played by boys, and in many classic theatres of the world—in Kathakali, in Noh, in China, in Tibet, in European medieval theatre—men alone (in general) played all the parts, yet these were specialized theatres. The common players, whose early beginning is such a mystery, did in fact sometimes have women in their companies, and such women were alluded to as actors. Thus Miss Cicely Radford points out [53] how Robert Busse, abbot-elect of Tavistock, suffered in the year 1324 a series of accusations, one of which was that 'in the space of two months at Exeter he gave away trinkets to the value of £60' (at least £600 nowadays), 'the property of the house' (abbey) 'and gave them *ystrionibus maribus ac feminis ac meretricibus et personis aliis levibus ac inhonestis.* This Latin seems unavoidably to mean 'to stage-players, male and female, and to whores and to other loose and disreputable persons'.

EARLY NOH

Some care was taken above to notice the similarities that can be found between the performance of the Tibetan Festival Play in the round and the English and French medieval plays in their Rounds. It seems very likely that this particular similarity is not a chance thing, but that the phases in development in the theatre have a sort of similarity in whatever part of the world they occur. This appears to be true however great the superficial dissimilarities in detail or in period that are imposed by different lines and different rates of culture. We may go to the other side of the earth and find theatre under the cultures of the Far East growing up in ways that are not strange but entirely familiar. For instance, the famous Japanese Noh theatre grew up just like any other, and had its stage originally set in the centre of an open 'Place' thronged with audience and bounded by 'scaffolds' for the nobility (Fig. 24).

Indeed, it seems that instead of the theatres of the world offering a bewildering diversity, there is in reality a surprising similarity. It is necessary, however, first to avoid local and superficial differences, and all the minor and unimportant 'facts' that a history of dates and individuals is likely to confuse us with. Instead there must be some understanding of the natural phases of development that the theatre normally undergoes as a human art linked with the march of human civilization (such, for instance,

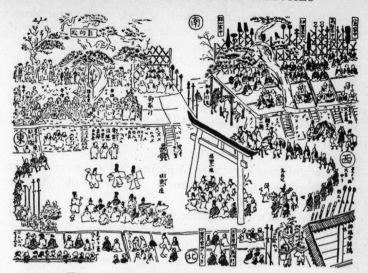

Fig. 24. A Japanese performance in a dry river-bed

as we have tried to outline here). Then it may very well be claimed that any reasonably good history of the theatre in any part of the world is a quite dependable and informative guide to understanding the history of the theatre in any other part of the world.

In one way indeed, study of this sort has a special advantage, for the local interests of one country may uncover much information about a particular aspect of the theatre that the different interests of another country have led it to overlook in its own history. Thus a new light may be found at home (as it so often may be) by looking through a stranger's eyes. This is no more than Brecht's theory of *Verfremdung* extended from theatrical practice to theatrical history.

A practical example of this is to be found in the curiously complicated and puzzling mixture of elements out of which the Noh performance arose in the 14th and 15th centuries. Among them are several musical forms—various styles of singing and dancing, including *Kusemai*. Much study is given by Japanese scholars to the task of unravelling the subtle differences between these many forms; and two drawings (reproduced in P. G. O'Neill's *Early Nō Drama*) show a *Shirabyōshi* with the same types of fan and drum as a *Kusemai* dancer. . . . What is immediately to the present

point, however, is that the English, in their study of the Elizabethan drama, constitutionally make much less of the place of
music in its origins than the Japanese do for their Noh. Yet there
were diverse elements in the Elizabethan origins (for instance, the
'jig' and the *Kyogen* may bear comparison), and there was in the
performance taken as a whole a musical component, with a
pictorial record comparable to the two drawings of *Kusemai* and
Shirabyōshi players—namely, the two prints showing Tarleton
and Kemp, both Elizabethan actors, and both with a hand drum
and pipe—and Kemp especially was famous for his Morris dance.
Such elements may have played a greater part in the make-up of
the Elizabethan performance than we commonly hold—as they
did in the creation of the Noh.

But apart from such details, the growth in the shape of the Noh
theatre itself runs through phases remarkably similar to those we
are discussing in this chapter. In the open-air 'subscription', or
public, performances (as opposed to performances in temples or
at the houses of nobles) as early as the 14th–15th centuries, raised
boxes were built 'which formed the perimeter of the auditorium'
(possibly in more than one storey) and 'served to accommodate
people of rank away from the crowd and to shut off the performance from the view of anyone outside the theatre' [48]. They
were built in a circle whose size averaged some 100 ft. in diameter,
and 'the stage itself was set in the middle of the arena'. The means
of access to this stage was interesting as foreshadowing the
famous method of entrance to the Noh stage today; it was by a
bridge. At an occasion in 1349, two bridges were used converging on the 'back' of the stage like a V from two dressing-rooms,
and apparently each built in a curving arch, like a hump-back
bridge. These were the forerunners of the *hashi-gakari* (*see* p. 206).
The two bridges was perhaps an unusual arrangement, and on
other occasions a simpler, single, asymmetrical 'bridge' was used.

An early theatre festival of this nature included between its
serious scenes certain comic (or human as against divine) interludes, called *kyogen*. A full performance might be made up of three
or five separate Noh plays, carefully chosen to give a developing
dramatic effect, and two or three *kyogen* interspersed between
them for relief. Maybe in much this way the group of human
plays which the Western World calls 'Interludes' arose.

So much for the theatre of this earlier period in Japan. Later, in the 16th century, the stage was to move to one side of the Place, as we shall see it do also in the Elizabethan public playhouse, and developments occurred to the *hashi-gakari*, which take us into the phase of the 'organized stage' that we have to discuss in the next chapter but one. But in the main, the solution of the Japanese professional player, when he had reached the stage of having to present great outdoor festivals of several days' duration to vast audiences on specific religious occasions in the year, was so similar to the solution of other players facing the same situation in other civilizations, that one learns of it with a feeling of friendliness and complete familiarity, and finds the minor differences of so much the greater interest because they are set in a frame that is completely sympathetic.

CAMBODIA AND THAILAND

As has already been shown, any one system in any one phase of theatre development may itself reach an elaborate height of complexity without transgressing the bounds of that phase. One form of the theatre in Cambodia well exemplifies this. So far as technical arrangement goes, it is in essence closely like the system of the Tibetan festival with which we began this chapter, but it takes the development of the central canopy to a very elaborate level indeed; and it also demonstrates another feature of growing theatre (which we shall have to consider in more detail at a later stage of this history), namely, the development of the aristocratic spectator's tent into a place of royal eminence for a king or prince to watch from.

The royal theatre, or princely theatre, forms another of those extreme chapters in the story of the theatre's fortunes, where the wheel turns to the exact opposite of Rogues and Vagabonds, to give one more example of the intrusions which the patient theatre has suffered—the intrusion of those who would turn it into a princely pleasure.

It is remarkable how, at almost all stages of theatre, performance before a High Person is as normal as performance before the Ordinary People. For all its potential vulgarity there is a surprising catholicity about theatre, and again and again we find, through Europe and Asia, that one of the high spots of courtly pleasure and demonstration is to select among the players and

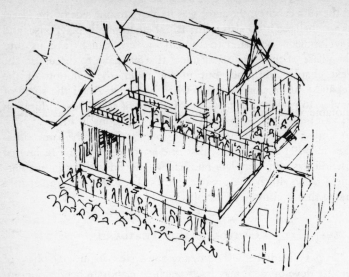

Fig. 25. A royal dancing-place in Cambodia; the roof of the main dancing hall and part of the galleries have been removed to show the interior. The king's seat is on the far side

sponsor a 'Command Performance'. Much of the players' revenue comes from the rewards of the rich who seek to outdo each other in the realm of spectacle, and many of the most ingenious theatre devices and richest verses came into being in answer to that particular demand. Here is, indeed, the great influence that we shall find supplanting the religious influence as we proceed into the next phase of theatre.

But the interest of this especial manifestation in Cambodia to the present study is to show how the primitive means of the Tibetan arrangement can be developed to royal richness merely by perfecting the elements, and without introducing any novelty in method or any significant change at all. In this way, but for the whim of history, might the Tibetan festival have developed.

The central 'theatre' is an oblong, columned hall, with roof but no walls (*see* Fig. 25), in essentials like the Tibetan awning. One end of the hall is closed by an actors' house, the other by a property store. The sides are open. Along one of these sides is a double pavilion, half of which is occupied by the King and his court; and half, beyond a partition, by the Queen and her ladies. In a narrow strip between the double pavilion and the 'stage' are the lesser notables of the court. Along the opposite side sit the body of the guests.

The roof above the oblong, central performing-area is like the Tibetan canopy in principle but its support is different in a notable way. Just as we are taught in the West that a proper dancer's costume should be free for movement, and find to our wonder how many traditional dancing costumes of the world are apparently exceedingly hampering to movement, so we are taught that a proper acting-area should be free and unobstructed— certainly unobstructed by such things as columns. But the Cambodian theatre-canopy is supported by columns, and not by few but by four deliberate rows of them, arranged to give two side aisles and a wider central aisle, down the length of the whole place. In each row there are no less than eleven columns—and thus a total of forty-four. The length of the roofed area is some 175 ft. and the width some 33 ft., and its floor is raised about 18 in. above the ground.

But the end-result of this forest of columns is not to obscure the performance. Rather it endows it with a peculiar flickering dignity, as of figures flitting between trees, and among these stately avenues the Royal Cambodian 'corps de ballet' weaves its stories.

The actors' house at the end gives by a door either side on to the acting-place, and between the doors is a stairway rising to first-floor level. At this level, a catwalk hung from the roof runs the length of the hall, which is used to aid effects of flying in the performances.

Some indication of the nature of these performances, of the richly stylized costumes, and of the subjects of the plays (all from Hindu religious epics), may be studied in Adhémard Leclère's *Le théâtre cambodgien* [41].

A similar relation between corps de ballet and royal patron exists in Thailand, which possesses a varied tradition of theatre, and where, beside the five categories of the Khon performances, there is a notable Nang, or shadow play.

In the Thai theatre a technical feature of some importance is that [15] 'stage hands who carry accessories on to the stage are

Fig. 26. A Greek theatre

required to adopt some kind of theatrical dress while performing their duties if the duties necessitate their appearance on the stage. The reason for this is obvious when one considers the fact that the stage is open on three sides instead of one and intrusion is much easier here than on the western stage. Neglect of this formality is regarded as discourtesy to the traditional Master of the Dance or Music.'

As in Kathakali, no performance is permitted to end in tragedy. If a leading character is killed, the play must go on till he is restored. Indeed resemblances to Kathakali are not uncommon and the Khon may be closely related with it in origin.

GREEK FESTIVAL THEATRE PROBLEMS

Just as we have for the Lucerne Mystery performance a detailed record of the scenic arrangements but no indication of the position of the audience, so for the Greek theatre we have the opposite—a wealth of detail about the place where the audience sat but no dependable record at all of how the scenic arrangements in fact worked.

Our uncertainty about the Greek theatre makes it difficult to classify it. On the one hand it is pretty certainly an example of the Great Religious Festivals and, in so far, belongs to the second phase with the other festivals in the present chapter. On the other hand it may be found that it has some claim to belong to the 'Organized Stage' phase in the next chapter but one. But unfortunately our knowledge about the background (or *skene* building) behind the actors is exceedingly conjectural; we do not even know that there was a stage at all (in the sense of a raised platform) as early as the great Classical period of the 5th century B.C.—or whether the actors performed on the same level as the chorus in its circular *orchestra* (Fig. 26). Sir Arthur Pickard-Cambridge [51] examines such problems with the greatest care. But he is forced to the conclusion that in regard both to the matter of a raised stage and to that of 'whether the temporary buildings included paraskenia or side wings projecting from each end of the background' we must accept the fact that 'archaeological evidence is wholly wanting for the fifth century'. For later periods some suggestions may be found; but for the period of the great tragedies and comedies that we know as Greek Drama, we have nothing. It seems then more important in the present review to state our ignorance than to discuss later information, and fall into the error of suggesting (as so many theatre histories do, probably quite unintentionally) that that information is any good at all in helping to reconstruct the show as it appeared in the 5th century.

As an example; there are some descriptions in Pollux and Vitruvius of the *periaktoi* (though even these are obscure) but 'there is no evidence at all that they were used in the Classical period' [51]. The *periaktoi* were those revolving, prism-shaped pieces so often referred to in theatre histories.

Again, the *ekkyklema* is another famous and oft-mentioned machine, yet 'the word itself is not found before the second century A.D.'. For all this (whatever the *ekkyklema* was—and we are far from certain) its earlier use is deducted from the writings of later commentators on the plays—but even here the nearest we dare go to certainty is the statement that it appears that 'Aristophanes of Byzantium (2nd cent. B.C.) believed that the ekkyklema was used to bring Phaedra out of the house' [51] in Euripides' *Hippolytus*. . . .

The same applies even to the actor's appearance. The same author tells us again at the very beginning of a chapter on Costume [50] that 'the general descriptions of the actor's appearance which have come down to us are all late, and their applicability to the

Fig. 27. A Greek mime stage

actors of the Classical period often very doubtful.' We learn
that the early masks were probably not noticeably grotesque, that
it is very unlikely that they had a megaphone effect, and that the
celebrated high *onkos*, or hair dressing, is not found in the 5th
century. And even regarding the *kothurnoi*, or thick-soled shoes,
'there is no evidence at all of the use of such thick soles until late
in the Hellenistic age' [50].

With these cautious restatements of the limitations of our
knowledge, it seems to me preferable to await a new development
in study before adding any general summary of the Greek classical
theatre to such a review as this.

The Roman theatre was based so closely upon the Greek that
our hesitance to attempt a detailed picture of presentation upon
the stage extends to it also. The evidence is confused; and we
await the further research of such specialists as W. Beare [10] who
are gradually penetrating the forgotten territory.

There is remarkably little that can be taken safely as genuine
pictorial evidence on the Classical Greek theatre; on the other
hand there is certain, very vivid, pictorial evidence of a form of
Greek stage that is not apparently connected with the classical
theatre—this is the small mime stage, of which several vases
bear curious details. Here our lack of information is reversed; we
do know something of the stage (Fig. 27), but we do not know
where it stood nor how the audience was placed with regard to it.
It is a genuine raised stage with a fairly elaborate background,
and as such it would certainly appear to belong to our Fourth

Phase—the 'Organized Stage' phase. But it is worth the including here because of its very early date, and because it is just faintly possible that it might have had a formative influence (perhaps through the mimes of Byzantium) on the booth stage to be discussed in the next chapter but one. It is also not outside the bounds of possibility that the forces that brought to being the shows performed by the Greek and Italian mimes on such stages may have been similar to the forces which produced the Interludes, which form the subject of our next phase.

Allardyce Nicoll has a stimulating picture of the mimes [46] but our knowledge is still too slight to discuss in any detail the use of this stage, and we can go little farther at present than offer our tentative reconstruction sketch to serve as a herald of things to come.

THIRD PHASE

The Rise of Professional Playing

THIRD PHASE

The Rise of Professional Playing

The Third Phase in the development of the theatre is a comparatively short phase but it had very long results. In it the foundations of modern plays were laid. It is a phase which sees the crystallization of professional players into small performing companies. During it their technique of presentation was to be notably extended.

The second phase of the theatre which we have just discussed was marked by great size—cyclic plays; universal conceptions; large casts; vast audiences; sweeping actions; cosmic subjects—and all taking place out of doors. But it must not be forgotten that running beside that phase, as beside all phases, there was the line of the minstrels or one-man entertainers. These would almost certainly maintain a kind of showmanship different from the whole intention of the great Religious Festival Plays. It would now seem that these men emerged from their solitude and began to band together.

For in the third phase, the appearance is practically the reverse of the second—very short plays; confinement to a single theme; small casts (or much doubling to spread many roles over few players); no more spectators than gather for supper; far greater emphasis on intimate dialogue; compact plots or even no more than a whimsical idea; considerable development in human characterization. And a great many of these performances take place now indoors. It is into this phase of the development of the theatre that what is called the English Interlude comes.

THE INTERLUDES

We have seen how, in the Tibetan theatre, certain short

episodes were sandwiched into the main play in a different language, and with a lighter and more homely note. They were particularly attractive to the ordinary people of the audience and offered some relief from the long seriousness of the religious epics.

Again, we saw that something of very much the same kind occurs in the classic Japanese Noh theatre, where what are called *kyogen*, being short popular comic scenes, are inserted as a relief among the graver plays which make up a full Noh programme.

It may be that the English Interlude had a similar origin. But no one has yet been able to put forward an explanation of why the word 'interlude' came to be used to name these plays in England. It has been suggested that an Interlude was a short play in the intervals of a longer play such as a Mystery play (perhaps on the analogy of the Italian *intermezzi*), but the typical Interlude as we have it is clearly not this, because from internal evidence of the scripts it is obvious that the place where the Interludes were played was quite a different sort of place from the place where the Mystery cycles were played. Also some Interludes, at any rate, were played at night.

Some authorities have suggested the Interlude signifies a short play between the courses of a banquet, as an 'interlude' in the feasting.

Again, since some printed Interludes bear on the title such a phrase as 'compiled in the manner of an interlude', it may be that our surviving Interludes are a form of play based on an earlier form, itself called 'interlude', but of which all examples are now lost. (Except that the fragment of the *Interludium de clerico et puella* of about 1300 may be a survivor of such a class; *see* [17].)

The English Interlude is an essential part of the development of the English theatre; it afforded the transition from the great tradition of the Mystery cycles to the complex poetry and characterization of the Elizabethan drama. It offered an especially suitable field for the study of people and humours. This does not imply that there was no deep characterization in the Mystery and Morality plays, but there such a thing was present chiefly to serve another purpose—in the Mystery plays, that of telling the Bible story; in the Moralities, that of expounding a philosophical scheme of man's life. With the Interludes, the canvas is so reduced that the scale of a Bible story, or a philosophy of the life of the times, cannot be attempted. A single episode, or a single idea, is all that can be compassed. On the other hand, in the Interludes, every appealing or convincing human touch in the portrayal of character offers yet another means for enlisting the sympathy of the audience, or for amusing them while the germ of the discourse is implanted in them.

It would appear from our survey that it is not inconceivable that the experts are wrong in tracing back the origin of modern playwriting to the Medieval Festival plays (and ultimately to the *Quem quaeritis* episode in part of the Easter church service). It seems more likely that it rose out of the Interludes which came between those plays, or which ran beside them, or which sprang up with the professional players as these plays fell into desuetude —Interludes which, at any rate in some parts of the world, were in the vernacular when often the main Festival dramas were in a recondite language.

The English Interlude writers took full advantage of the human possibilities of the new form. For instance, the sharpness of the conflict between the adolescent sexes is most understandingly portrayed in Redford's *Wit and Science* (which is indeed a fascinating and deeply observed young-love story). The spiritual uncertainty of a fair-minded young man, spurred on by a shrewd and ambitious mother with good intentions, to a course which can be read as of questionable honesty, is most delicately studied in the anonymous *Jacob and Esau*. And towards the end of the period, the double thinking that cannot be avoided by a character placed in Orestes' dilemma of deciding between a 'just' vengeance and maternal affection, is capable of as interesting a staging in the Interlude *Horestes* by John Pickering, as is the similar problem in *Hamlet*.

These essays in the vivid representation of the play of human character are isolated in the Interludes and free to be developed without the competition of a vast theme, so as to offer their own absorbing theatrical interest.

PLAYING IN HALLS

Another feature in which the Interludes lead the way from the Medieval performance to the Elizabethan performance, lies in the technique of their presentation; and this we must examine in some detail.

The Interludes introduce a new idea into theatre practice in

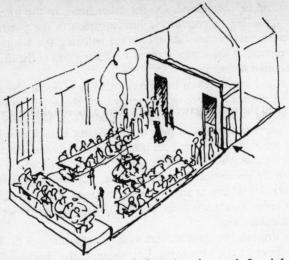

Fig. 28. A Tudor Hall showing the beginning of an early Interlude played before the Screen

that both in their lines of dialogue and in their marginal directions they make reference to 'doors'. Where could any door exist in the Medieval Place-and-scaffold system? Or in the system of the pageant-waggon? Clearly we are on the threshold of a fresh phase of theatre here. What were these doors? Where were the Interludes played? If they were indoors, what was the building?

This raises another of the problems to which we have found no solution. There may have been many types of interior in which the interlude players performed. But one building in particular is indicated—the Great Hall of a gentleman's house, after dinner, at night.

The situation here is something that we can with some reason reconstruct. It can be resumed in Fig. 28.

The master of the house sits, with his family and special guests, on the dais across the nearer end of the Hall. At one end of the dais may be an oriel window, at the other the door of entrance. The remainder of the household, with retainers and so forth, are seated at two long tables down the sides of the Hall. In the centre between them is the hearthplace. At the far end is a particular scene of bustle caused by the passing to and from the kitchen of the serving men carrying the material of the banquet.

This end of a Great Hall or Houseplace is constructed in a particular, traditional manner; at the end of either of the side walls are two doors, facing each other across the Hall; both lead to the open air. One is the 'front door' or entrance to the building from the outer world; the other is a sort of back door leading into the courtyard behind the house, and maybe to the orchard. These doors and the space between them form a thoroughfare across the building, called the 'entry'.

Beyond the entry lies the kitchen or buttery, where the meal is cooked. The kitchen is partitioned-off from the Hall by a wall, and approached by one or more doors in this wall which are reached by crossing the entry.

Now, there are obviously two disadvantages to comfort in the arrangement described so far. The first is that one could see from the main table down the Hall and directly into the kitchen. The other is that anyone opening either entry door will allow the outside air, with wind and rain in their seasons, into the Hall itself. Therefore a special feature is installed—a *Screen* across the Hall in front of the kitchen wall and at the nearer side of the entry (so transforming the entry into a sort of passage). Access to the kitchen is obtained by going round the screen at either end, and crossing the entry to the door of the kitchen (*see* Fig. 28).

Thus it is that what the spectator sees, looking down the Hall from the dais end, is neither a glimpse into the kitchens nor an open passage across the Hall, but simply a central wooden screen with spaces at either end for access to the entry and the kitchen beyond.

We have now to ask what these two 'end spaces' flanking the screen were called. Were they called doors? It is possible that they were, irrespective of whether they were or were not closable by some sort of leaf or curtain. The word 'door' was equally applicable in the Middle Ages to what we should call the doorway and to what we should call the door itself. Thus it is possible that these two spaces at the ends of the Screen were called 'doors'.

However that may be, it was these two openings which afforded entrance for players to come into the Hall at their cue in a performance.

To resume, now, our picture of the meal; it is through the openings in this Screen that there pass the streams of serving-men to and fro. By them also, there gather standing retainers in clusters and the general hangers-about. The passage behind the Screen may be roofed in such a way as to offer an upper gallery across this end of the Hall where musicians might possibly play. The fire is burning in the hearth; the candles illuminate the dimness of the Hall; the plates are pushed back; the confusion of clearing is going on. And then there is an interruption. (What follows now is taken from the script of an early Interlude called *Fulgens and Lucrece* [42].)

FULGENS AND LUCRECE

A man enters, in appearance much like any one of the company assembled. There is no special preparation; no stage; no curtain; no scenery. People are still clustering near the doors and talking. In this particular situation the man speaks. He will have to enter pointedly and speak commandingly to arrest attention.

He exclaims:

> *Ah! for God's will——*

and, if he knows his job, there will be sudden silence as all turn to the newcomer. He probably moves in a little farther to take a position; he comments on the silence and goes on, and the gist of his speech is:

> *What mean ye, sirs, to stand so still? . . .*
> *Have not ye eaten . . .*
> *And paid nothing therefore? . . .*
> *Ye are welcome each one*
> *Unto this house . . .*
> *But I marvel . . .*
> *That . . .*
> *There are no words among this press . . .*
> *But . . .*
> *Here ye stand musing*
> *—Whereabout I cannot tell:*

Then he has the effrontery to appeal directly to a member of the audience standing near and, not knowing his name, says:

> *Tell me, What-cal't, is it not so?*
> *I am sure here shall be somewhat ado,*
> *And I wis I will know it ere I go . . .*

At this point a second newcomer, called B, very notably dressed, enters—possibly from the other Screen door—hears the question and answers it with:

> B   *Nay nay . . . man, I undertake . . .*
>   *Thou mayest tarry . . .*
>   *Among other men and see the play . . .*
> A   *. . . I pray you tell me that again,*
>   *Shall here be a play?*
> B   *Yea, for certain.*
> A   *. . . I am glad . . .*
>   *I trow your own self be one*
>   *Of them that shall play.*
> B   *Nay, I am none;*
> A   *. . . I thought verily by your apparel*
>   *That ye had been a player! . . .*
>   *There is so much nice array*
>   *Amongst these gallants nowaday,*
>   *That a man shall not lightly*
>   *Know a player from another man.*

It is a fresh and audacious beginning. Two actors enter pretending they are audience but they assume a fine and familiar arrogance towards the spectators, and one affects to mistake the other for an actor because of his bright clothes!

Here it is worth noting that (besides a chance of satire on fashions) we have a good example of particular and designed use being made by the player of that one technical adjunct to himself which is always available on such an occasion—the costume in which he appears, and which so especially serves to establish the character of his role, and to lift him from a person to the player of a person. So fundamental is this conception of costume to theatre that it is almost a fundamental of art—a player must not be a man (for that is in fact what he is, and would be tantamount to naturalism); he must *seem to be* a man. Which is the difference between fact and art.

To return to our two players in the Hall. A supposes that B can tell him something of what the play is about. B has indeed been told and he recounts the plot at length, in fact for fifty lines of verse. Lucrece, the daughter of the Roman senator, Fulgens, had two suitors for her hand—a nobleman, Publius Cornelius, and a virtuous commoner, Gaius Flaminius. She decided to wed him that could be shown the more *truly* noble. The decision was referred to the senate, who preferred Gaius Flaminius despite his low birth.

At once A exclaims that this will not do at all, and the end must be changed. B claims that the play will prove the justice of the verdict. A says he hopes indeed it will or he will see they are made sorry they began it. But, he says, A and B themselves are not really concerned since neither is virtuous or gentle, and thus:

> . . . *in this matter we have nought to do.*
> B *We! no, God wot, nothing at all,*
> *Save that we come to see this play,*
> *As far as we may by the leave of the marshal.*

Thus we are informed that such proceedings were under the charge of a marshal who controlled right of entry of the audience. After some further dialogue, B interrupts with the exciting words (after all this build-up!):

> *Peace, no more words, for now they come,*
> *The players been even here at hand.*
> A *. . . I pray you tell me where I shall stand.*
> B *Marry, stand even here by me . . .*
> *Give room there, sirs, for God avow!*
> *They would come in if they might for you.*

Thus we have a movement of bustle to add to the mounting expectation, a collision with genuine bystanders and a summary ordering of them back out of the way to clear the Screen doors which is a prelude for an actor's entrance as old as the Mummers' Play itself. Then A asks:

> *Who is he that now cometh in?*
> B *Marry, it is Fulgens the senator.*
> A *Yea, is? What, the father of the foresaid virgin?*
> B *Yea, for sooth . . .*
> A *And where is fair daughter Lucrece?*
> B *She cometh anon, I say; hold thy peace!*

—and Fulgens, the father, now begins to speak. Surely, now, this is as good an introduction as a play might wish to have! And equally surely it is an introduction by an alert and amusing mind, by no means unacquainted with the task of handling an audience. So, the situation is here skilfully prepared; the actor performing Fulgens can now make his entrance to the Hall. Presumably the space before the Screen is now relatively clear, and possibly some further part of the floor between the Screen and the hearthplace also. So far as we have indication, no other preparation of any sort is made; the Hall is normal (save for the expectancy raised by this scene of build-up from A and B), and into this scene—a quite real scene of life, not a fictitious scene—walks Fulgens in his costume.

The play then proceeds to be acted out on the floor of the Hall, in the Place, with no particular technical speciality that calls for our attention. But in later Interludes, as the style develops, there are experiments and advances in technique that are of great significance.

DEVELOPMENT OF THE INTERLUDES

To run very briefly through the period: In John Skelton's *Magnyfycence* (about 1516) several directions in the script mention 'the place' in the sense of the old Place of the Rounds, but an exclamation in the dialogue to one of the characters (line 1725) has—'Hence . . . out of the doors fast!' So the play was indoors, and possibly on some occasions in a Hall.

In John Heywood's *Love* (about 1525), a delightful and amusingly subtle wrangle about the various forms of love, there is a direction concerning a character who 'cometh in ronnynge sodenly aboute the place——' but we have the exceedingly interesting addition immediately following in the next words '—among the audience.' Thus we know that, in Interludes, the Place was not a stage but somewhere where both actors and audience could be mingled together—namely, the floor of the Hall.

In Heywood's *Weather* (about 1527), a character (the 'Vice' who opens the play), in much the same situation as described above in *Fulgens*, cries to the spectators: 'Frendes . . . let me go by ye; thynke ye I may stande thrustyng amonge you there . . . ?' Thus we have further evidence of the closeness of actor and audience. But in this play we have something more; we have a human and truly jovial Jupiter who has a *throne*. Not only has he a throne, but there is a very curious direction informing that at a given point 'the god hath a song played in his throne'. The last three words are strange. The suggestion could be that the 'throne' is a canopied and perhaps curtained seat, extending its ambit to a confine large enough to admit a minstrel playing at the foot of the throne. A convenient position for such a scenic object would be centre-back, between the two doors in the Screen, exactly as we see such a thing placed in Plate 6.

If this might be by any means a true suggestion then the following puzzle could be solved: For the 'Vice' becomes Jupiter's door-man, and when the suitors come to intercede with Jupiter about the weather the Vice allows (at his discretion) some of them access to the God, and these presumably go up to the throne. But some he forbids and decides to settle their problem himself. After which he dismisses them. But what did Jupiter do during these pieces of cheek? It would seem that he must have heard nothing of them—and *be seen* to have heard nothing of them (or else he loses his godhead). Was then Jupiter's curtain drawn during such scenes?

In *Calisto and Meliboea* (roughly contemporary—about 1527) another slight step forward is suggested. Calisto says: 'To pas the tyme now wyll I walk up and down within myne orchard . . . Thus farewell my lordys for a whyle I wyll go.' (l.312). Then he leaves (presumably by a door), having first *established the dramatic fiction* that there is an orchard outside. (Or is this an example of early realism?) These doors are increasing in their theatrical significance under the growing skill of the new playwrights writing for such conditions, and learning how they can exploit them to create a new idea of playwriting.

(I must say that it seems to me that these playwrights were acting in the same way with regard to an emerging new conven-tion as Ionesco or N. F. Simpson or John Arden—and others—are acting today in what may turn out to be a similar problem in the psychological field to what this was in the physical field . . .)

In *Godly Queen Hester* (probably about the same date, 1527) we have several striking new problems.

The first is that the directions to the players (and this applies to many of the Interludes) are curiously sparse and curiously general. An instance of the one is that very frequently entrances and exits are not marked at all. An instance of the other is in the marginal note during a scene between 'King Assuerus' and his court, which reads—'One of ye gětyllmě [gentlemen] must answer, whyche you will.' This leaving-it-to-the-player is apparently slovenly craftsmanship. But when one reflects on the circumstances of these early Interludes, some reasons for such apparent casualness begin to manifest themselves. Chief of these is that it is obviously no good being meticulously clear in directions to the players if you are not, as a playwright, meticulously clear about where the play is going to be acted. It may be correct to suppose that many performance would be in Halls, but even if this were true, there is no certainty that all householders would have Screens in their Halls, or that, if they did, all the Screens would be of exactly the same pattern. And beyond this again, the players might often have to perform in other places than Halls. Thus, too specific a script would be a burden; something had to be left to the moment of performance. Only main generalities in the matter of directions would be suitable to the conditions; much had to be left to the players' improvisation. The reason being that the conditions of playing had not yet become regularized.

A second problem is particularly interesting. After the King has given directions to his court (including his chancellor, named Aman) to find a suitable Queen, the King turns away to leave them to their business. Then we get the remarkable marginal note (l.140)—'Here the Kynge entryth the trauers & Aman goeth out.' Now, 'Aman goeth out' is clear and simple; we suppose he merely exits as best he may—presumably by a door in the Screen, if there is one. But the King is specifically given something different to do; he does not *go out*, but *enters the traverse*. What is a traverse?

Let us again be frank: We do not know. But it does seem that, as the Interludes develop, certain special features gradually come to be imported, the purpose of which is to make the understanding of the action somewhat easier for an audience, and their experience as spectators somewhat more alive and varied—and to make the scope of the playwright wider. Thus, some sort of 'traverse' is brought in, of a nature such that a person 'entering' it would be doing something different from simply 'going out'. One is reminded of a draw-curtain on a scaffold. Did the King retire to a 'tent' or 'house' representative of his palace and consisting of some sort of curtainable space in front of the Screen?

Hester and Aman have a scene of meeting 'in ye place'. She is picked to be a candidate for the Queenship. Then 'thei go to the Kynge' and at once Aman addresses him with no direction to suggest that the King *entered*. Thus, the idea that he had not left the scene but merely retired temporarily behind the traverse, is strengthened.

The play goes on, and the King chooses Hester for his Queen. He makes Aman lieutenant of Israel and (very characteristically) invests him then and there with robes and wand. This done, the action comes to a pause and the King heralds it with a speech entirely reminiscent of Calisto's in *Calisto and Meliboea* (but with a most engaging final phrase!) He says (l.634):

> For a season we wyll to our solace
> Into our orcharde or some other place.

Where does he go? By a most unusually lucky chance we are not in this instance left in any doubt at all. He does not enter any door but:

> Here the Kynge entreth the trauerse and Hardy Dardy
> entreth the place.

Notice the word 'entreth' is used *both* to describe the King's *going out*, and Hardy Dardy, the Vice's, *coming in*. The King goes out by entering the traverse; Hardy Dardy comes in by entering the Place.

Much of the plot now ensues. But at length we come to the climax of the play where Hester entertains the traitorous Aman to a meal in the presence of the King to unmask him. Now we have a striking direction:

> Here must be prepared a banket in ye place.

At this banquet she unmasks Aman, who is haled off to hanging, while Hester rehabilitates the Jewish people under Assuerus.

Already it may be seen that in the space of a couple of decades (since *Fulgens and Lucrece*), a forging ahead in the construction of dramatic presentation and in the exploiting of the seemingly unpromising means available to Interlude players, has taken place, and so markedly that one looks back on the phases of primitive ritual and religious festival performances as things almost of another class. Here manifestly are the seeds of a new age of theatre—the age of pure playwriting—beginning to shoot green above the earth.

Interlude follows Interlude, and space forbids our considering anything like a fair selection of the seventy-odd that remain to us. But six more out of the total have invaluable items.

John Redford's *Wit and Science*, about 1540, we have already mentioned as a delightful play. It has been called a dull morality; this is nonsense. Just because a young man is named 'Wit', and the young woman he is wooing is named 'Science', and because the action indicates that 'Wit' cannot win 'Science' if he misuses 'Honest Recreation' and falls into the lap of 'Idleness'—and so forth—it does not follow that the playwright cannot devise a very delicate, very sensitive and wholly intriguing love-affair. Redford does this, and produces first-rate entertainment with all the highlights, such as fights and low-comedy, as well—and he does not fail in shrewd psychology of character.

But his technical exploitation of the means available to him as regards staging is especially interesting to us at one point: Here, the situation is that Instruction is offering the young man, Wit, a second chance to fight the demon, Tediousness; he instructs Wit to

> . . . *turne on your right hand*
> *Up that mount before ye shall see stand* . . .

The problem is; to what does 'that mount' refer? One might suppose that it is something imagined off-stage. But this is what follows: Wit fights Tediousness, manoeuvres him off and kills him off-stage, then comes in again and 'bryngth in the hed vpon his swoorde'. At which, Confidence informs him that the young lady, Science, is glad and *has watched all this* from

> *vpon yonder mowntayne on hye.*

Wit sends Confidence off with the head as a present for the lady, in the approved fashion of heroes, but immediately Confidence comes running back again, saying that Science is in fact about to enter in person. Whereupon a pleasant piece of group-singing takes place (which gives her the time to reach the entrance) and leads on to the closing passage of the play, which is introduced by Wit, 'standing in the myddell of the place', as a hero should for a peroration.

This mountain seems to pose that particular problem, which we shall meet again, of action 'above'. Was the young lady, Science, really raised up for this scene? If she were, then upon what was she raised? A specially-built elevation standing there from the beginning of the play for that purpose? Possibly. But another solution is of course to be considered—especially as the lady seems to be given some short interval to descend out of sight of the audience before she makes her eventual entrance to Wit—namely that she surveyed the scene from the gallery above the screen.

So far we have no evidence either way—a built scenic 'mount' or the use of an existing gallery are both consistent. Maybe we shall never be able to be certain of more than one thing in all this—that is that the consciousness of a possible technique in play-making is beginning to grow among the new, coming playwrights.

The anonymous *Jacob and Esau*, of about 1550, offers still further evidence of growing technique.

To begin is a note after the list of players, telling us that they 'are to be considered to be Hebrews, and so should be apparelled with attire.' Thus we find that the common notion that early players had no sense of costume is disproved as far back as the mid-16th century.

But the Hebrew element in the plot brings another technicality; the characters can in the circumstances make reference quite naturally to *tents*. We now have the very curious uncertainty whether any given reference to a 'tent' (and there are several) is a reference to a regular property-piece, or is a 'dramatic fiction' referring to no more than a door in the Screen. Thus, we have the direction, 'Esau, entering into Jacob's tent, shaketh Ragan off' (Ragan is Esau's servant).

These frequent references to 'tents' come both in the directions and in the lines of the dialogue, but none of them is such as to enable us to decide whether the tents were real tents or not. Now, is there any reason for this? It is not at all impossible that the growing awareness of the playwrights is leading them to frame their scripts so that they could be played equally effectively in plain, small Halls with no facilities for elaboration, or in larger and princely Halls where display would be both possible and looked for. At any rate, it would seem from a careful study of the script of *Jacob and Esau* that this is exactly what the ingenious and anonymous author has in fact done.

Such ingenuity is quite on a par with the general quality of the play. Throughout, it is marked by an alert mind, well awake to the oddities of a psychological situation, capable of a crisp, pregnant line wherever needed, and at all points quick to see how the peculiar circumstances of such early presentations could be turned to dramatic account.

Thus, to the apparent use of a raised place or the gallery above the Screen, we add a quickness to see the possibilities of a double play on 'tents', and a masterly command of the available means for expounding a plot.

There follow now in the matter of time such great and varied examples in this form as the dignified and scurrilous *Ane Satyre of the Thrie Estaits* by Sir David Lindsay, about 1552 (expanded from a lost 1540 version); *Respublica*, a vivid play about political thugs of 1553; *Gammer Gurton's Needle*; *Ralph Roister Doister*; and *Jack Juggler*, all of about the same year.

With J. Phillips' *Patient Grissell*, about 1559, all the elements of the rising style are mixed with a technical competence to plan dramatic entertainment that must have contributed much to the founding of the great Elizabethan school of playwriting soon to come to the full. But there is one small item in this play, of particular importance. After Grissell's temporary disgrace, one of the courtiers decides to visit her at her father's humble dwelling. He uses a celebrated theatrical convention for taking a journey—that is, he walks to and fro. But the direction contains a special word; it tells him to

> *Go once or twice about the staige* . . .

Thus we meet unmistakably, if for the first time in this present story, the vital word *stage*. Can it be used merely to refer to part of the floor of the Place? Or does it essentially imply a raised platform? If the latter, then we are already on the threshold of the acceptance of a new technique.

In the anonymous *Apius and Virginia* of about 1560, we have a definite statement on this question in the direction at l.854:

> *Here let Virginius go about the scaffold.*

This *must* be a raised stage.

In John Pickering's *Horestes* of about 1567 (only nine years before Burbage built his Theatre), we have a major orchestration of all these things.

To begin, the playwright has taken the old Interlude form and used all its familiar tricks to present a profound psychological conflict, that of Horestes torn between affection for his mother and the knowledge that she is guilty of an act punishable by death.

There are references to Place in the old technique, but now growing less specific in implication, as when Horestes cries:

> *Idumeus, that worthy kinge, doth com into this place.*

There are undoubted references to a stage as in the direction:

> *Horestis entrith with his bande and marcheth about the stage.*

But there is far more. There is indisputable evidence of the use either of the Screen-gallery as a castle wall, or of the existence of a traverse-curtain to represent a wall, over the top of which an actor can speak, for Horestes tells his soldiers he will storm 'yonder citie' (the city where Clytemnestra is); then follows the direction:

> *Let ye trumpet go towarde the Citie and blowe.*

What, now, does Clytemnestra do? All is carefully directed:

> *Let ye trumpet leaue soundyng and let ye Harrauld speake and Clytemnestra speake ouer ye wal.*

Here would be all we needed to establish the fact that a new and nearly perfected system of devising plays was on the point of coming into being; yet we cannot resist one further quotation. This is a stage direction illustrating that curious form of address to the players in the second person, that sometimes enlivens the scripts of Interludes; namely,

> *Go & make your liuely battel & let it be longe, eare you can win ye Citiei and when you haue won it, let Horestes bringe out his mother*

by the armes, & let ye droum sease playing & the trumpet also, when she is taken; let her knele downe and speake.

And the play goes sweeping on to as bold and wide a solution as ever marked the great mood of historical dramas in the Elizabethan age.

Our own immediate problem, however, is—What is this 'scaffold' or 'stage'? As with the 'traverse', we do not know. One of our main causes of uncertainty at present is—If a raised stage were in fact built in the Hall against the Screen, what was done about the 'dores' in the Screen? Were they suppressed and blocked by the stage? Surely not, for directions still refer to their use.

The unavoidable alternative is that the early stage was only a small platform (perhaps what is called a 'foot pace') and was built between the two doors (where possible), leaving them clear for direct entrance into the Place at floor level, as in the old days. The stage would then be reached from the Place by 'going up' some specially placed step or flight of steps.

In fact we have some slight indication that this was so, for in Thomas Garter's play of *The most virtuous and godly Susanna* (written about 1569) there is a specific direction in the court scene that a character 'goeth up'. Up to what? Presumably up on to a dais. Later in the same scene we have:

> *Here the Cryer goeth vp agayne, and maketh an O yes.*

Furthermore, early in the same play is the very curious line from Voluptas:

> *Come in Mayster Sensualitas I pray thee,*
> *Reche me thy hande and I will help thee. . . .*

There is, it seems, nothing in the scene whatever to justify Voluptas's offer of a hand to help Sensualitas to 'come in' save that Sensualitas is fat and has to climb steps.

So then, until further and more specific evidence is found which will point to some other conclusion, we may roughly diagrammatize the arrangement in a Hall for later Interludes as being something like that shown in Fig. 29.

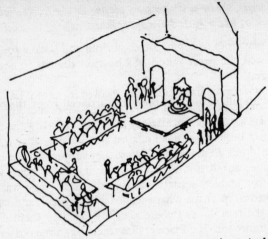

Fig. 29. A Tudor Hall with a small stage and a central curtained throne for later Interludes

Court Mummings and Maskings

Parallel with the English Interlude there ran another story. Right back to the 14th century and farther still there had been ceremonious ridings of gentlemen in disguise to pay visits of courtesy on an occasion such as a prince's birthday, and ending in a bestowal of gifts or the entertainment of a game of dice. Glynne Wickham [77] has made a detailed study of tournaments and Mummings and their relation to early English theatre.

These private and courtly occasions of entertainment themselves grew in technique; for instance, in 1501 (not far from the year of *Fulgens and Lucrece*) there was a wedding feast at Westminster Hall where a castle on wheels was drawn into the banquet, bringing eight ladies inside it [22]. It was followed by a second car like a ship, bringing two messengers to ask the ladies of the castle to capitulate to the 'Knights of the Mount'. Upon their refusing, a third car came in bearing the Mount itself with eight knights who descended, set themselves in array, and stormed the castle. After which there was dancing. Many sorts of device such as this decorated court life, both in the banquet hall, in the streets during processions, and on the tournament field.

From 1511 onwards we have vivid records of the entertainments, mostly called 'pageants', under Henry VIII [14]. For example; at a joust at Blackfriars a 'forest' on a car, 26 ft. long, 16 ft. wide and 9 ft. high, was drawn by a property 'lion' and 'antelope'. In the evening of that day a pageant was drawn into the hall at Whitehall for an entertainment called *The Golden Arbour in the Orchard of Pleasure*, wherein the arbour was constructed with pillars and wreathed with artificial vines, the orchard was planted with fruit trees of various sorts, and the whole device carried 30 people, moved, turned about, and broke the floor.

For Christmas 1511 there was a pageant of *The Dangerous Fortress*, including a castle with battlement and gates, and associated in some way with a *travas* or (?) traverse curtain. The next year saw a fountain drawn by a horse. In 1513, at Greenwich, was *The Rich Mount*, drawn in by 'wild men' with six lords upon it, and which opened to disclose six ladies within. Two years later at Greenwich comes what may be a variation—a Pavilion upon a 'pas', which may indicate a 'pace' or 'footpace', or low rostrum; it had four 'brickwork' towers at the corners with a lord in each.

The pageant suggested (but perhaps not carried out) for May of 1515 was to be 36 ft. long, 28ft. wide and 10 ft. high, with ten towers, and designed to be 'borne by men'. At Eltham in 1516 a castle of timber was prepared *in* the Hall—and thus presumably was not wheeled or carried in. But in 1516–17 at Greenwich, *The Garden of Esperance*—a railed garden with a floral pillar in the midst—was brought in and out. And for 1522 *The Château Vert* had a cloth which was strained on a floor beforehand to be painted (as continental scenepainters paint backcloths today), and there are references to 'spattering' and painting with stars—but whether for scenery or for the decoration of the hall is not certain. Though we have to remember that before the days of 'scenic illusion' there was no division made between scene and auditorium, and thus no particular distinction between the decoration of the stage and that of the hall itself.

To move on; in 1572 (a couple of years after the Interlude of *Susanna*) there took place at Whitehall an entertainment of this kind which, beside the costumes and the allegorical figures and the dancing (and a prison set up in the hall called 'Extreme Oblyvion'), had speeches specially prepared for the characters in verse. It was thus well on the way to being a complete piece of theatre. This show extended over three nights, with a Castle (called the 'Court of Plenty') being built for the second night, and an orchard (with golden apples) being drawn in for the third. A full contemporary description is quoted by H. R. Evans [22].

Such occasions as these were in no sense public entertainments. They were private and ceremonial amusements; most of them were performed by the courtiers themselves.

EARLY PROFESSIONAL PLAYS AT COURT

But professional players also came to court to give entertainments, just as they went to any other gentleman's Hall. And when they came special arrangements were made to provide a 'setting' for them. These arrangements were in the hands of a court official known as the Master of the Revels—therefore they were not, apparently (and this is an interesting point), in the hands of the players.

This is worth comment. A company of professional players, when it had the prospect of taking a play-production to court, would clearly need to rehearse it first. Indeed, one of the reasons given against enforcing the ban on public players in London was not only 'to relieve the poor players', but also 'to encourage their being in readiness with convenient matters for her highness's solace . . .' Again, it was held 'that without frequent exercise of such plays as were to be presented before her majesty her servants could not conveniently satisfy her recreation and their own duty' [49].

Thus it would seem that, as we should of course suppose, the players perfected a presentation before they brought it to court. But it seems also that when they got to court they were faced with a new 'setting'! Now, did this mean that their production had to be revised? Or had they already used a kind of 'setting' of which the court setting would be some replica—though a more elaborate one? This is to ask (though not answer) the question: Can the ordinary professional performances be supposed to have been staged in a way similar to, if more economical than, those at court? If so, court procedure would be a guide to the ordinary procedure before the public.

These things are at present mysteries to us. But one question to which we can supply a partial answer is: Of what sort were these settings for plays at court? And the partial answer is interesting, though how much it reflects the stage technique of performances outside court we do not know.

We draw the material for it again from financial accounts, those left us by the Master of the Office of Revels of Queen Elizabeth I [20]. The subjects covered in the accounts are well summarized in the opening lines of the 1571 expenditures; they are—for the apparelling, disguising, furnishing, fitting, garnishing and orderly setting forth of men, women and children in sundry tragedies, plays, masques and sports, with their apt houses of painted canvas and properties incident, such as might most lively express the effect of the histories played . . .

We have here the use of the phrase 'orderly setting forth' to cover the business of the visual presentation of a show; we have indication that women performed in some of the shows (but no indication which); we see that the shows included plays on the one hand and masques on the other—masques being presumably the descendants of the court's own private tradition of Mummings and Disguisings, and plays presumably deriving from the Interludes and being performances by boys or by invited professional companies of players. And finally we have the direct evidence that in this setting-forth *apt houses of painted canvas* were used. What were these 'apt houses' like? And where did they stand for the performance?

What they were like we can partly deduce from the details of the accounts. Where and how they stood in a show is more difficult to decide.

We find that the painters and their assistants worked on the canvas that made these houses, and did so both in the Office itself (which was at the old hospital of St. John of Jerusalem near Blackfriars), and also when they were brought to court (wherever that might be at the time—Hampton Court, Reading, Canterbury or elsewhere).

We learn that the canvas was 'framed, fashioned and painted'. The meaning of 'framed' is clear enough; today we frame-up the canvas to make the 'flats' with which a scene is put together. 'Fashioned' is more difficult to interpret, but it would seem to refer to the final shaping of a complete 'house'.

We find that the frames were made up of 'spars'—presumably just as ours today are made of 'battens'. There are entries for payments to men going to court to 'set up' frames, and numerous references to the carriage or transport of the frames. Once there, the separate frames appear to have been assembled and joined by long 'vyces'—possibly as we might use cramps.

The frames seem to have been capable of various shapes, for we have an entry for timber for a rock and 'for other frames' for players' houses. This suggests that a rock might be generically classified as a 'house', and that the frames might be of quite irregular shapes if they were used in the framework of a rock—which is again a perfectly familiar idea to a stage carpenter today.

Several of the details of expenditure relate to items in plays by the Earl of Leicester's Men as far back as 1572-3—that is when they were performing as a travelling company three years before their leader, James Burbage, built The Theatre.

But running all the time beside the items for players' use are items which more likely refer to masques. One of these, it would seem, is the payment to John Ross (gent.) for making a chariot 14 ft. long and 8 ft. wide with a Rock upon it and a fountain therein. And it is interesting to see that no less an artist than Hans Ewart made the design and the colour-sketch for it. Related to this item is a Castle for Lady Peace to sit and be brought in before Her Majesty.

Among the painters of these works, by far the outstanding name is William Lyzarde, whose technique is revealed to us in great detail by several long lists of colours and size and general materials such as paper for *papier mâché* work [63]. One item notes that he painted the houses with gold, silver and sundry other colours. And in particular the following is informative: Lyzarde received 10/- for painting a castle, 10/- for a rock and a church; and for one specially splendid architectural piece, whereof the pillars, architrave, frieze, cornice, and roof he gilded with gold and fine silver, he received 100/-, with another 10/- for adding the arms of England and France upon it. He also made a prison for Discord, and since this was in the year 1572 it is just possible that it was for the occasion at Whitehall referred to above on p. 143.

To return to plays. For the season 1579-80 we have an unusually full list of plays and their details. It includes:

The Duke of Milan, with a 'country house' and a 'city'. For this play 'all' was furnished by the Office of Revels—some items new; some 'much altered' from existing materials.

Alucius was wholly furnished by the Office and included a 'city' and a 'battlement' with rails, painted by Lyzarde.

The Four Sons of Fabius had a 'city', a 'mount', in the framework of which 'hoops' were used, and which was also painted by Lyzarde—and apparently also a 'prison'.

Scipio Africanus required a 'city' and a 'battlement'.

An unnamed play by the Earl of Leicester's Men had a 'city' and a 'country house' which again Lyzarde painted.

Portio and Demorantis, by the Lord Chamberlain's Men, had a 'city' and a 'town'.

The Soldan and the Duke needed only a 'city'.

Serpedon, again by the Lord Chamberlain's Men, was provided with a 'great city', a 'wood' and a 'castle'. Apropos of such scenes as the 'wood', we find an item for the Provision and Carriage of trees and other things to the court for a wilderness in a play.

A little later we see that for a certain 'Antick play' there was only needed 'one house'.

From the above we find a reasonable steadiness in the sort of character required of a 'house'. In the greatest number of cases it was something to stand for a 'city' (presumably such as 'Rome', 'Paris' or 'Mantua'). We are reminded of an item noted for money 'given to a painter for drawing the city and temples of Jerusalem and for painting towers . . .' as far back as 1565 [44]. But the architectural element was not invariable, and the 'mount' is often needed; and a variant of a 'wood' occasionally.

In this 'furnishing' of plays from the Revels Office there are some qualifications, however. For example, when the Earl of Leicester's Men did A Pastoral or history of a Greek Maid at Richmond, it was furnished only in respect of 'some things' in this office—not 'wholly', or 'well furnished in this office with many things'—and the possibility is that the Earl of Leicester's Men had brought some of their own stuff.

Again, items were on occasion borrowed by the Revels Office from theatres or companies, as was the case with a cloud, which was damaged in use and had to be repaired before it was returned. Further we occasionally find the pleasant phrasing—some things 'translated', some 'new made'.

So far we have noted things such as might be expected in our story. But there are certain others which are perhaps not expected;

Fig. 30. A 'Castle' and a 'Mount' for court performances

some of them are going to herald a new era. Chief of these is the mention of *clouds*.

These clouds were, sometimes at least, cut out of elm board and were painted. They were thus what we in the modern theatre would call 'profile' clouds. But what is so very especial about them is that they moved. We have items for pulleys for them, and for cords to draw them up and down. And we have one particular item paid to John Ross for long boards for the 'steer' of a cloud. This 'steer' can be nothing else than a 'way' or 'groove' to guide (or steer) the cloud in its movement. To this in a moment we must return.

To find lines 'to draw a curtain' is not unexpected; it was an old requirement. But to find a 'scaffold' mentioned is highly puzzling as late as this—is it a stage? Or is it a provision for audience-seating? There is no deciding. But we are clearly moving with a growing technique.

Of this technique there are one or two things to say of importance to our history. In the first place, whatever the ordinary professional players used in their visits to everyday Halls—or, after 1576, on the public playhouse stage—we know that when they came to court to perform they had special 'apt houses' set up for their plays.

But we have no information about where or how these houses were set up. We can find scarcely any hint at all that might indicate the use of a raised stage, and we are thus inclined to think (at present, anyway) that the 'houses' were set up on the floor of the hall.

We may try to express this diagrammatically, so as to fit in with

Fig. 31. The court performance of the Ballet comique de la Reine

the rest of our diagrams, but it is soon clear that we may not safely go any further than the apology in Fig. 30. Here is a Castle and a Mount. They probably stand clear on the floor of the hall; but immediately we represent them so, we recognize the fact that we are entirely lacking any knowledge of how the players got to the 'houses'. Did they walk across the floor to them from some door in the wall of the hall—perhaps one of the Screen doors? Did they climb into them invisibly from below by means of trapdoors in the hall floor? That would seem to involve too much structural preparation. Or were they hidden in them before the play began? Surely not the last if there was much doubling of the roles and, hence, changes of costume. We have to realize that our picture of the 'setting forth' is incomplete.

Again, where did the audience sit? At one end of the hall, facing the 'houses'? Or at one end and along two sides of the hall as for the earlier Interludes—partly embracing the 'houses'? Or on all four sides of the hall, with the 'houses' set up in a central clearing in the middle of the spectators?

It may be that the solution would be the same solution as is found in a French court production of 1581, known as the *Ballet comique de la Reine*, of which we have a description and a picture. Here the king sits at one end of the hall, with audience down either side in two galleries and also possibly behind the king. The 'houses'—a wood and a bower of clouds—are planted midway down the hall (Fig. 31), one either side; a third piece—a fountain —is planted asymmetrically near the far end. So far this is consistent with what we have visualized. But an extra item is present beyond all this that we have not expected; across the far end of the hall, opposite the king, is hung a great painted backcloth with a cut-out triple-arch piece in front, and below a low 'footpace' or rostrum, fronted by a little balustrade.

Now, there are in the accounts of the Revels Office in England some references to the painting of 'great cloths'. They are insufficient for us to guess what the cloths were for, but they may have been used as in the *Ballet de la Reine*.

The last item of importance to our history is going to develop into the most revolutionary. It is the introduction of *movement* into settings. We find two varieties of movement—that of a cloud moving in grooves, and that of a piece (say a mountain) opening to reveal something within, until then hidden.

But arrangements for movement involve machinery—sometimes simple but sometimes highly complicated. And no really free use of complicated machinery can be made without a firm basis and screens to hide the secrets. Movement for *effect*—that is, movement to arouse wonder—must conceal 'how it is done'. For this reason the new feature brought into the means of the theatre must be in the manner of an *illusion*.

Such a thing demands an organized stage; and so far in this history we have not met an organized stage.

We drew attention above to the cloud that moved. From the movement of this cloud there is to arise an astoundingly complex system of machinery for moving all the items of scenery so that *scenes* can be *changed*. Organization of means clearly must come about. But it will not come about without opposition.

It is very important for the understanding of what is to follow later in this history, to realize there is already present here the possibility of a fundamental split in ideas.

The object that is urgently needed by performers in all forms of theatre at this time is an organized stage. But on the one hand the professional players are seeking for an organized stage which will offer them an instrument to simplify their problems of acting and presentation. On the other hand the court and princely circles are seeking for a stage organized so as most effectively to contain the greatest variety of means of illusion.

Thus we are now to be faced with two courses in theatre's history, and must for a time follow them separately—even if this means abandoning the wideness of our view of the rest of the world.

FOURTH PHASE

The Organized Stage

FOURTH PHASE

The Organized Stage

THE REQUIREMENTS OF A STAGE

We now go back a little way. We have seen first non-professional performers in various primitive rites, and the emergence of a primitive play; next the expansion of performances under a religious revolution into highly elaborate festivals; next the gathering of small groups of self-supporting, professional players into companies travelling with short secular plays, and acting before the general public as well as occasionally at court. These companies now begin to form theatre into an organized craft.

In this organization they are faced with the need to take a considerable technical step; they have to systematize the modest, primitive 'tent' into an extremely compact, essential tool to incorporate at least six hitherto scattered necessary aids to their work. In short they invent an organized working stage to answer to their needs, and with this invention they open a Fourth Phase in the development of the theatre—a phase which could never have come about but for the needs of these newly-organized professional players.

Looking back on the forms of presentation that have been described so far, what are the six most important items that players might wish to provide for, as they begin to found a professional technique? It is important to remember the economic problem that they will have to face; it will be no longer possible to contemplate any kind of show on so vast a scale as a religious festival. These have always been expensive things and their costs have had to be borne by municipalities or by groups of trade guilds. The professional shows to come must depend on the income from their own receipts and must limit their expenses accordingly.

At any rate this must be true as far as unsponsored, public performances go—however the case was altered when a summons
came to play at a court. So then, with this need to reduce to
essentials, what items in their presentation are early actors likely
to class as the most important for their professional work?
Probably the following:

First: a place of entrance. The dramatic value of an *entrance* is a
basic item in the art of playing. One might almost divide an
actor's essential technique into three things; an effective entrance;
followed by a good performance; and concluded by a well-timed
exit. And it is remarkable how important the first and the last are
in practice! A good performance that leads off with a bad entrance
and ends with a bungled exit is incalculably lessened in its
effective quality. In fact, it is almost impossible to imagine a good
performer allowing such a thing, so detrimental is it to his work;
rather will he insist that the means of exit and entrance must be so
managed that he can make at least some effective use of them,
before he consents to give a performance at all. He owes this to
his work. This then is one matter which the developing professionals have to look to.

Second: a background. In this question of the value of a *background* to a player's performance, some people today may be a
little biased by experience of theatre-in-the-round, and suppose
that a background is of no importance to a player. I believe there
is a great deal to be said for this point of view, but a student of the
theatre cannot afford to limit his study to one point of view only.
There is another, in this matter of background; and to explain it
I cannot do better than quote André Barsacq [8]. The quotation
is the more to my particular purpose since the situation it happens
to describe is exactly parallel to the situation of early players at
the dawn of their technique.

'It was in June 1937. We, Jean Dasté, Maurice Jacquemont,
and I, had just founded our first company, La Compagnie des
Quatre-Saisons. We had arrived at a spot kindly offered to us by a
touring association of Cheminots, and we wanted to thank them
for their hospitality. So, on the anniversary of their organization,
in the heart of the forest of Rambouillet, we proposed to offer
them our first show, Molière's *Le Médecin volant*. We had been
brought up in Copeau's school which extols the return to first
principles in our art, and we rejoiced in the chance that was

offered us to make our first stage adventure in conditions so simple and so primitive. Arriving early at the place of our performance—a clearing in the wood—we began to put together the elements of our show. Backing against the trees, we built a trestle stage some 14 ft. square and 3 ft. 6 in. high; then we arranged the "auditorium", some felled tree trunks lying on the ground served for seats for the front rows; the people behind stood on the grass which sloped gently down to the stage. And the rehearsal began. In proportion exactly as the elegant turns of Sganarelle began to grow on the stage, a vague discomfort began to spread over me. I wasn't being interested in the action. Behind the player the forest went on living its own life, and our presence seemed unwanted in those surroundings. . . . It was absolutely necessary to do something about it—to find some solution which would give back to my poor actors the lustre they had lost into the emptiness.

'In despair of finding what had happened and moved by a vague intuition, I decided to knot together two sheets that we had with us, and to hang them across the back of the stage on a rope. Suddenly, then, the miracle of the theatre happened. Immediately, about the clearing silence fell, a silence of expectation, a waiting for something about to happen. . . . The empty scene, the very acting-space itself seemed to be waiting. Behind the curtain that we had just hung up there had become condensed together a different world unknown to us, of which we awaited the revelation. Then through the centre slit appeared the opening player. *Coming on in this way he made his appearance to tell us what was passing behind in that hidden world whence he emerged, and which none but he had the right to penetrate.* Then other actors appeared, and each time their entrances were rich with significance. The eyes of the crowd were no longer distracted by the encircling forest; they were drawn, fascinated, towards this new world which had just been created—*the world of the mystery of the theatre.* . . .

'This experience which will seem perhaps over-simple to some helped us, all the same, to understand the evolution of theatre architecture over the centuries. The rudimentary elements of my stage at Rambouillet—a raised acting-area limited at the back by a curtain or some other backing containing one or more openings— are something we shall rediscover in all epochs of the history of the theatre.'

How often discoveries are only re-discoveries!

A background, then, can do two things; it can defend the players, as a cupped hand defends a match, from the wind of distraction, and it can afford a means for entrances. Thus, two of the needs are unified.

Third: a raised stage. Once professionalism comes in one has to be ruthless; one takes short cuts. There are several ways by which an actor can come to dominate an audience, but the quickest of all, when there is a crowd (as the scaffolds of the Rounds had shown) is to lift him well up on a platform above the crowd. There he can 'pomp'. Now that he is alone to sink or swim by himself and his art, and now that he is before a crowd no longer patiently awed by a religious occasion, he cannot afford to forgo the pulpit-eminence, the prow-over-the-waves elevation of a raised stage.

Fourth: a dressing room. The most immediate adjunct, outside his own person, to an actor is his dress. He must get that right, and must, in order to preserve dramatic effect, set it to rights in a place beyond the audience's view. In the Rounds he dressed in a pavilion outside the circle. He had then to make his way to his entrance through or behind the people, but he needs to dress more immediately on the spot, and he needs also to have a very immediate place for a quick change, or for a switch from role to role if he is doubling.

Fifth: a property store. The professional player is now making use of secondary aids to his acting—chairs, thrones, a bed, even a tree! Where can these be stowed when not needed on the scene, and still be very close to hand?

Sixth: some means to act 'above'. A curious feature (as we have seen in the Interludes) of early organized playing is the pleasure and the effect to be gained by a scene acted between one player below and another aloft—in a window, on a wall, at a balcony. Such a minor delight always tends to cost much on the stage because of the need for a solid and stable structure to take the weight of the raised player. 'Levels' can be a producer's joy, but an eminence which wobbles is a player's curse, and an eminence which is firm is a carpenter's task. How to solve this problem?

One might perhaps add a Seventh requirement, though it is so nebulous a thing: namely, that however all these needs are met, they *must* be met so that the smoothness and the effectiveness of

Fig. 32. *An early booth stage*

the show are not one whit impaired—rather so that the show is improved and enriched. No 'amateur' solution will do. There is even some dimly-conceived notion that the result ought perhaps to be beautiful—at least, gay! It has to attract the crowd. And it must be cheap. And it must be portable. (How unmistakably we are entering the realm of professional theatre—at least, of unsubsidized professional theatre!)

THE BOOTH STAGE

Certainly by about 1542 they were well on the way to settling all these things. This statement can be made because we have records going back to this date. But there may well have been pioneer solutions before then that Fortune has left unrecorded. So we may say that *at the latest* by 1542 these things were well in hand.

To this year belongs a drawing in the Library at Cambrai, and with it our Fourth Phase of Theatre, that of the 'Organized Stage', is begun.

Fig. 32 is a diagram of the stage shown in this drawing. Here is the players' solution to their problem. It would appear to be a solution devised purely by the theatre people themselves, almost as a solution is arrived at in folk art, and with no element contributed by any outside specialists—whether architects or painters or engineers.

It provides the simplest entrances possible—gaps in a curtain; one at either end of the curtain and one in the middle where the two halves of the curtain join. Thus the players are provided with a technical replica of the circumstances they were used to in the two doors at either end of the Screen in a hall. The centre entrance is a curious addition which is to cause historians some difficulty in a later development. Was there such a thing in a Screen? Do players need a central entrance? If there was no central entrance in a Screen, did the players invent a small retiring-place in this position (such as a 'tent' set against the plain wall), and is the centre opening in the Cambrai curtains a logical descendant of this? In Pieter Balten's painting of a similar stage (*see* Plate 4) no such opening appears to be present.

Having provided the entrances by this simple arrangement of a traverse curtain hung on a rod at the back of the stage, the players have simultaneously of course provided themselves, like André Barsacq, with their much-needed background, and by identical means.

The third requirement of elevation, they supply by a raised stage. Often this was simply a floor of boards supported on large barrels—both perhaps borrowed locally. In most stages built to serve a standing audience, this floor is fairly high—between five and seven feet—well above the shoulders of the people. In this picture the supports of the stage floor appear to be covered in with strips of varicoloured curtain, or stage hangings.

The fourth requirement of a dressing-room, they ingeniously meet by erecting two poles a little behind those supporting the curtain-rod, running cross-pieces of wood round the top, and walling in the whole with hangings, so supplying themselves with a small booth adequate for dressing, for changing, for waiting for an entrance, and for concealing the prompter who kept the players to their script.

The booth of course also serves the fifth requirement, a property-room. In it can be stored all the furniture for the show, and from it pieces can be thrust out on to the stage or withdrawn into concealment as required. At need, as it would seem from Balten, an assistant might peep through a side curtain and take in an odd stool from a helpful member of the audience.

And finally, as Balten and many others show, this booth offered the simplest means for playing 'upper' scenes. This was no more than a ladder (so familiar already as an access to scaffolds in Round theatres), now placed in the booth itself and enabling an actor to climb up, pop his head over the top of the background curtain and settle his elbows on the curtain-rod, to declaim a scene from a balcony, or fling down a challenge from the walls of a city. When not needed, the ladder might—in order to leave the entrances unobstructed—be turned round and leant against the back wall of the booth.

There are lacking only two things to enable the whole of the canon of Elizabethan drama (when we come to it) to be adequately presented on this 1540 booth stage, so far at least as technical requirements go—and these two things are traps in the stage floor, and a shade or cover or awning above the stage, with which to throw a shadow on the background and from which to engineer flying feats.

So valuable is this booth as an actor's instrument that we may name this form of stage after it—the *booth stage*.

The performance done, the hangings are stripped in a few minutes and packed with the costumes in baskets, the poles unmounted, the planks, ladder and barrels returned whence they were borrowed, and the actors are on their way again.

The Cambrai picture adds even a few enrichments. The badge of the company (as it may be) hangs in the centre of the crosspole; a curious sheet of paper (?) with what appear lines of script on it is pinned to the curtain like a window; and at either of the two front corners of the stage there project cressets on poles, perhaps to light a performance at night.

This booth stage is the essential technical element of a complete section of theatre history. It spreads all over Western Europe with or without minor developments. It extends forward in time to our own day and we see its descendant, decked in festoons of electric lights, at the pierrot show on the sands. It would not be unjustifiable, perhaps, to look back and see its antecedents in the puzzling stage of the Greek mimes as portrayed on the Phlyax vases, as in Fig. 27.

In the Low Countries there are many early records of it—even some which, interestingly, show its back. Pieter Balten left a large painting of a fair (from about 1550), now in the Rijksmuseum,

Amsterdam, which portrays the details of the stage with more than photographic faithfulness—even representing the tapestry pattern on the end curtain (*see* Plate 4). Of this painting there are several copies.

The same system could be adapted for use indoors, and Adriaen van de Venne shows, in an etching of 1635 [69] as precise as an *Illustrated London News* engraving of the 1890s, just what it looked like when set up in, perhaps, an indoor tennis court (*see* Plate 6).

At Drottningholm Theatre Museum near Stockholm is a painting of about 1660 which shows exactly this sort of stage, but developed now to a pitch of perfection so far as concerns the booth and its façade at the back of the stage. Here any play in the Elizabethan canon could be performed—save perhaps those that called for traps or flyings (*see* Plate 7).

THE BASQUE PASTORALES

In Tardets in the Basque country they put up even today an almost exactly similar stage for their *pastorales*. The survival of the remarkable *pastorale* plays in the district of Soule has two especial interests at this point; the stage arrangement and the conventions of acting.

The stage is a perfect example of a large booth stage. Even today it is illustrative of almost every feature that we have listed as characteristic of a booth stage. A rough diagram of it is given in Fig. 33, and photographs of performances in progress by Rodney Gallop can be referred to [26] and by Violet Alford [2], who also has given descriptions of the plays [1].

The stage floor is in sections laid either on barrels or on trestles, both traditional supports. Curtains are draped round the edge of the stage to hide the space underneath making a typical example of stage hangings. The stage floor is approached by a flight of six steps in the centre front, and is some 4 ft. 6 in. high. From photographs it would appear to be some 40 ft. long and 25 ft. deep.

Across the back of the stage is hung a curtain about 9 ft. high. A little way in from either end is an opening. These openings form the two chief entrances; the one on the stage-right is traditionally reserved for the good characters, the other for the bad. This curtain is not brightly coloured or patterned but is—a little surprisingly—plain white relieved only by greenery, and perhaps

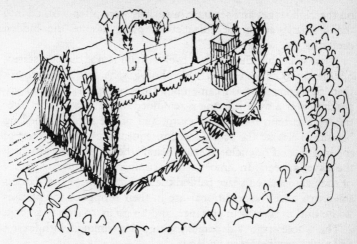

Fig. 33. The Basque pastorale stage at Tardets

a gilded and tasselled hanging at the centre. Though the side openings are the usual entrances, it is particularly interesting to find that there occasionally is employed a centre door of gold and white, but reserved for special purposes—for angels and for the dead entering Paradise. This possibility of a central opening for special effects may throw some light on the formation of the tiring-house façade on an Elizabethan public playhouse stage.

Rising above the back curtain in the centre is another interesting feature—an elevated platform, arched over with leaves and flowers, which forms a small musicians' place. Its position here is reminiscent of several things: for example, Jasper Mayne's approval of Ben Jonson's laying 'no sieges to the Musique-Roome' (*Jonsonus Virbius*, 1638), and Wilson's echo of this in his reference in the play *The Cheats* (1663) to 'tedious sieges to the Musick-Room'; these now seem to have a clear meaning for if troops (such as those in the *Horestes* Interlude) were to attack a city-wall portrayed by such a back curtain, no phrase could better describe their action than a 'siege of the music room'. Again, the musicians' position here is reminiscent of that of instrumentalists in the gallery over a Hall-screen. A further enlightening fact is that despite this special place for the music above the Basque stage, the player of the traditional pipe and stringed drum sits actually at the back on the stage itself. The instrumentalists do so on the Noh stage; and separate musicians were often worked into the dramatic action of Elizabethan plays despite the hidden orchestra that was available.

What is behind the Tardets back curtain is not directly stated, nor clearly to be seen in available photographs. But in the remark that 'the Voice of God came once from a top-hatted head appearing over a wall' [2], one is reminded of the appearances over the back curtain fronting a booth, and of the ladder leaned up behind to elevate the actor, and consequently of the existence of the booth itself or enclosed space behind the curtain, out of which the player appears. In almost certain confirmation of the existence of such an enclosed space behind the back curtain of the Tardets stage, we have the traditional use in their scripts of the phrases 'to go out' to signify an entrance, and 'to go in' to signify an exit.

The whole stage is decorated with poles trimmed with leaves, and with swaying green garlands.

The audience is accommodated before this stage on specially erected, 'towering', scaffolds or groundstands. These, beside facing the stage, curve forwards at the sides to carry the audience round opposite the two ends of the stage as well, making a true example of open-stage formation. This provision of a deliberately built, stepped auditorium is a special development in this particular phase of the primitive booth stage.

The audience travelling in across country to take its place on these stands repeats another tradition in that it brings its food with it, in preparation for what may be a six- or seven-hour session.

As we have been led to expect from our earlier study of the booth stage, a simple minimum of furniture is used at Tardets: a group of stools or ordinary chairs is brought on when needed and removed as soon as a clear stage is required. No doubt much in the same tradition as 'a bed thrust out'.

But in the Tardets performances, perhaps one of the most valuable pieces of information on stage technique comes in a certain development of this simple stage furniture into a genuine 'scenic object' in as pure a form as any investigator could wish to find. There is an example in a play dealing with the life of François I, and the object permits the presentation of a scene where he is in prison. The method used appears to be a striking example of how such a scene might well have been presented on an Elizabethan public stage. It is very simple. It consists of no more than a tall, upright wooden cage, some 7 ft. high and 3 ft. square, brought in and stood on one side of the stage (*see* Fig. 33). The cage door is opened and into the cage the actor walks and stands. There is the setting for a prison scene.

(Miss Violet Alford in a written communication to me kindly adds: 'Other scenic objects I have seen are the Cathedral of Rheims about 4 ft. in length burnt off-stage and a church into which somebody crept on his hands and knees.')

Here, then, are survivals today of a scenic system that is probably very reminiscent of the system used both on the Elizabethan public stage and in 16th-century performances of plays at Court. These objects seem to be in the same category as 'mounts', 'cities of Jerusalem', 'apt houses' for players, and 'bowers', and 'tents'.

It would appear that still other means of entrance to the stage are possible. Indeed this is already indicated by the presence of the steps in front. For example, there is a group of special figures called Satans, who have various functions in the performance as we shall see. When a distinguished visitor joins the audience, the Satans dance 'backwards in front of him, from the gate to his seat' [2]. They must then turn and mount the stage. This last they do with traditional difficulty, for they are bound to the regions below and have to struggle to achieve any higher level.

Into the space between seating and stage-front (a sort of reminiscence of the Place) horses are sometimes ridden by some of the approaching characters—just as horses were ridden into the Place in some of the medieval Round performances, and as (*see The Conversion of St. Paul* in the Digby plays, l.140) Saul 'rydyth forth with hys seruantes a-bowt the place, [and] owt of the pl[ace]'.

One of the plays relates the story of Abraham and in it, since this is a pastoral country, sheep are driven on to the stage.

The style in which the actors perform is never realistic. Formal movement regulates the fighting, and a kind of recitative the speaking. 'The whole performance depends on rhythm' says Miss Alford [1]. 'Without their rhythm these shepherds . . . could never succeed in playing their play. Anything approached realistically is a failure . . . When the village actor is taken by the rhythmical tide he launches himself upon it, forgets himself and his fear of forgetting his part and his difficulties with his arms and hands. He shelters behind the rhythm which protects him . . .' and we are reminded of the psychological problems of a player before a public that were referred to in the introduction to this book.

The attitude towards costume is remarkably informative in connexion with that vexed question whether or not early actors wore contemporary dress for historical scenes. Costumes on the *pastorale* stage are not historically accurate, but neither are they merely unrelieved contemporary dress. All the 'soldiers'' roles wear uniform—a kind of Ruritanian, frogged tunic, with striped riding breeches and riding boots—even François I and Napoleon. But their helmets (at any rate those of—interestingly enough—the evil soldiers) are decked with flowers and offer the impression of survivals from an earlier rite.

All these are conventions reminiscent of those we suppose governed 15th- and 16th-century stages. There are many others—for instance a sheet is laid down when a figure has to fall and die. After a wholesale battle with perhaps twenty or more participants on the stage, there remain many corpses. The problem is raised (as it was on the Elizabethan stage), how were these corpses removed? Here the solution is found in the band of Satans; this agile chorus runs on and carries them away. The Satans serve too in some sense as interlude-providers, coming on with a whirling ballet at pauses in the action, much as the triangular-masked, yak-tailed dancers did in the Tibetan Festival Play. They are the agents by which is made possible yet another feature which presumably resembles the Elizabethan players' technique—namely, that the Tardets shows can be presented with no breaks or waits in the action at all.

The plays have very large casts, and therefore seem to belong rather to the more ancient phase of amateur, religious, seasonal, festival performances than to the phase of professional players such as we are especially treating in this chapter, but the performance as such has progressed out of the usual central 'Place' system of action in a way that many theatres must have done, but which few have left records of, and it has taken into its method the booth stage of a slightly more formalized technique that brings the shows very near to the advanced systems of the eve of the Italian Renaissance. The *pastorale* performances seem to offer a *multum in parvo* of three phases of theatre development, boxed together.

Some further points are that:

The script of a play reposes in manuscript form in the hands of a family, of which a suitable representative acts as the *pastoralier* or *instituteur*, and would seem to correspond with the medieval 'book-holder' or 'ordinary'. He it is who supervises rehearsals and performances.

The subjects of the plays are immensely varied and (like the Tibetan Festival scripts) range from religious legends, such as that of Abraham, to recent histories, including those of François I and Napoleon, and even extending so far as a version of the 1914–1918 war (presented in 1929). And yet, whatever the subject, one feature is invariably introduced, and that is the marching, counter-marching, and formalized conflict of two armies—that of the Christians and that of the 'Turks'. Thus a mass strife takes the place of the individual strife that formed the essential of the Mummers' Play; but the subject is analogous, the conflict of . . . and still we are undecided how to name these two opposed forces; they might be good and evil, or light and darkness, or life and death, or something still more human and more deep.

Angels are brought into the action on occasion, and they are played by small children in white garments. One is closely reminded of the little figures sitting at the top of the heaven ramp in Fouquet's miniature of the Martyrdom of Saint Apollonia. But these performances at Tardets are so particularly interesting for our purpose as examples of history, because they demonstrate beyond gainsay that the sources of such shows cannot be just unmixed Mystery plays; they clearly have much that must be traced farther back still and springs from primitive ritual itself. Here once more we realize that a sort of duck-billed platypus of a survival can exist in the modern theatre world exhibiting traces of several phases of otherwise forgotten evolutional history.

To take another point: the speakers of the banns of medieval Mystery plays (the banns were preliminary announcements of performances) either actually were, or were accompanied by, flag-bearers called *vexillatores* (*vexilla* is a little flag). In the Basque performances, the speaker of the Prologue to the show is still supported by two traditional flagbearers (and the Basques have developed the waving of a flag to a ceremonial art).

Again, somewhat vaguely described 'guards' (who call for silence) are present at the performances; and the memory of the medieval 'stytelers' is brought back.

In short there seems no feature in these *pastorale* performances that has not some echo either in the rites of primitive celebrations, or in the occasions of great religious festival presentations, or in the technique of the first exponents of that new instrument of theatrical art, the booth stage. And here and there we are reminded of a possible parallel with the culminating Elizabethan stage itself, still to be studied.

THE INFLUENCE OF THE BOOTH STAGE

What does stand out apropos of the above observation is the intriguing question: What is the *age* of the Basque *pastorale* stage? Did it first come into existence in the 18th century (whence we have our first written descriptions of the performances)? It has features that seem clearly older. Did it then first come into existence in the 17th century? And if so, in the earlier or the later half of the century? If the later half, then it is subsequent to the Elizabethan type of stage, and may have derived its features from that type of stage (though by a path that is not immediately clear to see). Or, on the other hand, did it first come into existence in the earlier part of the 17th century—or even before then? Or, to offer a further alternative, did it come into existence as a late 17th- or early 18th-century development of something which itself was in use before that date?

If either of these last two possibilities is in fact the truth, then we shall have to conclude that the Tardets stage belonged to a type which itself was the *source* of the Elizabethan stage, not that the Tardets stage was a debased descendant of the type of the Elizabethan stage. Its evidence would thus attain a still greater importance. But, alas, on such questions as these we still need more facts. What we can say, however, in conclusion is that we are enabled to compare: on the one hand, a survival which still exists today and of which we can therefore check all the details by direct inquiry; and on the other hand, a form of performance in the past of which only some of the details are known to us.

The first thing we learn is that a number of the details which *are* comparable in the two shows are so alike that we can conclude the modern performance is in some degree a faithful reminder of the old. And that in itself is something.

But there is more. If the similarity is so close on known points, then it is not impossible that it might also be close on 'not-known' points, that is points which cannot now be compared because they are entirely missing from any record of the old show. We can thus to some extent venture tentative reconstructions, and supply matters which we should not even have dreamed existed, had we not indisputable proof of them in the survival before our eyes.

This is one use of survivals in aiding us to reconstruct a lost theatre form. It must be employed carefully. It is clearly not an infallible aid. But this observation must be made about it; it is a better method than reconstructing a lost theatre-form purely on the basis of personal ingenuity—as when the investigator says 'Clearly one way in which this could have been done was that they could have easily——' etc., etc. (It is in such a way as this that most of our reconstructions of classical Greek staging have been made.) At least by working from parallel survivals, the investigator can be certain that the suggestions he draws from the survival *are practical theatre procedures*, and thus he is automatically debarred from propounding a system that is theatrically just not workable at all—which the other investigator so frequently manages to do.

An extremely important query that arises about the booth stage is, How widespread was its use? This we have still to decide, but at the moment one is faced with the reflection that there seems no reason to suppose such a stage as this would not be the type used by travelling companies of professional players in England—at any rate, when they played out of doors or in an inn-yard.

We do not know how far they may have erected something like this indoors when they played in a hall but, as we have seen, there are effects in some of the later Interludes which seem to need some special arrangement being put up; and it is to be remarked that the features of this booth stage show exactly the kind of arrangement that would be suitable.

From this arises a special question.

Were there, about 1575, many professional companies of players working through England in this technique?

Or were the professional companies chiefly working in the technique of wheeled pageant-waggons? It should perhaps be noted here that if they were, then the pageant-waggon system, which we have supposed was a system restricted to Guild performances—that is amateur performances—must have been taken over by the professionals at some occasion of which we have no record. Moreover, we have not been able to learn that there was anything about the pageant-waggon that can be said to have constituted any special organization of its parts into a regular working stage, suitable for performing any available play upon. The great theatrical difficulty about a pageant-waggon (see above, p. 109) is that it seems to have been at best no more than an acting platform with provision upon it for playing *one scene only*. Unlike the booth stage, it possessed no general background adaptable for any performance. It was designed for a specific scene and presumably could not be used for staging any other scene without radical reconstruction.

Or, thirdly, was there another technique of presentation in England which so far has escaped our notice altogether, and which was employed by professional players?

The purpose of these questions is very direct. Somewhere among the professional companies was one particular one called the Earl of Leicester's Men; and it would settle some of the most acrimonious arguments in the field of theatre research if we knew what technique of presentation they used, because in 1576 the leader of this company took a step that revolutionized English theatrical practice for nearly a century, and revolutionized the theory of theatre throughout the civilized world up to the present time—and beyond.

The vital question, before we discuss this revolution, is however: What system of presentation was this company normally familiar with before 1576?—The booth-stage system? The pageant-waggon system? Or another system which we know nothing about as yet?

To this question we do not, apparently, know the answer.

The present writer finds himself forced into a corner. He cannot bring himself to believe that this company used the pageant-waggon system, because he presumes it was developed (at any rate in England) for religious cycle plays, and the Earl of Leicester's Men did not perform in the religious cycle-play tradition.

Secondly, he cannot with confidence embrace the idea that they performed in a mysterious, lost, third technique—simply because a study of the theatre suggests that there is no such thing as a lost technique.

And thus he is forced to the conclusion that the Earl of Leicester's Men acted in the booth-stage technique. If they in fact did, then it is surely most likely that the booth-stage details which they were used to would influence the design of any new stage they might come to build later.

This may of course be a most signal piece of unreason, but such a conclusion informs all that part of what follows which deals with the stage background. And it is only fair to advise the reader of this.

For we have now to enter perhaps the most puzzling and controversial field of modern theatre history (as opposed to 'ancient' theatre history).

The leader of the Earl of Leicester's Men, beside being a player, was a business man and a joiner. He decided for the first time in the modern world to build a specific, wooden playhouse to enclose his stage, and to accommodate a regular, paying, ordinary public audience, and in which to present to them a policy of new, highly attractive, five-act plays, independent (so far as we know) of any princely command, or of any widely-spread religious intention. And to present this policy purely as a business venture which had to pay its own way. Taking all these things into account, he may be called the first man ever to do such a thing in the world—ancient and modern included.

He was, of course, James Burbage.

Of his playhouse we can guess much concerning the auditorium. But about the details of the stage which was built in that playhouse, we remain as ignorant, and consequently as irascible, as about any theatrical item in the world.

THE ELIZABETHAN PUBLIC PLAYHOUSE

To put as much order, as briefly as we can, and with a very

pious intention to avoid bias, into this major problem of the theatre in the Elizabethan period, the first point to be made is that there were three forms of theatre:

   i. the public playhouse,
   ii. the private house theatre,
   iii. the court theatre.

Taking the public playhouse first; there appear to have been some ten of these playhouses in London during the period (including in this figure two that were burnt and rebuilt), and they come chronologically as follows:

1. 1576 James Burbage built *The Theatre* in Shoreditch (possibly with a removable stage).
2. 1576 or '7 *The Curtain* built nearby.
3. *c.* 1587 *The Rose* built on Bankside.
4. 1595 Francis Langley built *The Swan* on Bankside; sketch of interior by De Witt *c.* 1596.
5. 1598-9 *The Globe* built on Bankside from the timbers of the demolished *Theatre*.
6. 1600 *The Fortune* built in Cripplegate by Henslowe and Alleyn, a square playhouse but with details based on *The Globe*; the builder's contract survives.
7. *c.* 1600 *The Red Bull* built in Clerkenwell.
   1613 *The Globe* burnt.
8. 1614 *The Hope* built on Bankside by Henslowe and Maid; a mixed playhouse and bearbaiting arena, shape based on *The Swan*, stage removable, the builder's contract survives.
9. 1614 *The Globe* rebuilt.
   1621 *The Fortune* burnt.
10. 1623 *The Fortune* rebuilt.

In this list three pieces of direct contemporary evidence about the playhouses are mentioned—a drawing and two builder's contracts. Taken together these three items form the more or less essential basis to which any other evidence must be related.

Let us begin with the two builder's contracts. Their information is not as full as we would like, but presumably it is factual. One initial difficulty about them is that they are wordy documents couched in somewhat obscure, legal language. On the whole, once they are studied in detail what they say is fairly clear so far as it goes, and it will perhaps be of help to the general reader to give now a rendering in modern language of the essential contents of each before they are discussed. (The numbers in curved brackets refer to the notes which follow.)

THE FORTUNE CONTRACT

This contract was made 8 January 1599 between (a) Phillip Henslowe and Edward Alleyn, and (b) Peter Street, a carpenter of London (1). It agrees that Peter Street should set up a new house and stage for a playhouse (2) on a site near Goldinge Lane (St. Giles without Cripplegate) in the following way:

The frame of the house to be set square (3), and to measure 80 ft. square outside and 55 ft. square inside; with sure foundations of piles, brick, lime, and sand, both for the outside and for the inside walls; the foundations to rise at least 1 ft. above ground.

The frame to be in three storeys; the first to contain 12 ft. in height, the second 11 ft., and the third 9 ft. Each storey to be 12 ft. 6 in. broad, 'besides a juttey forwards in either of the saide twoe vpper Stories of Tenne ynches of lawfull assize' (4), with four divisions for gentlemen's rooms (5), and sufficient other divisions for Twopenny rooms (6), with seats in these rooms and throughout the rest of the galleries (7). And with stairs, 'conveyances' [passages], and divisions like those of the Globe (8).

With a stage and tiring house made in the frame (9), with a 'shadow' or cover over the stage—the stage and staircases to be as shown in the diagram [now missing]—the stage to be 43 ft. 'long' (10), and broad enough to come to the middle of the yard (11). The stage to be boarded in below with new oak planks, and similarly the lower storey of the frame on that side facing the yard, and this to be also 'layed over' and fenced with iron pikes (12). The stage in all other dimensions to be like that of the Globe.

With glazed windows to the tiring house; and the frame, stage, and staircases to be tiled (13), and be provided with lead gutters to drain the water from the covering of the stage to fall backwards (14).

The frame and staircases to be lathed and plastered (lime and hair) on the outside, and the gentlemen's rooms and Twopenny rooms to be ceiled with lath, lime, and hair; and the floors of the Galleries, Storeys and Stage to be covered with new deal boards where necessary.

All this to be as in The Globe, except that the principal and 'main' posts (15) of the frame and stage 'forwarde' (16) shall be square and made as pilasters, with carvings of satyrs on top of each; and except also that Peter Street shall not be responsible for any painting of frame, house or stage, or for plastering or ceiling any rooms beside the gentlemen's rooms and the Two-penny rooms and [those behind the] stage (17).

Peter Street promises, at proper charges and with good work-manship, to set up the above frame, etc. in new timber on the above site (having free access to the site for the purpose) before 25 July next. He shall also provide all workmen, timbers, joists, rafters, boards, doors, bolts, hinges, bricks, tiles, laths, lime, hair, sand, nails, lead, iron, glass, workmanship and other things needful. He shall make the frame in every point, for 'scantlinges' (18), larger in size than those of the Globe. He shall begin and continue reasonably and without distraction till the work is finished.

In consideration of the above Henslowe and Alleyn promise to pay £440 as follows; £220 within seven days of the timberwork being set up, and £220 within seven days of the work being finished. Provided that whatever money is advanced before beginning shall be counted as part of the first payment, and all such money advanced during work shall be counted as part of the last payment. In witness whereof the parties set their seals.

P.S.

witnesses; William Harris, scrivener.
   Francis Smith, apprentice to above.

Notes on the Fortune Contract

(1) Peter Street assisted the Burbages when The Theatre was demolished and the materials transferred to Bankside to help build The Globe.

(2) That the playhouse was specified to consist of a 'house' and a 'stage' seems to suggest that the stage was considered as an item in its own right, not as a mere adjunct.

(3) Most of the theatres other than the Fortune appear to have been 'round', or more probably polygonal (with perhaps sixteen or more sides).

(4) This passage is given in the original words of the contract because it is not clear what it means. The 'jutting-forward' may

have implied two jutties, or projections, one in the second storey and one in the third; or it may mean only that the second and third storeys together jutted forward over the first, but were themselves in vertical alinement.

(5) The Gentlemen's Rooms were presumably arranged two either side the stage. They were almost certainly 'boxes' (*see* the Hope contract). It is to be noted that they are termed 'divisions', and thus were in some way 'divided' from the rest.

(6) The Twopenny Rooms were presumably the 'rooms' in the remainder of the galleries. It is clear that they were called 'rooms', and like the above, also had 'divisions' or partitions (*see* the Hope contract) between them.

(7) These rooms and the 'rest of the galleries' (hence by implication some part of the galleries *was not* divided into rooms) were provided with seats.

(8) The Fortune, despite its square plan, was to be based on the arrangement of the Globe; thus the present contract is some tentative indication of the form of the Globe.

(9) The intention of these words is not clear. They may mean 'with (*a*) a stage (separate from the frame) and (*b*) a tiring house incorporated *in* the frame'. Or merely: that inside the surround of the frame a stage-and-tiring-house was to be made in one unit and both separate from the frame. The *frame* is the skeleton structure of the total ring of the auditorium, and the *tiring house* is presumably where the players dressed and whence they made their entrances on to the stage. Leslie Hotson in his *Shakespeare's Wooden O* argues that the tiring house was beneath the stage.

(10) The dimension '43 ft. *long*' is to be read as referring to what we should call the 'width' of the stage;

(11) its 'breadth' (what we should call its depth) came to the middle of the yard, and by calculation would amount to some 27 ft. 6 in. The *yard* is the ground, corresponding to the medieval Place.

(12) The *iron pikes* were presumably spikes along the edge of the lowest gallery balustrade to prevent the groundlings from climbing out of the yard into the rooms without paying their extra penny.

(13) Tiled—instead of thatched as the first Globe was.

(14) The arrangement of the gutter-pipes to fall backwards is not entirely clear. To direct rain water back towards the frame so

that it did not drip in the yard is surely necessary. But whether, when it reached the frame, it fell or was conducted down in pipes, and whether, in either case, it was discharged on the outside or the inside of the frame, is a puzzle.

(15) The *principal and main posts* of the frame were presumably the columns separating the galleries on the yard face (for other posts, *see* the Hope contract).

(16) The stage 'forwarde' is a great puzzle; it may mean the stage-front.

(17) Thus, the Gentlemen's Rooms, the Twopenny Rooms, and either the stage or the rooms behind the stage (whose use is not specified), were ceiled. The rest of the galleries were then presumably not ceiled.

(18) *Scantling*; a term referring to the dimensions of timber.

THE HOPE CONTRACT

Agreement 29 August 1613 between (*a*) Phillip Henslowe and Jacob Maid, waterman, and (*b*) Gilbert Katherens, carpenter.

Katherens promises that he will at his own cost, before 30 November next, pull down the Bull- and Bear-baiting House and stable on Bankside, and will also before that date build 'one other same place' or Playhouse, fit both for players and for baiting (1), and also a fit Tiring House, and stage to be removable and to stand on trestles (2). And he will build this playhouse or gamehouse near or upon the place where it stood before.

And will build the playhouse of such compass, form, wideness, and height as that called the Swan in Paris Garden (3). And shall build two staircases outside and against it in such places as shall be most convenient for them to be (4), and of such size and height as those of the Swan.

He shall build the Heavens all over the stage so as to be carried without any posts set on the stage (5); and all gutters of lead necessary for carrying such rain as may fall on it.

He shall make two Boxes in the lower storey fit for gentlemen to sit in (6). And make partitions between the Rooms as they are at the Swan. And shall make turned columns upon and over the stage (7). And make the principals and fore front of the playhouse of oak; no fir to be used in the lowest or middle storeys, excepting the upright posts on the back wall of the said storeys (8), (all binding joists (9) to be of oak).

The inner principal posts (10) of the first storey to be 12ft. high and 10 in. square, those in the middle storey to be 8 in. square, and the innermost posts in the upper storey to be 7 in. square. Prick posts (11) in the first storey to be 8 in. square, in the second 7 in., and the uppermost 6 in. square. Also the bressumers (12) in the lowest storey to be 9 in. deep and 7 in. thick, in the middle storey 8 in. deep and 6 in. thick. The binding joists of the first storey to be 9 in. and 8 in. depth and thickness, and in the middle storey 8 in. and 7 in. depth and thickness.

Item, to make a good foundation of bricks to at least 13 in. above ground.

Item, to build the said Bull-house and stable with good scantling timber, planks, and boards and with partitions fit to hold six bulls and three horses, with mangers and a loft over as at present.

He shall also newly tile with English tiles all the upper roof of the Playhouse, gameplace, and Bull-house or stable and supply all lime, hair, sand, bricks, tiles, laths, nails, workmanship, etc. necessary.

The Playhouse to be made in the form of the Swan (the scantling of the timbers, tiles, and foundation as mentioned, without fraud).

Henslowe and Maid promise Katherens that he shall have all the timber, benches, seats (13), slates, tiles, bricks, etc. belonging to the Bear-house or stable and also all such old timber as Henslowe has lately bought from an old house in Thames Street, most of which is now in the yard of the Bear Graden.

Also to pay Katherens for doing the work £360 as follows: £60 acknowledged already received, and £10 each week for the first six weeks during which the workmen shall be on the building, for their wages (if they total so much), and when the playhouse, bull-house and stable are built, to make up those wages [to?] £100, and when the playhouse, bull-house and stable are built, tiled, and walled to pay a further £100, and when the playhouse, bull-house and stable are fully finished and done to pay another £100 in full payment of a total of £260 (14).

Katherens binds himself to Henslowe and Maid.

G.K.

witnesses, Moyses Bowler
      Edward Griffin.

Notes on the Hope Contract

(1) The Hope, then, was a dual-purpose house.

(2) Again a double reading has been claimed. The passage either means 'a fit tiring-house-and-stage (in one unit) built to be both removable, and when in use both supported on trestles'. Or it means Katherens will build '(*a*) a proper tiring-house and then (*b*) separately and in addition, a removable stage itself to stand on trestles.'

(3) The evidence of the Hope, then, can to some unspecified degree also relate to the Swan, of which we have De Witt's sketch. It is therefore just possible that what is described here in the Hope contract may have looked like what we see in that sketch, and thus that the sketch partly illustrates the contract.

(4) The staircases, then, were outside the frame and were presumably contained in the two adjoining towers visible in some exterior views of the theatres on Bankside.

(5) In this respect differing from the Swan.

(6) The Gentlemen's Rooms, then, in the Hope were at or about stage level.

(7) The distinction between 'upon' the stage and 'over' the stage is not clear.

(8) The posts opposite to the inner principal posts; that is, the posts separating the galleries in the *outer* wall of the frame.

(9) Binding joists; horizontal joists binding the inner wall of the frame and the outer wall together.

(10) *See* 8.

(11) Prick posts; possibly intermediate posts set between the inner principals and the outer principals to help support the floors.

(12) Bressumers; horizontal timbers spanning from one principal post in a face to the next principal post.

(13) Whether the separate mention of both benches and seats in the abandoned Bear House implies that there could be a more comfortable form of seating than benches, is not certain.

(14) The figures are difficult to reconcile.

THE DE WITT–VAN BUCHELL SKETCH

Here, then, some encouragement is offered to begin the reconstruction of a playhouse. Can this information be safely supplemented from any other source?

The authenticity of the facts reported in the De Witt–Van Buchell sketch is widely debated. But it would seem that the following things are categorically stated and presumably have to be accepted:

1. There appear to be two flights of stairs leading into the frame at points either side the stage. These are labelled *ingressus*; they would then seem to be the access from yard to galleries.

2. The three galleries are named. The name on the lowest may refer not to the whole gallery but only to that part beyond the steps. The name is *orchestra*; on an analogy with the best seats in a Roman theatre, it may here signify the Gentlemen's Rooms. The middle gallery is labelled *sedilia*, lesser seats. And though seats are also shown in the top gallery, this is labelled *porticus* which means a roofed walk-way. The suggestion is that (since sight-lines would only allow two rows of benches up here as against five rows in the lowest gallery) there must have been a promenade-space behind the seating. These and other suggestions are studied in some detail in the present writer's article in *Shakespeare Survey* No. 12, entitled 'On Reconstructing a practicable Elizabethan public playhouse'.

3. The part of the theatre at the back of the stage is labelled *mimorum aedes*, the house of the players.

4. The two great columns supporting the Heavens appear to be classic columns of the Corinthian order. Further, the row of small columns lining the balcony along the façade of the players' house, as well as those supporting the galleries, appear to have bases, possibly also capitals (but these are hidden by the overhang), and certainly that form of curvature of profile known as *entasis*, which is a characteristic of classic columns. The general conclusion might perhaps be drawn that this is an interior decorated in Renaissance style.

5. The stage floor itself bears a possibly unexpected name, but this is going to have a considerable influence on our interpretation of the future developments of theatre planning. It is called *proscaenium*. Thus the first time we meet this momentous word in our history we find it applied to the floor on which the players act—it is the stage.

What may be called negative, or puzzling, facts in the drawing are as follows:

1. The two shaded shapes under the stage either side have defied all interpretation so far.

2. It is very difficult indeed to imagine in what way the wall of the players' house is meant to be joined to the adjacent galleries. Certainly it seems to be a flat wall, but does it stand in advance of the curve of the galleries, or is it set back so as to be 'flush' with them?

3. The character of the persons represented in the balcony behind the stage has never been determined. They have been called: other actors taking part in a scene; other actors, but only watching at a rehearsal; not actors, but musicians; neither actors nor musicians but audience. On the whole perhaps the likeliest explanation is that they are drawn there to represent the plain fact that some of the audience could indeed sit there. The rest of the auditorium is left empty simply because the draughtsman took it for granted that anyone looking at the drawing would know that spectators sat there also, and thus he did not bother to put them in to spoil his careful benches.

4. The greatest and most disturbing puzzle in the picture is the uncompromisingly blank wall below this balcony, and between the two doors. Here, one school of reconstructors claims to be certain that there existed the 'inner stage' with its convenient traverse curtain. But De Witt gives not the slightest indication that he saw anything remotely resembling such an arrangement. He ignores the 'inner stage'.

If he was right, an awkward question crops up. Where, then, did the Elizabethan 'discoveries' take place? Richard Hosley has studied this question [30]. He shows that discoveries were possibly much rarer than might be generally supposed, and is perfectly prepared to accept De Witt and to plant 'discoveries' either at doors, or behind a curtain hung across the front of the tiring house façade. May it not also be possible that, in the approach made in the present book by way of the staging methods of Interlude players before Hall-screens, we have ourselves found justification for supposing the Elizabethan player was quite capable of rigging a 'discovery space' in circumstances like those shown by De Witt, if he wanted to? Indeed, the whole history of the booth stage would seem to lead up to giving him just that knowledge.

A matter about which there is positive evidence should be added to the above. We have various statements that the interiors of the Elizabethan playhouses were 'beautiful to look at', were 'painted', and were marbled in a fashion skilful enough to deceive even a curious bystander.

BOWERS, TREES AND BEDS

One only of the many problems of staging can be referred to here, it is the problem indicated by the (almost classic) phrase— 'a Bed thrust out'. What is implied here?

The approach made in this present review has often brought to attention the idea of players making use of an 'extra thing'; indeed the whole class of 'secondary resources' now available to an actor might be divided into *fixed* things (like the stage and its background and entrances) and things extra or *brought on* to help the action of one particular scene only. These things may possibly be removed again for the next scene, or they may stay in position and be tacitly counted as not existing during following scenes in which they are not needed.

Examples of the first type of secondary resources—the fixed things—are the *pandal* in Kathakali, the awning in Tibet, and the whole booth stage itself. Examples of the second type—extra things, or things brought on—are a chair set in an Interlude, the enclosure of red cloth for a house in Tibet, the curtain used for a city wall on the Chinese stage, the scenic properties of the Noh stage and the prison in the Basque pastorales.

To what extent were such resources used on the Elizabethan stage and how were they managed? Formerly, the opinion seems to have been that they were not widely used. Perhaps because the idea seemed too unfamiliar and 'crude' to be associated with plays so advanced in literary style as the Elizabethan. Instead, the notion of the 'inner stage' was invented and exploited widely, by means of which all such needed things could be set in place behind a curtain (as on a modern picture-frame stage) and then 'discovered' when required, by opening the curtains on to what was in effect a little inset scene. This method has the great disadvantage that action played around objects so placed must be far away and 'lost' at the back of a large empty stage.

One of the results of the approach made in this review, however, is that it no longer seems inconsistent for players to use 'pretence' in a performance. They are and always have been quite content to say 'Let us pretend this chair is a palace'—and go on with what mattered; the acting. Again, it has become clear that players never found any objection in the idea of a servant, or stage-hand, bringing on such a needed object quite simply and openly, and putting it down and leaving it for the action, and then coming on and removing it when it was done with. It's all part of the show. If these are true opinions, then a more practical and effective use of a 'scenic object' is not to lose it in an alcove, but to have it brought on, taken well downstage (if necessary) and set where the action could be seen by all. This would leave the discovery space at the back for use only when some special effect was needed, and even then only for as short a time as possible, taking the first opportunity to bring the action out of the removed space and go on with it forward on the stage proper.

Thus it is likely that not only were beds 'thrust out' on to the stage, but also prisons (as at Tardets) and tents and many other similar needed items of that kind. So also in the case of what might be called the Mystery of *The Spanish Tragedy*. In this play Thomas Kyd makes much of the arrangement by the two lovers, Horatio and Bellimperia, to meet in a 'bower'. It is repeatedly mentioned in their preliminary talk in Act II, sc. 2. In sc. 3 there follows a separate discussion between the king and an ambassador; and then sc. 4 opens with the lovers again and Horatio says 'Let us to the bower', and there follows straight away a love scene obviously *within* the bower for Horatio says:

> *The more thou sitt'st within these leafy bowers*
> *The more will Flora deck it with her flowers.*

Later, murderers attack the ill-fated Horatio and the stage-direction runs—*They hang him in the arbour*. Bellimperia shrieks '... Murder! Help, Hieronimo ...' One of the murderers retorts 'Stop her mouth ...', and then follows a general exeunt. Next, Horatio's father, Hieronimo, enters (having heard the cry for help) and exclaims '... Alas, it is Horatio, my sweet son!' and cuts him down.

Now all the above might seem to be amenable to performance in one of those distant 'inner stages' which were presumed to exist at the back (save that it would surely be lamentably bad presentation not to make the most of such an action). And yet we have a

Fig. 34. From the title page of The Spanish Tragedy (*ed.* 1633)

remarkable illustration on the title-page of the 1633 edition of
The Spanish Tragedy. What importance ought we to attach to it?
It seems to show something very different, (*see* Fig. 34). Here are
the three figures of Hieronimo, Bellimperia and Lorenzo with
legends coming out of their mouths bearing almost identical
words to the lines quoted above from the play; and on the
reader's left hangs the body of Horatio in a stage arbour so like
the Tardets prison in principle that the belief is absolutely unavoidable that this scene could have been played entirely without
the use of any putative inner stage at all. When we add that there
is no use of the term 'inner stage' in all Elizabethan literature,
and that the illustration to *The Spanish Tragedy* is a contemporary
fact, the thought is inescapable that here we may have a scenic
'house' or 'tent', and that it was brought on just as a bed was
'thrust out'—by stage-hands.

George Fullmer Reynolds [56] gives valuable hints about such
scenic items—even trees [57]—brought in and stood on the stage.
With regard to the latter item, trees, it is a remarkable fact that
in Van de Venne's etching (*see* Plate 6) we can see peeping up
above the back curtain on the stage the tops of certain trees. This
might be no curiosity if the stage were out of doors. But it is not,

it is an indoor theatre. Therefore it is inescapable that the trees we see must be property trees and waiting to be carried in and set up on stage for a passage in the action—say a wood or a heath.

There are, beyond the points mentioned above, many sources of information less certain in their application, or applicable only to certain theatres, or to the theatre at certain periods. There are accounts by visitors to the playhouses; there are the hints contained in the diatribes of the opponents of the theatres; and there are the many bewildering implications in the scripts of the plays.

But on the whole we may perhaps be forgiven for summarizing a general impression of all these things in the form of a sketch-diagram of what the whole might have looked like for comparison with our other Figures (*see* Fig. 35).

And we add a final opinion that the Elizabethan playhouse was the culmination of a long period of steady development, one that we have laboriously tried to outline above—and that it was not a self-born, sudden brilliance, heralding an unknown modern age still to come.

THE ELIZABETHAN PRIVATE HOUSE THEATRES

Of the second form of Elizabethan theatre we know, from the practical point of view, very little. But there are one or two suggestive points to serve as a basis for future research.

Most of the available information is summed up in W. J. Lawrence's essay 'The Elizabethan Private Playhouse' [40], and in William A. Armstrong's pamphlet *The Elizabethan Private Theatres* [7].

In 1574 an Act of Common Council of the City of London laid certain considerable limitations on the performance of plays, but added:

'Provydid allwaie that this Acte . . . shall not extend to anie plaies . . . shewed in the pryvate house . . . of anie . . . gentleman . . . for the festyvities of anie marriage, assemblye of ffrendes, or otherlyke cawse, without publique . . . collection of money . . .'

Here was a loophole for shrewd managers. True the ban on money-taking seemed final, but this was got over in time. Cuthbert and Richard Burbage opened Blackfriars on these terms,

Fig. 35. A reconstruction of the interior of an Elizabethan public playhouse

letting it as a private house to the boy players. In 1609 they went a step further and used it themselves—the first time a troupe of professionals had played in a 'private house' theatre. So the law was got round.

Some preliminary feeling of the way into the mysteries of the kind of scenery used in the Blackfriars as a private house theatre is offered by W. J. Lawrence in his essay 'New facts about the Blackfriars' [39]. The most seizing point here is that Lawrence claims the stage was limited to showing only three 'mansions' or houses for three different simultaneous scenes—centre, left and right; any further scene needed by the play had to be left 'unlocalized'—that is, played between the mansions. Thus we get an early suggestion of the division into located (or represented) scenes, and scenes of a much lighter localization, where the action of the players on a stage was raised once more to the chief scenic interest, rather than their pretence at being in some other spot. This split convention lived on into the Restoration when, as we shall see on p. 242, there is an echo of it in the construction of the Dryden-Purcell operas.

A Stage for Masques

If the foregoing were the entire story of the opening of the 'organized stage' phase, theatre history might have taken a different course and the theatre of today been of a different shape. But it is not the entire story. Another group of people were organizing another stage and with other intentions.

The professional players with their own dramatists serving as practical members of their companies would presumably have been content with the stage we have described, since in fact it was the stage they built, and by it they raised at any rate the dramatic theatre to one of the heights of its history. But the courtly amateurs had another view.

They organized a stage not for acting and drama, but for spectacle and scenery; and generally speaking the word 'spectacle' used in this connection means one particular new branch of theatre—the *opera*.

This bifurcation of stage function is possibly the most influential factor in the creation of present-day theatre that has happened in theatre history—the bifurcation into the acting-stage and the scenic opera-stage.

The origins of the scenic stage lie in court performances in the 16th century. They became especially influenced by developments in Italy; but it is convenient here to take, as an example of the story the events which happened in England. In England in the early 16th century, the performance of a play at court had, as we have seen, many items in common with the performance of a play in any great house. But the masques are different. The form of entertainment developed from maskings was peculiarly adapted to court taste, and offered a specially suitable vehicle for satisfying an ancient court appetite for chivalric allegory. The masque was always a show with a limited appeal. No masque-writer ever wrote for the general public. In spite of some of the most amusing occasional *divertissements*—for instance James Shirley brought on the stage-hands in the middle of his *Triumph of Peace*, Whitehall 1634, to argue about, and claim credit for, separate items of the setting, and at length to insist on staging a pseudo-impromptu masque-dance of their own; which is excellent fooling—in spite of such things, the masque primarily set itself to please and to flatter royal spectators. It was an elaborate, clever, learned, 'modern', and exclusive entertainment. And since courtly entertainment must frequently be international entertainment, it was expected of the masque that it should, beside extolling the host and his country, impress foreign visitors as outstanding in splendour and in brilliance.

Moreover, it had to create these impressions in a world of new thought, starred with inquiring intellects and the exponents of a rebirth of learning. It is therefore perhaps understandable that the brightest minds of the time should be encouraged to do something that Andrea Pozzo, in 1700, was to phrase as 'making the spectators themselves see a thing which they denied could be done' ('quo tandem assecutus sum ut illi ipsi factum conspicerent quod negebant posse fieri' [52]). Andrea Pozzo was an Italian expert on Perspective. And it was in Italy that the first explorations were made into the mysteries of revising the presentation of court entertainments. They produced three results; they made the entertainments fit the contemporary idea of the methods of the Ancient Classical World; they demanded that the entertainments should employ perspective, for the sake of its marvellous effect; and they stressed the elements of singing and music.

These new endeavours went back in Italy to the late 15th century. By 1551 Sebastian Serlio could produce the first treatise on building scenes for a theatre (translated into English in 1611). It was very notably not the treatise of a professional player, but of an intellectual and an architectural theorist. It proposed backgrounds for theatrical performances but for performances in no respect like the shows of the English Interlude players. It took no account, in fact, of the plays to be performed at all—except to offer three varieties of scene; a tree scene for 'satyrical' plays (which were comparatively rare); and two street scenes (identical except for the buildings composing them), intended one for any 'tragedy' and the other for any 'comedy'—no interior scenes being provided for at all. These varieties were made on the basis of the classical drama. There was no consideration of any method of scene-changing. So far as can be seen, Serlio's scheme had little effect on the development of the living theatre.

What were to have a much more far-reaching effect were the devices of Buontalenti (1536–1608) and the brothers Giulio Parigi (d. 1635) and Alfonso Parigi (d. 1656), and several other such, for movable scenery for the setting of operas.

This effect was exerted, so far as English theatre is concerned, through the following channel:

INIGO JONES'S 'HOUSES'

There exists, from about the years 1605 to 1640, a document of outstanding English interest—a very considerable number of designs for costumes and for scenery (together with some plans of stages) for performances at the Stuart court from the hand of the architect, Inigo Jones. What they show is the complete revolution which took place in the scenic method of the masque, including the introduction of a specially organized stage, designed to accommodate the novelties. Jones's designs begin with a style of setting very like that we had reconstructed from the Elizabethan Revels Accounts, but in 1606, and again in 1613, he went to Italy (bringing back certain of the Parigis' designs). Thereafter the story is different.

I propose to take two examples from this series; one from the beginning of Jones's work showing its link with tradition and one from near the end, to illustrate the change. Jones's earliest surviving drawing for masque scenery is for Ben Jonson's *Masque of Queenes* at Whitehall in 1609. It shows a scenic 'house' of just the sort we have imagined at the end of the previous chapter, though perhaps a little bigger and a little more elaborate. The house is two-storeyed and would appear to be some 20–25 ft. high. It represents The House of Fame, and the 'house' itself is almost all that is shown in the drawing. But when we seek to make a rough diagram of the setting as it must have appeared, referring at the same time to Jonson's own account of the performance which accompanies the printed copy of the masque, we are forced to make certain conjectural additions. These are suggested in Fig. 36. Of this diagram, only the central part—the house itself—appears in any detail in Jones's sketch. But it can just be seen in his sketch that he did in fact indicate something else; for in the very slightest lines he has added a couple of reclining figures above the house, one on either side, seeming to be separate and lying on clouds. And from each there fall two faint,

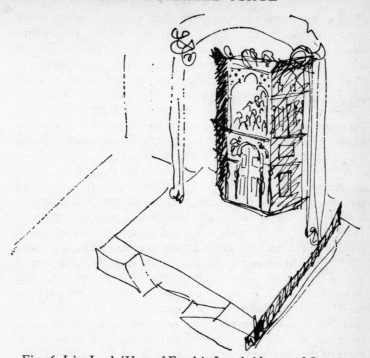

Fig. 36. Inigo Jones's 'House of Fame' in Jonson's Masque of Queenes

loose lines down to the ground—suggesting the folds of a curtain.

Taking, now, Jonson's description [22], we may extract the following to help reconstruct the performance:

'. . . His majesty then being set, and the whole company in full expectation, the part of the Scene which first presented itself was an ugly Hell; which flaming beneath, smoked unto the top of the roof . . .' It was the abode of witches, and 'These witches, with a kind of hollow and infernal music came forth from thence' to the number of twelve. And after making their entrance they recited spells and began to dance, moving 'contrary to the custom of men, dancing back to back, and hip to hip, their hands joined, and making their circles backward, to the left hand . . .' They thus presented the 'anti-masque', a sort of 'foil, or false masque' to set off the true masquing dance of the Twelve Queens (all noble ladies of the court) that was to follow.

Now the moment of the great effect was ready; there was a 'sound of loud music . . . with which not only the Hags themselves, but the hell into which they ran, quite vanished and the whole face of the scene altered . . . in place of it appeared a glorious and magnificent building, figuring the HOUSE OF FAME [*see* Fig. 36], in the top of which were discovered the twelve *Masquers*, sitting upon a throne triumphal, erected in form of a pyramid, and circled with all store of light. From whom a person by this time descended, in the furniture of *Perseus*, and expressing heroic and masculine *Virtue*, began to speak.'

After his speech—'here the throne wherein they sat, being *machina versatilis*, suddenly changed [that is to say, the throne in the upper storey of the house, bearing the twelve queens, was built on a revolve, which now turned]; and in place of it appeared *Fama Bona* . . . she after the music had done, which waited on the turning of the machine, called from thence to *Virtue*, and spake . . .' Thus, the queen-masquers in the upper storey, being turned out of sight, were given an opportunity to leave their seats and descend unseen in readiness for the next effect; Fame's speech, together with further music, gave them the time to do this. So we may 'by this time imagine the masquers descended and . . . mounted into three triumphant chariots ready to come forth.' Four of the queens mounted a chariot drawn by eagles, escorted by four torch-bearers and trailing four witches bound prisoner behind; another four queens got into the second chariot drawn by griffons, and similarly accompanied; and the last four queens (including now the Queen's Majesty herself) mounted a 'more eminent' chariot drawn by lions, with six torch-bearers, and similarly trailing captive witches; and a troupe of musicians brought up the column. Then the double doors were thrown open and with 'a full triumphant music' this noble procession entered and 'róde in state about the stage'. (At this mention of a 'stage' our interest is especially sharpened to see what follows.)

There was another song. Then they 'lighted from their chariots and danced.' (But we are not told where.) There followed a second dance. And then the great essence of the masque-occasion came—'they took out the men' (that is to say each lady masquer invited a gentleman from the audience to dance with her) and together they danced 'the measures' for some hour. Now, this part of the entertainment must have taken place (as indeed it did

Fig. 37. The players entering from the House of Fame

in other masques) on the dancing floor of the Hall itself—not on any stage. There next followed a song 'to give them rest', accompanied by 'the music which attended the chariots'—and then a third dance by the queen-masquers—then galliards and corantos—'and then their last dance . . . with which they took their chariots again, and triumphing about the stage, had their return to the House of Fame, celebrated with their last song'.

We have two problems in this. How was the first scene of Hell made and caused to disappear? And what is implied by 'stage'?

Let us turn back to Fig. 36. The 'house' appears to be, as we have hinted, a perfect example of the sort of thing itemized in the Revels Accounts. It is very likely made of three 'frames', canvassed, 'fashioned', painted, and set up. Maybe the frames are joined with 'vices'. It is presumably quite as resplendent as anything William Lyzarde 'gilded with gold and fine silver', and particularly is it made brilliant with glistening lights.

It would appear, however, that it is unlikely to have been a free-standing house, clear by itself on the hall floor. This is chiefly because of the very considerable procession that has to be arranged behind it, and has to enter through it. Thus we set it against one of the walls of the Hall in front of a door—but whether against an end wall, or in the centre of one of the sides, we have no evidence. It must, however, have been a little away from the wall to allow the projection backward, and turning, of the revolve.

We have now to consider the two mentions of the word 'stage'. If these are to be taken literally (and there appears no alternative), then we must add something of the nature shown in the Figure. It cannot be a small stage; but it was probably not a very high one. It cannot be small because it had not only to accommodate three chariots with their teams of draught animals—but to permit of the 'riding in state' and the 'triumphing' about that stage as well. And beyond the chariots there are twelve witches, fourteen torch-bearers, Perseus, and a troupe of musicians and singers— to say nothing of the twelve Queens sitting in the cars—all moving on the stage at once. That is getting on for fifty people in all—a kind of throng that has to be pictured at least as extensive as the suggestion in Fig. 37.

The stage is not likely to have been very high because of the dances. By which is meant that though we have no information on where the Queens danced—whether on the stage (which of course was still encumbered with their waiting cars and the rest of the throng), or on the floor of the Hall—we yet have, on the other hand, the certainty that the Queens must have come down to the floor of the Hall in order to go and 'take out the men' for the great masquing dance. And thus there must have been some form of ramp or steps to the stage to allow of their descent.

Finally, we turn to the scenic problems at the opening. How was the Hell done? And how did it vanish?

It is possible that Jones's four faint lines hanging from the clouds above, offer a hint. Jonson's words about the Hell are that, 'flaming beneath', it 'smoked unto the top of the roof'. This bringing-in of the idea of the hall-roof may suggest that the thought of suspension was in his mind. And indeed there pre-

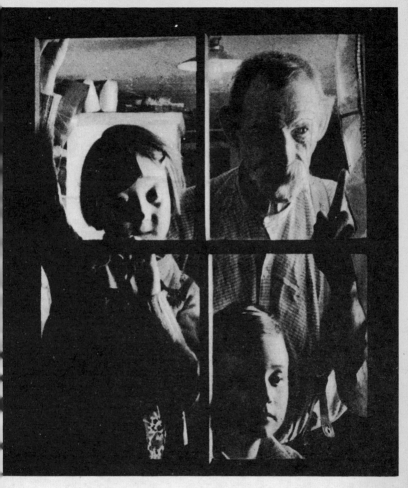

Primitive audience: a Bavarian cottager and his grandchildren at their window awaiting the approach of the Wild Men.

2a. A Kathakali dancer from the Kerala Kalamandalam Institute (*cf*. Fig. 12).

2b. A view of a Tibetan performance in Batang (*cf*. Fig. 18).

3. A Balinese *barong* making an entrance into the acting area.

4. Detail of a painting by Pieter Balten showing a booth stage at a Dutch fair

5. Detail from a print by R. Booms dated 1618 showing an open-air stage in Holland.

6. Illustration by Adriaen van de Venne from *Tafereel van de belacchende werelt*, 1635, showing a stage that possibly resembles an Elizabethan stage, arranged indoors at a fair in the Hague.

7. Detail from an unidentified painting *c.* 1660 (perhaps by van der Meulen) at Drottningholm Theatre Museum, showing a stage possibly resembling an Elizabethan stage, arranged in a town square.

8. Photograph of a model now destroyed, formerly in the Nationalmuseum, Nürnberg. This photograph is our only record of a significant piece of evidence for the scenic system described on p. 225, and should be studied in conjunction with Fig. 49.

9. The complication of machinery above the stage in the 1766 theatre at
Drottningholm Palace near Stockholm.

10. The oldest surviving opera house in Germany; the Schlosstheater at Celle dating from 1670.

CONTINENTAL OPERA HOUSES

11. An old photograph of the Manoel Theatre in Valletta, Malta, built 1731, showing the ranges of boxes before alteration.

2. The 1748 Markgräfliches Opernhaus in Bayreuth, designed by Guiseppe and Carlo Bibiena.

CONTINENTAL OPERA HOUSES

3. The recently restored Residenztheater in Munich built in 1752 by François Cuvilliés.

14. A Chinese *ch'ing*, or great painted make-up; an actor in the part of the Earth
God in a play from the Monkey epic, *The Revolt against Heaven*.

5. A Japanese Kabuki player on the *hana-michi*; the celebrated actor Matsumoto Koshiro in the character of Shibaraku at the Kabuki-za Theatre, Tokyo.

16. A model by the author reconstructing the first theatre of 1716 in William[s]burg, Virginia.

17. A model by the author reconstructing the 1766 theatre set up insi[de] St. George's Guildhall, King's Lynn (see also Fig. 58).

. The two chorus singers in Bertolt Brecht's *Der kaukasische Kreidekreis* (1954) tting at the foot of the proscenium side (director, Bertolt Brecht; costumes Karl von Appen).

19. The interior of Le Théâtre en Rond de Paris; founded by Paquita Clau[
and André Villiers in 1954.

TWO THEATRES IN THE ROUND

20. The theatre in the Round at the Library, Scarborough, arranged for Sartr[
Huis Clos; founded by Stephen Joseph.

. The 'Arena Theatre' set up in a tent in Cannon Hill Park, Birmingham; founded by John English.

TWO OPEN-STAGE THEATRES

. The Shakespearean Festival Theatre at Stratford, Ontario, Canada, iginated in 1953 under Sir Tyrone Guthrie and Tanya Moiseiwitsch, architects Routhwaite and Fairfield.

23. A theatre adapted for the open-stage productions of the Cockpit Thea[tre] Club in 1952 by Ann Jellicoe (see also Fig. 65).

24. The dance-school at Dartington Hall, Devonshire, arranged for an op[en] stage presentation of Anouilh's *The Waltz of the Toreadors* in 1959 (direct[ed] Richard Southern; costumes, Iris Brooke).

sumably must have been some means of suspending the two reclining figures painted on clouds above Jones's house. The whole might have been a cut-out cloud border, painted like smoke, concealing a curtain track on which one of those oft-mentioned 'traverse curtains' ran—one that here was painted after the manner of a 'great cloth' to represent flames below and smoke above rising to mingle with the border clouds, and with certain openings in the lower part through which the Hags appeared—'first one, then two, and three, and more till their number increased to eleven', to quote Jonson's own words. (The Twelfth Witch made a separate entrance later.)

Then at the scene change 'not only the Hags themselves' ran back through the openings and so vanished, but upon the drawing of the curtain-line 'the hell into which they ran quite vanished' also—or gathered in two folded columns either side, to frame the gorgeous and glittering House which now appeared, with the twelve noble masquers seated aloft and 'circled with all store of light.'

This, then, would be a comparatively traditional kind of masque, if our reading of the evidence is a true one.

In which case it is not uninteresting to note that in Jones's drawing we have possibly the only actual illustration so far known to exist of a typical 'apt house' for players. Or at least, in this case, for masquers. It is not unlikely that we should be justified in accepting it as an illustration of a 'house for players' provided we were to imagine it less elaborate. And it is an important reflexion that the professional players would be completely content with houses that *were* less elaborate, while for the court-masque performers a setting that was *not* elaborate was no setting at all. Our approach through this history so far suggests that it is quite understandable that professional players would be more attracted to prompt an audience to 'piece out our imperfections with your thoughts'. Whereas we know that the greatest masque writer of all exclaimed against masques—and specifically against masques that Inigo Jones set:

> O showes! Showes! mighty showes!
> The eloquence of Masques! What need of prose,
> Or verse or sense, t'express immortal you?
> You are the Spectacles of state! . . .

So, Ben Jonson thought of masques in his bitter *Expostulation* of 1635.

We have spoken before of *intrusions* into the theatre from influences outside who saw in it a means for exploiting a conception of their own. In Ben Jonson's mind, Inigo Jones was a supreme example of such an intrusion, since under his hands the Poetry of the theatre was smothered by something

> *which by a specious, fine*
> *Terme of you Architects, is call'd DESIGNE!*
> *But, in the practiz'd truth, DESTRUCTION is*
> *Of any art, byside what he calls his!*

Thus, the move to elaborate the 'apt houses' was not to proceed without opposition.

INIGO JONES'S STAGE

There now follow in Jones's designs a great number of developing ideas of setting as he passes through experiment after experiment. At first his advances are modest. For Jonson's *Oberon* in 1611, Jones prepared a painted, cut-out mountain with a great cave in the centre. This cave was closed by rocks at the beginning of the performance, but at the scene-change the closed rocks parted and slid aside revealing a palace behind. This in turn gave way to 'the nation of Faies', though unfortunately we lack any drawing for this last scene and cannot guess what was involved in the change. But the significant point remains that we have here three distinct scenes succeeding each other by some method or other of primitive scene-change.

There follow more ambitious effects; greater marvels; the inception and development of a specialized machinery system. The path was not all roses. Jones's second visit to Italy in 1613 was a longer one, but on his return he would appear, on the very scanty hints we have, to have found an initial difficulty in picking up his thread again, and for several years the story is hard to trace. Then the marvels begin. But space forces us to pass over them until we come to the year 1635.

We are then unusually favoured. We have the designs for a show in the newest of Inigo Jones's styles; we have surviving drawings for all (save one) of the scenes involved in that show; we have two stage plans and two technical diagrams of the stage; we have on one of these plans something that is unique in all masque history, that is an inscribed plan of the disposition of the auditorium as well. And, finally, the show in question is especially interesting to this history in that it was not a masque but a 'pastoral' play—and thus one step nearer to orthodox public theatre. This 'pastoral' (or idyllic-shepherd play) was in French, presented by a company of French players under Floridor at Whitehall in December 1635, and entitled *Florimene*. It is an interesting reflection on the theatre of the times to see that a British designer prepared the auditorium, stage and scenery for a visiting French company. There would appear not to have been that concern then for the intimate integration of action, setting, production and play that we profess to rate as one of the essentials of theatre today.

The *Argument* of the play with a description of the scenes was published in English in 1635, but I have unfortunately not been able to hear of the existence of a copy of the play itself. From the Argument we find that *Florimene* is a play about shepherd wooing complicated by the most involved disguisings, mistakes and cross-wooings. It all takes place (save for the final scene) in one setting, a 'shutter scene' on the isle of Delos. But there are six scenes; and in the intervals between them, an Introduction and four Intermedii are played—more or less in the form of *ballets* with little to do with the plot—and representing a Temple and the Four Seasons. Each of these has different scenery and for each the shutters are opened and the whole depth of the stage revealed, with the temple or the views of winter, spring, summer or autumn arranged in cut-out planes as special spectacles—scenes in relief. Thus we have:

Sc. 1.   Delos (shutter),
Sc. 2.   'Introduction', Temple of Diana (relief),
Sc. 3.   Delos (shutter),
Sc. 4.   1st Intermedium, Winter (relief),
Sc. 5.   Delos (shutter),
Sc. 6.   2nd Intermedium, Spring (relief),
Sc. 7.   Delos (shutter),
Sc. 8.   3rd Intermedium, Summer (relief),
Sc. 9.   Delos (shutter),
Sc. 10. 4th Intermedium, Autumn (relief),
Sc. 11. A new scene of the Temple of Diana (shutter).

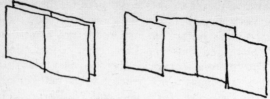

Fig. 38. Two pairs of 'back shutters'
Fig. 39. The opening of the first pair of shutters to reveal the second

('for' says the *Argument* rather proudly, 'no Scoene but that of the Pastoral was twice seene.')

At the end of the last scene 'Here the Heavens open, and there appear many deities, who in their songs expresse their agreements to these marriages.' For illustrations of all the scenes, with a brief note *see* [64].

There is one revolutionary innovation in the above when compared with all the performances we have so far outlined in our history—and that is the system of scene-changes and their method of working. We must make some study of this. Jones had seized on his system of *opening* a piece of scenery by drawing its two halves apart to reveal a new scene behind; he had elaborated it in the intervening masques, and coined a name for the two sliding elements, the descriptive name of *shutters*. He further incorporated the new and fashionable effect of the perspective vista, by framing his back scene of shutters at the end of an avenue of diminishing *side scenes*. These had a functional as well as a visual purpose; they covered up or 'masked' the space at the sides into which the shutters slid when they were opened, as well as helping the effect of perspective 'depth' of the back scene.

Fig. 38 shows two pairs of closed shutters, one behind the other. Fig. 39 shows the same save that the front pair of shutters is opened. Fig. 40 shows the framing-in of the shutters by an avenue of diminishing side scenes, and the whole mounted on a stage. Clearly we are now beginning to go a long way from the 'House of Fame' in *The Masque of Queenes*.

But the adventure is not yet complete. So far, this is no advance on Serlio. But the final steps are difficult. We require a heaven; how to conceal where it begins? And the crucial step is then taken. The framing side scenes are themselves framed in by a special front frame, which now provides a mask to the heavens-

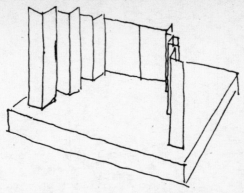

Fig. 40. Framing the back shutters with 'Serlian' side scenes or wings

edge by a strip across, hung from the ceiling. And the setting is now set behind a surround—suitably named by Jones, a *frontispiece*—and is viewed through and under this surround (*see* Fig. 41).

An unbiased observer would be free to comment at this point, 'But surely—though it is very interesting—this is a quite strange idea! Why should the simple and direct setting of plays that we have studied so far suddenly take on this remarkable complexity? What has it all to do with the presenting of the play?'

The simple answer must be given. On the face of it, and according to the facts we have, it does not seem that it had anything to do with the presenting of plays. It is understandable that, with the particular attitude in which court entertainments were regarded, it can have had a good deal to do with the presenting of masques. And of course this is what our history has demonstrated. No such system was ever employed, up to this time, by the common players in their public performances. It has been a purely court system. And even in the court it was never resorted to when the professional players came to give one of their regular plays.

But it possessed immense glamour. It was very splendid; it could be most satisfying as a demonstration of munificence. It might cost a great deal, but what was there not to show for it! And it was fashionable, in that all the princely courts of Western Europe were taking it up, and it incorporated the new intellectual and artistic achievement of the budding Renaissance world. It

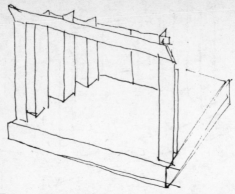

Fig. 41. Framing the whole scene with a 'frontispiece'

was impossible to avoid it because it was an emblem of the age.

And so, when *Florimene*—not a masque but a French pastoral play—came to court in 1635, Inigo Jones prepared a full theatre for it which can be represented diagrammatically as in Fig. 42. It is useful to compare this diagram with those in Figs. 29 and 36 to emphasize both developments and contrasts.

The auditorium was set up by building degrees, or steps, round one end, and the halves of two sides, of the Masquing Hall, leaving a space of clear floor inside. At the end of this clear space, the State or royal seat was placed. The degrees were, at certain points, railed off into rudimentary 'boxes'—one for the Countess of Arundel, another for the Lady Marchioness and so forth. Jones's plan for the seating (in Lansdowne MS No. 1171 at the British Museum; for reproduction *see* [61]) shows certain posts rising at points in the seating; whether these were to provide further rails or to support anything above, we do not know.

It is interesting to notice how, although a new system of staging (which we shall consider in a moment) is used at the opposite end of the Hall, yet the arrangement of seating is not such as would dispose the spectators most easily to face the stage, but is on lines exactly reminiscent of the old arrangement of spectators round the Place at an Interlude in a Tudor Hall. This is partly in deference to the King's position.

We turn now to the great, newly organized stage, brought into being to exploit the system of changeable scenes. The nearest part of the stage is still according to court tradition. It offers a

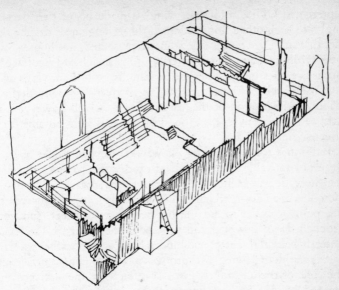

Fig. 42. The complete theatre for Florimene; *the borders above the scene are omitted for clearness*

small forestage with two flights of steps such as would allow masquers to descend for the taking-out dance in a masque.

Immediately behind this forestage is the great Frontispiece, whose opening was filled with a curtain at the beginning of the show but which served, as soon as the curtain was drawn, as a frame and mask for the scenery behind—to hide the necessary machinery and the actors waiting at the sides to make their entrances through the side scenes.

Behind the Frontispiece these side scenes stood in two converging perspective rows. They were, for this show, shaped on what it is convenient to call 'Serlian' lines—and a word about this is required. Serlio's perspective stage was chiefly concerned with showing a street scene, comprising two rows of houses running away and decreasing into the distance to give a greater sense of depth than the stage really had. Serlio built each house of two frames at an angle, one frame facing the audience to represent the near side of the house, the other running somewhat obliquely up-stage to represent the retreating side of the house. (The other two sides of the house were of course invisible and were not represented.) Thus a 'Serlian wing' is made up of two flats at angles to each other. Jones adopted this arrangement despite the fact that in *Florimene* his side scenes represented, not houses, but trees with 'here and there scattering, some shepheards' cottages'. But it is a question whether the Serlian disposition of wings ever lent itself well to the representation of trees— despite Serlio's elaborate description of the 'satyric scene', which however it is hard to reconcile with his ground plan that is only suitable for a street scene.

But Jones was still feeling his way. These side-scenes of trees were not movable; they remained exactly the same all through the show. It was behind the wings that the changes took place. Here the stage floor, which had been sloping gently upwards to this point in order to aid the perspective vista effect, suddenly dropped down one step and proceeded thereafter on the level. Directly behind this step, and hidden by it, a great timber was laid across the floor having two grooves along its upper surface. At the ends of these grooves, just out of sight of the audience and masked by the farthest wings, three slender uprights rose at each end, one from each wall between the grooves—thus presenting two narrow intervals. A similar grooved timber, facing downwards, connected the uprights at their heads, so forming a frame.

Into the intervals at either end of this frame the halves of the shutters could be inserted, and they could be pushed to and fro, provided proper care was taken to keep the grooves clean and well soaped. Men were stationed out of sight to push or pull these halves of shutters (they became appropriately called 'scene-drawers'), and so the shutter scenes were made to change.

But this was only the beginning of the marvels. Practically all the above had been done already as far back as *Oberon* but in a more modest and less organized way. There was a space on the stage behind the shutter scenes; what was this used for?

A scene that changed by means of closing a shutter was changed practically instantaneously, but the new scene which followed had perforce to be another simple scene, painted on the flat surface of the two fresh shutters. No time was allowed for the setting up of anything additional to the flat shutters—and no furniture could be placed. Now, it is important to realize that this condition was unavoidable owing to the nature of the new system, *for all such scene-changes had to have the effect of the magical*; they had to take place in front of the audience and, like the opening rocks in *Oberon*, maintain the element of wonder. Never, for over two hundred years, was scenery to escape the effect of this requirement. Never was any scene-change to take place except before the eyes of the audience. That was one of the essential functions of a scene-change—to be seen.

But a dilemma is created. The growing skill of the architect-designer is quite up to producing far more intriguing settings than a flat picture painted on a flat screen with a split down the middle! He can make up confections of all sorts of cut-out planes and shaped edges, provided he is able to get these arranged adequately on the stage without a complete anti-climax of bustling, struggling stage hands intervening in his magic, and provided he can disclose such scenes instantaneously.

The solution to all this problem is that he can set up *one* such complicated scene in cut-out planes, provided he does it at the back of the stage and reveals it when ready by the simple drawing, as usual, of a pair of shutters. And if such a course is taken, and the pair of shutters, upon drawing, reveals not just another flat scene as might be expected but a complete wonder of complication beyond it that had never been dreamed of—then that great mead of a Renaissance stage architect is his; the gasp of surprise.

But he has to make quite sure of one thing; the next scene to follow after this must be another flat scene, for you could not change a scene in planes before the audience's eyes—you had to hide it and take it down piece by piece.

Jones developed this second variety of scene which he called, again appropriately, a *scene of relieve*, a scene in relief. These relieves could be set ready for discovery in the space behind the shutters and changed while a shutter scene was proceeding in front.

To back these groups of cut-out pieces, Jones erected a permanent backcloth across the deepest part of his stage.

One problem only remained now to be solved. If you sat near the front of the auditorium and looked up through the frontispiece, you would see the roof of the Hall over the scenery. What is of particular difficulty is that you would see the top shutter-groove hanging across, empty, when all the shutters were drawn open. Jones did two things; he crowned each pair of wings by arching across a sky border, narrow and high in the centre but

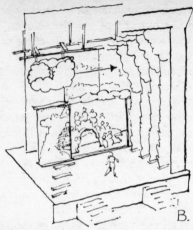

Fig. 43. The fully developed masque stage for Salmacida Spolia

with long, descending 'legs' at either end to reach down to the
wing tops. This was the first thing; it solved part of the problem
but it still left a hole in the centre, between the high arch of the
last border above and the grooves of the back-shutters below.

Then came the second thing and the crowning piece of characteristically 'wonderful' ingenuity. Jones added a pair of *upper
back shutters*, sliding in a higher set of grooves, and painted to
represent clouds. When *these* opened, you had your culminating
marvel—you saw clear through into heaven!

And so, behind the grooves along the top of the lower back
shutters Jones built a tier of seats for deities to sit in upon requirement—and they were of course frequently required. (In Fig. 42
the nearer half of the sky shutters is omitted to show these
seats.)

There was only one snag now; when both upper and lower back
shutters were open at once, still the whole effect was spoiled by
the sight of the empty top groove of the lower back shutters.
This there was no method whatever of getting rid of (at that time)
save by nailing a narrow strip of cloud across to stay permanently
there and hide it. This Jones did. He was (like Pozzo) quite happy
to paint 'air' on his scenery.

This was a 1635 performance, and it by no means displays Jones
at the height of his powers. In 1640, after Ben Jonson had

quarrelled with him, Jones collaborated with Sir William Davenant, and finished by producing *Salmacida Spolia*—by far the greatest of the masques from the point of view of spectacular entertainment. It was one in which both King Charles I and his Queen played the most superbly dressed and ingeniously mechanized parts. (A full description is given in *Changeable Scenery* [61], from which Fig. 43 is reproduced.)

And in 1649 the country was riven by the Puritan revolution, and the 'luxury-loving' king executed, the Commonwealth instituted, and all theatres—courtly or public—were closed.

THE CHINESE STAGE

The Chinese theatre had, at a period not very remote from this, been organizing a stage. It proceeded from a basis that was in many ways like the Tardets stage, with somewhat comparable conventions.

But it became a professional-player theatre, not an occasional, amateur's theatre, and thus these same conventions—such as the marchings, countermarchings and stylized combats—though they had the same basis, yet were allowed the opportunity to receive a technical polish, through centuries of sustained training-tradition, that has made them one of the wonders of the theatrical world.

On the simple stage which the Chinese organized (remarkably like the Elizabethan stage in its character) the costumed-player has still survived supreme. No scenery has ever insinuated itself there to vie with him.

Indeed, it does seem that it would be true to say that on all professional, non-scenic stages the Costumed Player of ancient days has been left to stay supreme. Perhaps that is the great virtue and the great charm of the non-scenic (booth) stage.

A troupe of the most highly advanced, classic Chinese players —such as the Peking Opera—will, when they tour and visit a foreign country today, play with a bare stage surrounded with nothing but plain curtains.

In themselves, and in their costumes and technique, the whole splendour and the whole magic of the show lies. No other effect is called for (*see* Plate 14). And what a splendour and magic it can be!

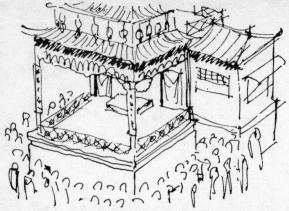

Fig. 44. An 18th-century Chinese classical stage

But the question of *convention* has got to be faced. Their playing is utterly non-naturalistic from top to bottom. It belongs on a non-naturalistic, conventional stage.

The Elizabethan public stage was non-naturalistic (since the players spoke verse) and conventional (since armies battled in groups of four or five). Later (as we shall see), with the coming of scenery and illusion a naturalistic period did later occur in European theatre; but on the Chinese classical stage, scenery never developed, and through the 17th, 18th and 19th centuries the techniques of conventional acting were left to expand, blossom and fruit unspoiled. They did so amazingly.

The stage they required took a form very familiar to us with the approach to theatre made in this book. It was (and is today wherever the old tradition maintains) a plain, open stage, railed at the edge, with two doors in a backwall, and often covered by a canopy. At the back may be some gorgeous hangings. But the riches lie in the costume, and occasionally in the make-up. The properties are (mostly) the simplest essentials. There is a deal in common between the Chinese stage and the Tibetan theatre. To Western eyes the Chinese stage is peculiar; no poet ever seems to have intruded into it; no architect seized upon it for his imaging; no theorist composed a canon of behaviour for it or formulated its ideas. It remains a theatre of the common player.

There has been made available in recent years some considerable amount of information about Chinese theatre make-up,

Fig. 45. A Chinese stage of the early 20th century

properties, costumes and musical instruments. (*See* for instance [4, 6, 35, 72 and 80].) But the Chinese stage itself as the place of the actor's performance has (like so many actor's performing places) been very inadequately studied or illustrated.

The Chinese offer us, however, a splendid example of the pure 'organized-stage' phase of the theatre. Their classical stage is among the simplest, although the richest, in the world. An open-air stage in Peking in the 18th century preserved ancient traditions and yet is very close to the theatres of the 19th century. It looked like Fig. 44. Its description is so simple as to be nearly 'perfect'; a square platform; a roof above supported on columns; two doors in the back wall (that on the stage-right for entrances, and on the stage-left for exits); a dressing-room behind; the audience on three sides. There could be no more complete (nor scarcely any more advanced) expression of the booth-stage tradition confirmed into a national form.

No theatrical action however involved, however sophisticated, however humble, seems beyond the range of this eternally complete solution. There is but one restriction; the action must be expressed in a convention, it cannot be naturalistic.

The close relation of the whole system with that of the Elizabethan stage is remarkable.

In Fig. 45 is the slightest sketch of how such a stage was incorporated indoors in the 19th-century Chinese theatres. This

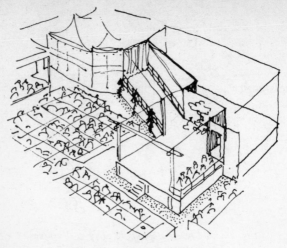

Fig. 46. A Japanese Noh stage

example is based on a curious but valuable illustrated article in—of all unexpected places!—*The Stage Year Book* for 1909.

THE JAPANESE NOH STAGE

The Japanese similarly evolved a non-scenic, organized stage. It arose from much the same kind of root occasion as did the Chinese stage, but acquired particular details.

Some description was given on p. 114 of the form of the early Japanese performances from which the Noh theatre arose. The developments in the position of the stage and in the means of entrance to it, which were hinted at there, were as follows.

The Japanese Noh stage is one of the very few asymmetrical stages in the history of the world. In the 16th century, while still an open-air stage, it moved to one of the four corners of a square enclosure. From a building on the opposite side the prince or dignitary watched it. Today it is incorporated in a building but retains many of its outdoor features (*see* Fig. 46).

It is a square stage situated in the audience's right-hand corner of the theatre, with the ancient *hashi-gakari* now slanting back across to the audience's left. It is railed as shown. The steps in front are now a mere survival. Behind the stage is an annexe where the musicians sit. To the actor's left of the stage is a similar annexe for the chorus. The entrance of the principal characters is from the Mask Room (where it is traditional to have a ritual moment in front of a mirror before entering) at the end of the *hashi-gakari*; thence, by means of a curtain raised like an awning, into the sight of the audience and to the first steps of a processional walk past three pine trees to the stage proper. The small strip of floor surrounding the open stage is strewn with pebbles in memory of its ancient outdoor use, and above the stage is still a decorative roof (omitted in the Figure). The dressing-rooms are behind the stage; and to the stage-left side of the musicians' annexe is a small, low door for hurried or magic exits, such as the disappearance of a spirit.

The audience sits mainly at the front and on one side of the stage, but a few seats exist on the other side also, so making a complete open-stage arrangement. On the very far side of the auditorium are some raised boxes for spectators.

At the back of the stage behind the players is a plain wall with a fir tree painted upon it. That is all the scenery. But upon particular occasions in the plays, certain very simplified scenic objects are brought in and stood on the polished stage floor—a mountain, a carriage, a bell tower, a well. They are close in spirit to the properties of the Tibetan theatre or the bowers of the Elizabethan.

Upon this stage, and in costumes of the richest traditional beauty, with masks for certain characters, the great plays of the Noh repertory are performed in a highly-stylized and ancient technique. Of their beauty some impression may be gained in the delicate translations by Arthur Waley [76]. The *kyogen* as comic interludes are still retained.

Both the last two theatres, Chinese and Japanese Noh, began in the open air but became incorporated into roofed buildings later. In this respect they anticipate our later story, for this present chapter deals only with the rise of the organized stage, and the origin of the roofed playhouse as a regular system has yet to come.

The great impulse to roofed theatres was given at the introduction of scenery from the court entertainments to the stages of public playhouses. But there are in history a few rare occasions when an organized, non-scenic stage has been conceived as a part of a roofed building from its inception. Two examples are the Teatro Olimpico at Vicenza, and the Classical Indian theatre.

THE TEATRO OLIMPICO

Palladio's Teatro Olimpico at Vicenza in Italy (finished by Scamozzi in 1584) can almost lay claim to being the most-illustrated building in theatre-history books. It survives today, a delight to visitors; it is recorded in an excellent documentary film; it is claimed to be the source of all modern playhouse construction.

Its interest is unquestionable. But its influence on later play-house design is so dubious (except as the demonstration of a path that was avoided) that it seems much more relevant to include it in this chapter as a culmination of the organization of the stage than in the next as the beginning of a new era of roofed theatres.

Its main feature so far as this review is concerned is its stage background. This was conceived, or so it appears, to provide the members of the Accademia Olimpica with a reconstruction of the stage background, or *frons scaenae*, of Classical times, so far as Renaissance research had then understood it. It would therefore seem to be unsuitable for any performances save those of Classical plays—or of new plays written in emulation of the Classical forms. In the event, the current of the living theatre did not follow strictly these lines; it had its own way to make.

Noble as the early performances in this theatre were as scholarly occasions (and a vivid contemporary description of the first night there of *King Oedipus* in 1585 is quoted by A. M. Nagler [45]), the theatre fell into early disuse. As often happens in history, when an architect leads the way with a new theatre form con-ceived on the drawing-board, the stream of professional playing found little use for it, and no school of playwrights arose to exploit the conventions it offered.

It is left to the period of 1958 for a distinguished theatre man of modern times, Oscar Fritz Schuh, recently director of the Kurfürstendamm theatre of Berlin, to refer to its possibilities. This he did in a letter [9] which it is perhaps very relevant to quote at a stage in this book when we are just about to enter a new

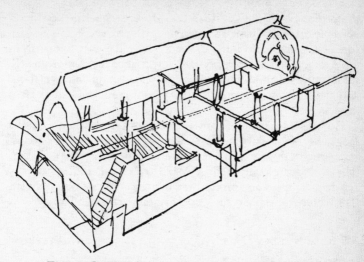

Fig. 47. Conjectural reconstruction of a classic Indian theatre

phase of theatre history and a rebirth of theatre architecture. He wrote:

'Obviously there are many possibilities open to theatre building at the present time. . . . We are at length clear that the picture-frame stage, just as it once sprang into existence, will similarly one day disappear again. And it is to theatre buildings from the Earliest Times up to the Renaissance—including the delectable Teatro Olimpico—that we must turn to build after in terms of modern methods.'

But the Teatro Olimpico has led us to anticipate.

THE INDIAN THEATRE

We await with some eagerness a clear study of the development of the Indian theatre. Of its styles of dance there is beginning to be some account in Western languages, but of the form of the performances and especially of any building specifically designed for the presentation of performances, we are sadly ignorant. How and when, for instance, were Kalidasa's plays for the Gupta royal court staged?

There exist translations of the great classic work on Indian theatrical art, Bharata's *Natyashastra* (said to date back to about the beginning of the Christian era): here is detailed description of three forms of theatre building grouped according to size (the first, some 200ft. long, the next 100ft., the next 50ft.—or, in other renderings, oblong, square and triangular). Unfortunately these translations encounter many difficulties in interpretation, and the final picture must be very conjectural on our present knowledge.

However, a valiant attempt was made in a special number of the magazine *Natya* devoted to theatre architecture [55], to reconstruct such a theatre; and a tentative sheet of plans was published. The notes were completed by Madhao Achwal from a study by the late Subba Rao, professor, architect and Sanskrit scholar. The picture these plans suggest is diagrammatized in Fig. 47.

THE COMMEDIA DELL' ARTE AND ITS STAGING SYSTEMS

The Commedia dell' Arte of Italy has certain curious features which make it a little difficult to place in this development of the phases of theatre. To begin with, it possessed much that was primitive; it was generally simply staged, and made its chief appeal to the ordinary public. On the other hand it has a curiously sophisticated and even brilliant side, which is clearly a product of Renaissance ideas and was capable of satisfying, with its spirited agility and wit, many of the most informed and educated minds of that time.

In some respects it belongs to the dawn of the professional-troupe period of Phase 3, and in some ways to the highly-wrought ingenuities of the latest court entertainments. But on the whole we may associate it more with the pre-scenic phase of the theatre than with the phase of the organized playhouses equipped for full scenery. For, after surviving briefly (and not without some *éclat*) in those new surroundings, the *Commedia* began to fade away.

Thus it seems well to introduce it here in our survey, in such a way as to serve as an instance of the transition between the non-scenic theatre and the scenic theatre still to come. And this particular function it serves to illustrate very well.

In the staging systems of the *Commedia* we find, in some sense, the whole story in little of the problem that faced professional players at the outset of the scenic phase of theatre development.

Commedia dell' Arte is the name of a particular sort of professional theatre that—despite several very significant differences—is fundamentally comparable with that of the Interlude players in England. The main similarity is that the core of the show was the performance of the costumed player in an entertainment for a relatively popular, or at least mixed, audience, with little dependence on any complexity of staging. The main difference (and a very interesting one) is that, lacking the curiously enriching development in their own language with which such human poets as Chaucer had blessed the English tongue, the words of the *Commedia* shows were—in some cases—not skilled and deliberate compositions like Medwall's, or Heywood's, or Redford's, or Pickering's, but were the result of the players' agreeing upon a plot beforehand, and then going on to perform the action straightway, improvising their dialogue as they went along.

It might perhaps seem to a reader of this outline of the theatre that such a course would be a very hazardous one, and that no significant form of theatre-presentation could come from such off-handed method. But this is not so. Just as in the Kathakali theatre a highly effective system of acting technique sprang from the development of silent gesture, so in *Commedia* a highly effective system of acting technique sprang from the development of what it is not improper to call improvised dialogue.

It might seem, too, that to suggest the possibility of such a thing as *technique* in a matter so apparently lacking in form as improvisation is a complete abuse of terms. But this again is not true. The improvisation was only relative. Despite the fact that *Commedia* players had not necessarily a written script (at any rate in the earlier part of their development), they yet had a surprising number of stock, agreed, verbal devices which served as keys to a store of accumulated successful effects. Such effects might be certain situations in a plot which always went well, and which through experience had come to have associated with them a pre-arranged sequence of verbal exchanges, or 'gags', or tricks. As soon as the improvised dialogue had led up to a point suitable for the introduction of one of these effects, a cue from a player would set in motion one of the well-tried *lazzi*, and everyone on the stage would recognize the hint and know the situation that was to follow.

Again (and taking into account the enormous theatrical value to a player of an effective exit, as we have already noticed), the technique of *Commedia* playing involved the knowledge of a fund of *chiusette*, or exit speeches; into one of these an experienced player, once he had exhausted the possibilities of an improvised scene on the stage, could launch, in order both to signal to the others the need for proceeding to a further stage in the plot, and also to give himself a build-up for a climax and, ultimately, a crowning exit.

Furthermore, this technique was so highly developed that a sort of surrealism was created in the use of words, so that a dialogue (or at least a verbal exchange) might take place between two players with an immensely dramatic effect, but using words and sentences in an entirely different way from that found in ordinary speech. This conception of dialogue is clearly difficult to understand from brief description and an example may be useful.

In A. Perucci's *Della parte reppresentiva*, published in Naples in 1699 (which is both a rich and a rare source of information about *Commedia* technique), several examples are given of brief dialogues for special occasions—such as 'Scorn and reconciliation', 'On a dropped handkerchief', 'Of love returned', and so forth. One of these is the dialogue of 'Scorn against Scorn'. In it a Man and a Woman speak. Some passages were perhaps given in echo, some simultaneously, some spoken as ordinary dialogue; some slow, some fast, for timing would be the essence of this sort of thing. And there would scarcely have been omitted the flashing eye, the hands on hips, the stamped foot, the snap and swirl as of castanets and the *flamenco* of Spain. Freely rendered, it runs:

The Dialogue of Scorn against Scorn

She cries These bonds . . .
and He These chains . . .
She . . . what do you cramp?
He . . . what do you bind?
She This soul!
He My heart!
She Break!
He Loose!
She If faith . . .
He If love . . .
She . . . has bound you—

He	. . . has forged you—
She	—Then Hate . . .
He	—Then Scorn . . .
She	. . . will break you.
He	. . . will cast you off.
She	The victim's delivered!
He	The slave is free!
She	Reason . . .
He	Duty . . .
She	. . . saved her.
He	. . . freed him.
She	Villain!
He	Slut!
She	What do you say?
He	What are you muttering?
She	I say I hate you!
He	I say I detest you! . . .

and so it goes on, till finally we have:

She	And you, O Cupid . . .
He	And you, O Love . . .
She	. . . toss off these bonds!
He	. . . destroy these chains!
She	I am free!
He	I am my own!
She	Freed from slavery!
He	Cleared of barriers!
She	The knot's undone!
He	The bond is broken!

These, and many other, stock dialogues were committed to memory by the professional players and drawn upon as the situation arose in the course of actual playing on the stage.

Sometimes more was written. Beyond the simple *libretti* come more or less complete scripts, but in general the player reserved the right to treat his material with the utmost freedom, adapting it (heedless of any author's intentions) to the sort of situation and treatment that he himself had found from experience he could most effectively handle.

The staging of *Commedia* performances was varied. Fundamentally it belonged to the pure booth-stage type, and took place on a high scaffold in a town square or elsewhere outdoors, with the backing of the traditional curtained booth. Sometimes the back curtain is painted (or even merely sketched upon in rude black lines) to represent a perspective street. Sometimes an interesting variant is made by breaking forward a section of the back curtain to give relief to the surface. Sometimes (it would seem) two such breaks-forward, one at either end of the back curtain, might develop into two independent 'towers' or 'houses' either side the stage, each with a practicable door, and a window above from which upper scenes might be played, as can be seen in the Receuil Fossard in the Drottningholm Theatre Collection, and with such an arrangement we seem to reach the transition from medieval simultaneous setting to the symmetrical scene, framed in side 'wings' that heralded the stages of the Italian Renaissance, and of the English Restoration with its 'proscenium doors', see later p. 237.

Sometimes again, we find a variation of the Sabbattini system, and are offered illustrations (as in the Corsini Codex) of full street scenes with three pairs of 'Serlian' wings and a backscene in perspective, though of a primitive type.

And sometimes we find, as for instance in France, in the latest period of the *Commedia's* life an apparently fully elaborated scenic effect, designed to accompany highly sophisticated confections of farcical plots full of tricks and acrobatics. Such sets may well have been identical in principle with the later ones at the Hôtel de Bourgogne described on p. 233.

But for all their richness of technique, a sort of Nemesis was rearing over the heads of the *Commedia* companies and—despite the learned and cultured brilliance reached by some of the most famous of the individual men and women who formed them—the obligation of a new form of theatre settled gradually upon them, and took away their virtue. The nature of the Nemesis we have to describe in the next chapter.

FIFTH PHASE

The Roofed Playhouse With Scenery

THE WORLD POSITION ABOUT SCENERY

THE SCENIC SYSTEM À L'ITALIENNE

AN AUDITORIUM TO SUIT

MAHELOT

THE RESTORATION IN ENGLAND

THE PROSCENIUM AREA

EARLY LONDON THEATRES

KING'S LYNN

THE CONTINENTAL OPERA HOUSE

THE KABUKI THEATRE

FIFTH PHASE

The Roofed Playhouse With Scenery

THE WORLD POSITION ABOUT SCENERY

The remaining couple of centuries or so of our review is scarcely more than a footnote, considered from the temporal point of view, to the great span that we have already covered. The main story is in effect now complete so far as concerns the greater part of the world. Only in comparatively few countries do we see a particular development which brings us to a fifth phase of the theatre, that in which special roofed playhouses are built designed to accommodate scenery. In these countries, the common player instead of being equipped with a small 'tent' or two, with which he could express Abraham's home, the City of Rome, or the Continent of Africa, has to assume the responsibilities of full scenery. And they entail very particular consequences, of which the chief was that (though at first it did not matter so much what was painted upon the scenery) it was absolutely essential from the beginning that this scenery *should change*; next, that the changes should be instantaneous; and last that they must take place *as a spectacle* under the eyes of the audience. Students of the effect of early scenery on theatrical method sometimes tend to overlook these three considerations.

We return now to consider this new development from the point of view of a professional player at the English court.

There may or there may not have been dismay in the hearts of these professional players when they saw, during their visits to act at court, three things; that the court was evolving its own, much more magnificent, form of entertainment; that even their own presentations were decked in a way beyond what they were used to in the public theatres; and finally that shows indoors were spared (as they themselves could never hope to be spared in the unroofed playhouses) the ravages of weather.

It would not be surprising if some of them reflected on the possibilities of a reform, involving the development of a scenic system on masque lines, and consequently of a newly-equipped sort of playhouse under a protective roof.

It would also not be surprising if a good deal of opposition were raised against such an innovation. There is a custom today in some circles to assert that if an Elizabethan playwright could have had at his disposal all the scenic resources of a modern theatre, he would never even have hesitated to abandon his 'booth-stage' habits and turn to writing for full scenery. I am not satisfied on the evidence of history that this is true. I would be quite prepared to find a great number of these playwrights take one look at the scenic method and exclaim: 'Not on your life! Just look at the limitations it imposes!'

On the question of performing indoors, the position is probably different. For one thing, the players were already well used to performing indoors when they did shows in halls. What would probably cross their minds was that they would be forced to choose for ever between two methods of lighting—the hard, revealing, but capricious light of day, and the dim, enchanting glow of artificial flames (which would be so remarkably costly).

There was also to be reckoned the rich and true sound of the actor's voice in open air (but with its burden of background noises) and the more isolated sound of it between walls with few distractions save those made by the audience which he might (given reasonable acting ability) make some effort to mitigate by his performance.

The choice is not easy to make. Except on one matter there is something to be said on both sides—and that one indisputable matter is (in northern climates) the unqualified evil of rain. Whatever the value or not of scenery, no one could deny the advantage to public players of a protection against the rain.

In the event (apart from this point of a roof) the resumption of the theatre story at the Restoration in England saw equal forces in either camp. But this even balance was not to be maintained for long.

From now on the whole story begins to change. The coming of

scenery and the coming of opera into the practice of the theatre together bring something that we have to study with the greatest care if we hope to understand it with any exactness.

Before giving details; what was the position at the opening of this phase in the rest of the world?

The phase is the phase of the roofed theatre designed to accommodate stage performances with scenery. It is the opening phase of our present era. If we seek to obtain an idea of the extent to which this phase spread through the world, we must guard ourselves from preconceptions; certain of the ground can be declared free of this phase straight away. For instance, it is obvious that no form of primitive theatre ever embarked on it, and similarly no form of pure, costumed-player theatre. Again, none of the survivals of great religious festivals ever attained it. (A possible part-exception may perhaps be allowed in the Oberammergau Passion Play, but this is a peculiar case, to some degree artificially brought 'up-to-date' in the interests of touring visitors, and even here the protection of a roof and the use of scenic illusion are only slightly developed.)

Furthermore, travelling troupes of players stemming from the old Interlude tradition made only very qualified use of this phase—as, for example, in the 18th and 19th centuries when travelling with 'portables', or movable theatres, was the vogue.

And lastly, no performance on the booth stage ever entered this phase. For though a booth stage may certainly be set up indoors, yet a booth stage both indoors and employing representational scenery would be a contradiction in terms—for a booth stage is not a scenic stage. Here again, to make our account complete we must recognize the occurrence now and then in the 18th century of certain travelling stages which were set up in public open spaces, and which did possess a proscenium frame, a front curtain, and some form of painted scenery at the back. But such stages are rarely found in unfavourable climates and never, to my knowledge, indoors.

Thus a very great area of the field of theatrical activity never became concerned with this fifth phase of development at all, and still goes on today without any connection with it.

Let us now take the matter by continents. India with Polynesia, and Australia (so far as native traditions go) almost never entered this phase. In Asia, China remained quite free so far as its own culture was concerned, while Japan on the other hand did develop a form of theatre which advanced far and freely into this phase. In the Primitive Americas it was unknown. But in Europe it took a great hold.

It is because of these facts that our examination of the development of theatre must here undergo a change. It is no longer a general story applicable to any community in the world where the act of performance takes place but from now on is restricted to happenings in Europe and Japan only. It would be possible to add of course that very late in time—that is in the late 19th and the 20th centuries—some form of imitation of, or derivation from, the European theatre began to spring up in certain Indian and Chinese and Japanese cities, and in those of North and South America, but these have mostly the character of pushful intruders. The exception, of course, being the theatre of the United States of America, where the intruder (like the English tongue) became naturalized.

We have then to consider development of this fifth phase of the theatre only so far as concerns Europe and Japan. In Europe itself we may consider certain of the countries separately to see what was happening in each at the beginning of the phase—the phase, let us repeat, of roofed theatres specifically designed to accommodate scenery.

In Italy about 1570, the existence of opposing, or at least opposite, forces is very obvious. On the one hand we see the *Commedia dell' Arte*, the remarkable and individual tradition in which the player and his performance were all-important, and the scenic spectacle and the dramatist's script or composer's composition, comparatively nil—or existing only as a sop to the Cerberus at the gate of fashion. On the other hand we have the aristocratic, private presentation in ducal courts of the dazzling new form of the age—opera, with perspective scenes, and machinery. It becomes a cult. Its exponents spread it through the whole of Europe, and admiring visitors take back to their homelands sensational news of the marvel.

In Spain the traditional native performances on cars, and the shows in the *corrales* or inn-yards, are rivalled by the imported Italian fashion at such palaces as Buon Retiro.

In Germany the shows of the people gradually give place to the wonders related by travellers like Furtenbach, who describes with diagrams his versions of the new scenic system.

In Austria Burnacini, from Italy, creates breath-taking spectacles at the court of Leopold I, such as *Il Pomo D'Oro* (The Golden Apple), with no less than twenty-four magnificent scenes.

In Russia, as late as 1758, Angelo Carboni is found preparing elaborately-detailed explanatory diagrams to show how the devices of the Italian scenic system could be set up at the palace of Oranienbaum near St. Petersburg [70].

In France an especially interesting transition movement takes place that we must look at in some detail below.

And in England the Restoration of the monarchy in 1660 sees an entirely new chapter of British theatre history open.

Looking over this immense mass of scattered and varied material there appear to stand out (so far as our present knowledge allows us to see) three important subjects which need discussion in some detail. They are: (1) the new scenic system *à l'Italienne* and the Italian opera house it gave rise to, (2) the peculiar compromise system that was evolved at the Hôtel de Bourgogne in Paris, and (3) the solution worked out to reconcile the foreign scenic innovations with the native dramatic tradition in England, and the individual form of playhouse that was produced there as a result.

THE SCENIC SYSTEM *à l'Italienne*

We have now to see in detail just what was this new method of staging court operas that arose in Italy.

We have already had some slight hints; we have referred to the primitive writings of Serlio and Sabbattini. But these were mere preliminary essays. So vast a revolution in method could not be planned in a generation. The final system of stage arrangement was a much more complicated thing. But so wide did it spread, and such was its influence, that in France today a normal traditional setting (that is a setting of what we should call the 'wing-and-backcloth' type) is still spoken of as belonging to the stage-system of *la scène à l'italienne*. What was this 'Italian stage'? What was the problem which its new device of scenery set out to solve? (Perhaps it would be useful to say here in order to prevent a confusion that often occurs, that the French word *la scène* means something different from the English term 'the scene' and is in most contexts much more near to what we call 'the stage'. In such matters it might be not unhelpful to consult *An International Vocabulary of Technical Theatre Terms* [54].)

Briefly, this Italian system was devised to enable an unlimited number of dazzling spectacles or scenes to succeed each other nearly instantaneously, and to facilitate the introduction into any or all of them of some quite dazzling effect of mechanical gymnastics.

We have covered so far in this book a period of, let us say at a guess, three thousand years. There is only left us, to come up-to-date, a small space of three centuries. Since we have in any case pointed out the narrowness of any purely chronological sequence in the theatre, it will be perfectly allowable for us to state that the position we have just described above is almost the same as is seen today in Germany, where the marvels of German (and Austrian) stage machinery in the 1950s and '60s echo that Italian movement. And, like it, seem to contribute as little to the fundamental art of the actor. Is this a fair thing to say? The reader must make his own decision. But there is this consideration: before both Italian Renaissance scenery and the German modern machinery, the common player might reflect—'Why must we have fantastically elaborate, ingenious machines? For two pins we could act our plays without any loss on the old booth stage of tradition. But of course we have one difficulty— people like scenery. It gives them a sense of trust. If the scenery is delectable, then they can rest satisfied at having had in some respect a good show. If there's no scenery, they have to judge the quality of the show by the effect made upon them by the skill of the player's art, and that's very much more strenuous an act of personal participation.' It involves understanding a reality, not an appearance—and appearances are always easier to understand than realities, since realities for ever retain that disturbing element of the double meaning in art, that we drew attention to on p. 24.

Let us, however, make it quite clear that the above is supposed to be the reflection of a performer of *plays*. For the participant in a performance of *opera*, the line of thought (at least until *The Rise and Fall of the Town of Mahagonny* in 1930, *see* p. 274) is quite different.

The Italians eventually solved the problem of staging early opera, and the scenery and scene-changes it involved, in the following way—and this is the *scène à l'italienne*:

To begin with they divided the scene-picture into three parts— side wings, backscene and borders above. Each of these parts was handled in a different way.

The sort of scenery that was demanded by the earlier operas was almost always an exterior scene. This means that all early borders were sky borders. The exception to such a rule emerged if a Hell scene had to be represented—for Hell was underground and had no sky. It is about the middle of the 1600s that we begin to find Hell scenes designed in Italy with a top-masking of arched rocks, that is as a subterranean cave. And before that time it is very difficult to find any other treatment of the borders than as sky. Palaces were frequent, but their wings were crowned with clouds. Only after about 1650 do we find palace scenes sometimes represented as taking place in a room inside that palace, and thus requiring some kind of architectural or ceiling border above.

The system for the side scenes—or in modern parlance, the 'wings'—was finally solved, perhaps about the late 1500s or early 1600s, in the following way. The Serlian angled wing was abandoned, and instead a plain flat piece, parallel with the stage front and with a profiled edge, was used. These were placed in pairs, one either side, and the pairs decreased in height as they went upstage, to give a sense of perspective vista.

At each wing position on the stage a piece of special machinery was installed to carry the wing and to change it. It consisted of a long framework sliding to and fro in a slit in the stage floor, with wheels at its lower edge that ran on a railway specially built in the basement under the stage. At least two (sometimes three or four) such frames were built at each wing position (*see* Fig. 48, A and B). The wing itself was hung on that part of the frame that projected above the stage. The lower part of the frame beneath the stage (which bore the wheels) was called the *carretto* in Italian, *chariot* in French, and *Kulissenwagen* in German.

The movement was at once simple to work and complicated to describe. Let us take the front *chariot* of any group (A in Fig. 48). To the inward edge of the *chariot*, below the stage, a rope was

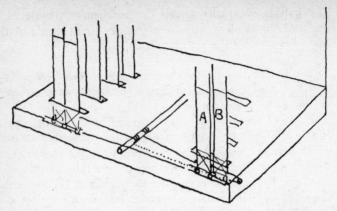

Fig. 48. The Italian system of machinery for scene-changing

attached whose other end wound round a central shaft. The opposite wing was similarly attached to this shaft. Thus the turning of the shaft would wind-in both ropes and pull both *chariots* towards the centre of the stage, into their visible position.

But these two *chariots* had also to be pulled off at the end of the scene. For this a second rope was attached to their *outward* edge, taken round a pulley in the side wall of the stage-basement and returned from thence to the centre shaft, but winding round it in the opposite direction.

Thus, the turning of the shaft one way would draw the wings on. Turning it the other way would draw them off. All the *front* chariots (A) at any wing position were rigged in this way and consequently one turning of the shaft would bring them all on simultaneously, or all off simultaneously.

But the *second* chariots in each wing position were also rigged to the same shaft, *but with ropes wound in the opposite direction*. Thus the total result of one turning of the shaft was to take all the wings of one scene *off* and, simultaneously, all the wings of the next scene *on*.

Any wing in the off position could be unfastened from its *chariot*-frame out of sight and replaced by a fresh wing ready for a further scene.

The next problem is more difficult. How is the large area of the backscene to be changed? It is not easy to find clear information about this so far as the 16th and 17th centuries are concerned. There seem to have been three alternative ways. One (usable on small stages), to divide the backscene vertically down the centre, mount each half on a frame and hang these frames on a special large *chariot* working like the wings. (On a large stage this would involve very big and unwieldy pieces of scenery.) Two, to frame up the backscene in one piece and lower it entire under the stage through a slit (or 'cut') in the floor by means of 'sloats' (see below). And three, to leave the backscene unframed— a sheet of loose hanging canvas—but to roll it up in the change in one of a number of ways.

One thing to be remembered about the backscene is that in this world of trick perspective the progressive decrease in height of the wings towards the back of the stage, and the progressive lessening of the distance between opposite pairs, reduced the size of the backscene needed, both in height and width, so that it would always be something smaller than it actually appeared. One unavoidable difficulty about this otherwise convenient economy was that the entrance of any actors near the back of the stage was to be avoided, since they would be out of proportion with the vanishing lines of the architecture of the scene at that point.

Almost the only considerable alteration in this system of the *scène à l'italienne* (and incidentally the only feature of it which survives today) was in this matter of handling backscenes. Some time in the early 19th century the method of rolling up backcloths in order to take them out of sight in a change gave place to the method of *flying*. This involved the raising of the roof above the stage and the creation of a kind of high loft into which the backcloths could be pulled up out of sight as they hung, without any need for rolling. Rolling can be damaging to a painted cloth. The new fashion spread and, by the year 1888, even a small provincial theatre such as that at Ipswich incorporated the idea.

The next difficult matter was the completion of the scene above—the representation of the sky or (very rarely) of a roof. This was done by means of a succession of hanging *borders*. A problem was to make these borders reach down to the wing-tops without lowering them too far into the scene. The solution (at

Fig. 49. A typical 17th-century scenic arrangement, showing upper and lower back shutters, side wings, high borders above, and 'cloudings' to join borders to wing-tops. Compare with Plate 8

any rate on some occasions) was to use rather short borders and to hang at either end of each a lower-hanging piece of cloud, giving something in the nature of an arch (*see* Fig. 49.) To change this, the centre part was pulled up out of sight, and the side pieces either drawn off in grooves or pulled back by means of a hooked stick.

A model, formerly in the Nationalmuseum, Nürnberg, dating probably from the early part of the 18th century, but now destroyed, used to show this system (*see* Plate 8).

So much for the elements of the scenery. For the machinery that moved it, there were two standard devices—the drum-and-shaft system and the sloat system.

The drum-and-shaft system worked on the lever principle. To roll a heavy, round log, a lever (as in Fig. 50, left) is a great help. If now instead of a log you have a round pole supported at either end as in Fig. 50, right, it can be most easily revolved by attaching a drum, of a greater diameter, somewhere in its length, and pulling upon a line (here called the 'working-line') wound round this drum. If now another line is wound round the shaft (called the

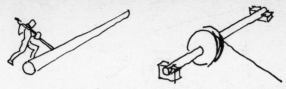

Fig. 50. *The principle of the drum-and-shaft machine*

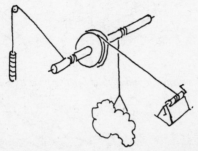

Fig. 51. *A cloud hanging from a counterweighted shaft*

'hanging-line') with the weight of a piece of scenery at the end, this weight can be moved by pulling or slackening the line round the drum (Fig. 51). A third line running round the shaft in a contrary direction can serve to carry a counterweight for the scene-load, and so lighten still further the motive effort. This principle was developed to a maze of elaboration and multiplication (*see* Plate 9), so as to work almost anything movable on the stage. Several hanging-lines could be attached to one shaft to move several objects simultaneously; or (and this was a pretty development) several hanging-lines could be attached each to a drum of a different diameter, fixed to the same shaft (*see* Fig. 52), and then upon actuating the working-line all the hanging pieces would move up or down at varying speeds, gradually spreading out as they sank, or closing together as they rose.

The sloat system was chiefly for raising pieces up from below the stage. A sloat is a vertical 'slot' with a specially designed tongue sliding up and down in it by means of a rope over a pulley in the head of the slot and attached to the base of the tongue. Fig. 53 shows three such sloats fixed under a cut in the stage floor, and bearing a long piece of cut-out scenery attached

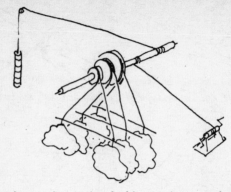

Fig. 52. A composite, opening cloud hanging from a graduated drum

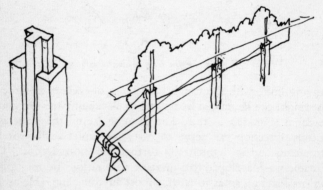

Fig. 53. Detail of a sloat, and sketch of the sloat system for raising scenery from below stage

to the exposed face of each of the tongues. Turning the winch to which the three working-lines are attached will raise the piece up through the stage.

These are the simpler, orthodox features of the *scène à l'italienne*. We have now to mention two other departments; that for cloud-effects and flying effects; and that for magic apparitions through the stage floor.

Fig. 52 has already hinted at the basic element for lowering a cloud screen, or a heavenly chariot from above. Fig. 54 now illustrates how a character could take to his wings from the stage, and fly diagonally upwards to disappear out the opposite corner

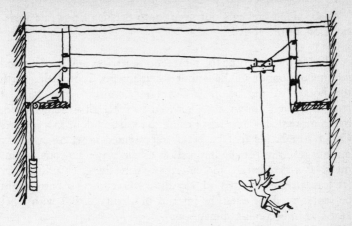

Fig. 54. An arrangement for a simple side-to-side flight

of the heavens. A rope fixed to a side gallery over the stage runs over a pulley in a little carriage, and down to the player on the stage. The carriage runs on a wire, or rope, track above the stage and is pulled by a line running to the opposite side gallery, where it is counterweighted. As soon as the 'check-rope' on the counter-weight is released, the carriage is drawn across above the stage and the rope holding the player pulled up, so that he not only rises from the stage but also moves sideways as he goes.

By permutations and combinations of this and other systems, almost every variety of trajectory of flight, and almost any direction, could be fixed at will.

For risings from below the stage, traps were used. A number of ingenious devices were found for opening the stage floor at almost any point. Below the openings so made, any kind of rising trap-platform could be rigged, from a single square capable of holding only one person to a 'bridge' as long as the stage was wide, and carrying a complete group of posed, infernal spirits wrapped in red fire and smoke clouds. And the speed of such apparitions could vary according to the loading of the counter-weights, from a slowness like the creep of time to a velocity that would shoot the player high into the air. (By a very curious quirk of Fate, the people who came to develop the highest and most daring and most skilful use of these Italian traps in the later 19th century were the English!)

Space alone prevents our going into details of possible variations on all the above.

All this was very fine for representing palaces and gardens and mounts of honour and hells; but was it any good for setting forth the homes of the people? Was not Abraham's now-familiar tent adequately shown by a scaffold in the Hall—even, indeed, by no more than a manner of using the existing door in a Screen? Could Abraham's tent be better represented now, or in a way more significant for the impression of the play? To some extent the *scène à l'italienne* could interpret such things. Occasionally (at least in the later period, say the 18th century) a barn might be represented, or even the interior of a cottage. But with what vast and unbecoming dimensions!

However, one might ask what occasion there was now for representing the ordinary homes of the people? And it is true that there was very little occasion in early opera. But there was in early drama. Beside *Jacob and Esau* needing a plain, people's tent in 1550, *Arden of Feversham* had required a typical townsman's room in 1590, and *King Lear* a hovel in 1605. But the system of the *scène à l'italienne* lent itself very grudgingly to such things. What was to be done? Alter playwriting? The question was not a grave one to the original exponents of the *scène à l'italienne*, for they had only to provide settings for the ideal opera, and so it never arose for them.

But it did arise in England and, to some extent, in France, in both of which countries a tradition existed of pure plays that might quite as easily as not include in their range a subject from ordinary contemporary human life (for example, Aphra Behn or Molière). This the *scène à l'italienne* was ill adapted to set. In fact it was simply not designed for such a thing, and only accommodated it at the cost of the greatest straining of effect.

Thus it was that in England especially and in France partially, the system of the *scène à l'italienne* remained more or less a stranger system. It is even likely that it was never fully installed in England until the 19th century, when in 1891, Walter Dando equipped what is now the Palace Theatre in Shaftesbury Avenue, London, with wing carriages, only to have them torn out again a few years later. But this is anticipating later history.

THE ROOFED PLAYHOUSE WITH SCENERY

An Auditorium to Suit

But we have not yet finished with the *scène à l'italienne*. The fifth phase of the theatre which we are now describing consists of enclosing an organized scenic stage in a roofed playhouse, designed to accommodate spectators to view that stage and its perspective marvels. Clearly nothing we have described so far in our review was adequate for this.

And so the design of the Italian Opera House was brought to birth.

On the whole it was much simpler than the stage. The early Italian opera house consisted of two main elements—seating on the ground floor in front of the stage, and seating in the walls enclosing this floor. But the whole was conditioned by one outstandingly demanding element; and that was the frame through which you had to look at the stage.

One thing is inevitable about scientifically designed perspective scenery, and that is that you can specify exactly the point from which the perspective effect can be best seen. But *there is only one such point!* All other positions, nearer or farther away, to the side or above or below, are progressively less satisfactory for viewing the perspective as it should be viewed—that is to say, so that its effect should appear to be correct; or as if it were not a *painted* but a *real* structure. (We note here that this is the second point at which the sense of *illusion* has crept into the theatre. The first was when trick effects were presented in such a way that you could not see how they were done. Scene-changing itself was such a trick.)

Thus it follows that the range of angle from which you can safely view a perspective scene is strictly limited. In fact, any but a right-line of vision is permissible only by the toleration of the audience.

For this reason—as well as for the need to hide all the drawn-off wings awaiting the scene change, and the actors awaiting their entrances, and all the numberless ropes and pulleys and shafts—there had to be built a frame to the stage-picture identical in principle with the frontispiece at Inigo Jones's masques.

To see through this frame, the audience on the floor had to be a serried mass clamped together in a close sector. They could receive one aid to better seeing, and that was the raking, or sloping, of the floor so that those at the back could see, to some extent, over the heads of those in front. Now, it is not uninteresting to notice the name given to this part of the Italian opera house. It was at once a very ancient name and a rather out-of-place name. It was the *platea*.

It seems strange, and yet not strange, that the name for the open space on which the medieval audience stood to watch a Morality, and to which the players descended by ladders from their scaffolds to take part in special spectacular actions among the spectators, should come to be the name given to what we would call the stalls-and-pit of a modern Italian opera house. But so it was.

The *platea*, then, was planned to face the stage-opening. In shape it was some variation of the horse-shoe. The walls beside and behind were tiered into shallow galleries one rising above another, perhaps (in high houses) to the number of five, and each divided into self-contained boxes; in French *loge*, in Italian *palco* (*see* Plates 19–13). These provided still less favourable seats at the sides, but had the social advantage of privacy, and of offering opportunity for entertaining oneself and one's friend, or friends, to refreshments.

Such then was the Italian system of scenery, of scenic machinery, and of opera house construction to suit. Now we add a comment which provides material for thought.

In 1952 there took place in Venice an exhibition of the birth of Italian scenic art, *Il secolo dell' invenzione theatrale*. A distinguished illustrated catalogue was prepared. The preface (by Gerardo Guerrieri) opened with certain words (of which I give an English equivalent) as follows:

'One of the paradoxes of theatre history is how the nation least productive of dramatic literature in the whole 17th century came to impose, in that same century, its own conception of spectacle upon all Europe. The theatre building of today, perspective illusion, the frame to the stage and the stage machinery, the auditorium with its boxes, and all which constitutes, even today, the 'theatre', do not spring from the England of Shakespeare, nor the Spain of Calderon, nor the France of Molière, Corneille and Racine; but are inventions, elaborated in Italy through nearly two centuries of experiments and projects and provisional schemes. And they were produced—which is no small curiosity—out of the world of architects and decorators rather than that of men of the theatre. . . .'

It is pretty clear, I think, that, the way things are going, we may expect to see the story of the theatre shortly come into a head-on row. But let us watch events.

(I reproduced the above passage in my *The Open Stage* [67], but include it again here not only because of its particular relevance but also in order to incorporate the correction of an error in translation in l. 3, which was pointed out to me by Dr. Leslie Hotson.)

MAHELOT

We have had to go somewhat closely into this development in order that succeeding events might be the more understandable. Now we leave Italy and turn back to France at the opening of the fifth phase in theatre.

England at this critical point in her theatre history had a hiatus; France did not. Equal in interest to Inigo Jones's great fund of drawings is the *Mémoire* of the designers for the company at the Hôtel de Bourgogne from 1633 to 1686 (though with certain breaks). These designers were Laurent Mahelot, Michel Laurent and some others. The document was illustrated and studied by Henry Carrington Lancaster [38].

This work offers a sort of historical link between the (apparently so divided) courses of the professional players in England and the court productions by Inigo Jones. It is not impossible that the system it discloses had some relation with the still obscure systems used in the Elizabethan private house theatres.

Mahelot's method of setting suffers development as he goes on; but in its early phases it appears to compromise between the divided, medieval or Tudor 'houses' system and the unified scene recommended by Serlio. But it is especially interesting because it is the scenic system used not by an architect designer to a private court but by a practising scene painter to a professional company—one of the first professional companies to employ scenery.

The *Mémoire* consists of notes for the staging of the plays presented by the company, together with most valuable sketches

Fig. 55. Diagram of Mahelot's early scenic system at the Hôtel de Bourgogne

to illustrate these notes and to serve as a record to the compilers of how such plays looked on the stage. The plays presented are the work of such writers as Du Ryer, Rotrou, Scudéry, Hardy and others.

The system of setting is very simple. It closely resembles, from the practical point of view, that of Jones for *Florimene*, but with one very important qualification; in Mahelot's earlier designs the side scenes are not members of a common, unified picture, but are each designed independently to serve as the setting for a different scene in the play—despite the fact that all stood visible together throughout the performance.

A typical example may be shown diagrammatically as in Fig. 55. As in *Florimene* these side scenes or wings are of the Serlian type, each composed (generally) of two flats set at an angle, but each wing is conceived as a separate 'house' somewhat in the way that the separate units in the Valenciennes Passion Play were conceived.

An interesting feature is that we can find evidence that the possibility of a certain confusion was recognized—a confusion about which scene of all those visible was the operative scene in use at a given moment in the play. This evidence is that we often notice, projecting on to the stage from these scenic 'houses', little short balustrade-pieces, serving to delimit in some sense that part of the stage near to the house, and mark it off as a separate area supposed to be especially related to that house or scene—and to no other.

Mahelot's sketches seem to suggest that the company kept in stock a number of scenic 'frames' (or flats), which they assembled as they chose, altering them or making new ones as occasion arose. Some of the 'frames' would appear to have been what we call archpieces, or open flats, some were plain or fully canvassed. On an occasion where two open or arch frames were used to form a wing representing an ordinary building, or palace, a black curtain might be hung in the arches to close them till the particular scene came; then the curtains would draw so as to reveal the 'interior' of that particular house—presumably suggested by a couple more plain flats behind, used as backings.

The backscene on Mahelot's stage was (like Inigo Jones's) of two storeys; and a couple of drawings show cloud chariots in use on the floor of the upper storey—that is to say in 'heaven'.

Separate in conception as were the different wings, or 'houses', in Mahelot's early drawings, yet in the course of a very few years they began to take a unified character, and the old, simultaneous-scene impression fades out. What is left is in effect a set of scenery much as we have it in the traditional wing-and-backcloth scene of today—that is to say, where all the wings belong to one set, and frame a relevant, matching backscene so as to form one unified picture.

THE RESTORATION IN ENGLAND

The situation in England when we last considered it was a sudden and total interruption, caused by the accession of the Puritans and by their condemnation of all theatres. Certain surreptitious activity took place during their régime (including at least one very important private production in Sir William Davenant's own home in 1656), but the break was so complete that when the monarchy was restored, an almost entirely new beginning had to be made.

Some curious legal conditions limited this beginning. When, in 1660, it became possible to open public theatres again, only two men were granted government permission to do so. They were Thomas Killigrew and William Davenant. Both were men of experience in the theatre; both had written plays that were earlier presented in the public playhouses. But Davenant had the particular experience of succeeding Ben Jonson as a masque-writer at court, and had worked with Inigo Jones at the summit of his scenic developments. Jones had left a successor in the person of his former assistant, John Webb; and Webb as a scene designer was closely associated with Davenant. Killigrew, on the other hand, had no such scenic connexions.

Immediately on receiving their patents, both men started to prepare playhouses in London. Both began with temporary measures and both decided to arrange indoor theatres. Each took over an indoor tennis court for his purpose. It came about, then, that the famous open form of the unroofed Elizabethan public playhouse—so famous at least to us today—was tacitly rejected by both men, and instead something more nearly related (so far as our knowledge goes) to the private house theatres was en-visioned.

But beyond this point the two men thought very differently Killigrew took the tennis court known as Gibbon's, in Vere Street, off what is today the foot of Kingsway in London, and equipped it with a traditional platform stage. This is an easy statement to make, and I think no authority would dispute its truth, but all the same we have only the vaguest idea of what this 'traditional platform stage' might have been like. It is our custom today to suppose that some at least of the private house presentations had a somewhat elaborate staging on 'simultaneous setting' lines, and perhaps resembled, to some undecided extent, the system used by Mahelot in his earlier work at the Hôtel de Bourgogne.

On the other hand we have the actual, and rather disturbing, record in the frontispiece to Kirkman's *The Witts* (1662). This represents an indoor theatre. One is hesitant to suppose it an imaginary theatre. It has been proved not to be (as was once supposed) the Red Bull. Is it then a picture of the interior of Killigrew's Theatre Royal in Vere Street? If it should be so, then our ideas on the private-house stage may need to be revised.

But whatever the case with Killigrew, our evidence is that Davenant in adapting Lisle's Tennis Court, at the south side of Lincoln's Inn Fields, took a different line in that he instituted a stage designed to accommodate full scenery. Our supposition is that his adaptation turned the tennis court into something basically not unlike a masquing house, such perhaps as that planned for *Florimene*. Our certainty is that he opened his new theatre with a revival of his own play *The Siege of Rhodes*, which he had earlier presented at his home in 1656. (For details of this *see* [61].) But it was a *Siege of Rhodes* with a difference; it was now expanded by a Second Part; played on the succeeding night, and in this Second Part the actors made their entrances by *doors*, not (as in the First Part) through the wings.

What had happened, apparently, was that Davenant had built his new stage not purely like a masque stage, but as a combination of the masque stage and the old public-playhouse open stage. On that open stage the players had entered by doors in the back wall giving upon the stage-floor, which (we must not forget) was called the *proscaenium*.

Davenant's action in designing the new stage seems to have been to bring the doors round to the sides of the *proscaenium* (so causing the stage to be partly enclosed by side walls) and to station the scenery well out of the way at the back of, or behind, the *proscaenium*. Since this *proscaenium*, or stage, had been relatively deep in the old days—it was 27 ft. 6 in. deep at the Fortune Theatre—there was clearly room for more than one door each side. What is interesting to discover is that in certain at least of the Restoration productions there were as many as three doors either side of the *proscaenium*. Thus the *proscaenium* formed quite a 'hall' for the players, with walls either end, a ceiling above, and perhaps six entrances to it—to say nothing of the scenery on the far side.

But a proper theatre in this fashion had yet to be built; so far we have only an adapted tennis court.

Certain events now followed closely. Killigrew's non-scenic shows could not compete in public favour with Davenant's scenic shows which, as a contemporary said, were so 'thronged after'. So in 1663 he opened a new house in a riding school in Bridges Street, off Drury Lane, and installed there a scenic stage. Davenant reacted by commissioning Sir Christopher Wren to plan a new and ornate spectacle house. Killigrew thereupon commissioned Wren to plan a fine new playhouse. The events need charting for clarity:

KILLIGREW and his company known as THE KING'S MEN	DAVENANT and his company known as THE DUKE'S MEN
1660. Opened at (1) Gibbon's tennis court, called Theatre Royal, Vere St. or Theatre Royal, Clare Market (*platform stage*)	1660. Opened at (2) Lisle's tennis court, called Duke's Theatre, Lincoln's Inn Fields (*scenic stage*)
1663. Opened at (3) a disused riding school, called Th. Royal, Bridges St. (*scenic stage*)	
	1668. (Davenant died)
	1671. Opened at (4) a new playhouse designed by Wren, between Fleet St. and Thames, called Duke's Th. Dorset Garden
1672. Bridges St. burnt. Company move to abandoned Duke's Th., L.I.F.	
1674. Opened at (5) a new playhouse designed by Wren called Th. Royal, Drury Lane	
1682. The two companies united at Drury Lane	1682. Duke's Th. Dorset Garden abandoned
	1695. Companies separate again, (6) New Th. Lincoln's Inn Fields opened

We have only sparse information about these six theatres (numbered 1 to 6 in curved brackets in the chart). Of the Theatre Royal, Bridges Street (No. 3) we are told by Count Lorenzo Magalotti, who visited it, that 'this theatre is nearly of a circular form, surrounded, in the inside, by boxes separated from each other, and divided into several rows of seats . . . a large space being left on the ground-floor for the rest of the audience'.

Of the Duke's Theatre, Dorset Garden (No. 4), François

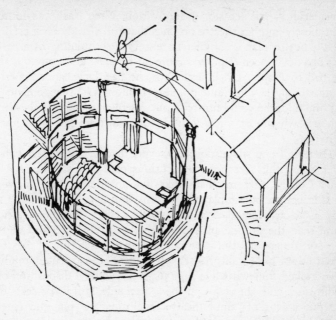

Fig. 56. Conjectural reconstruction of a plan of Sir Christopher Wren's for a theatre

Brunet in his *Voyage en Angleterre 1676* wrote that the pit was 'en amphithéâtre', and that there were only seven boxes, each holding twenty persons, on the ground floor, with an equal number above, and a gallery on top of all. We have then to imagine an auditorium with a large central box at the back and three large side boxes either side. The sumptuous proscenium with its carvings by Grinling Gibbons, and its distant scenes, is shown in five plates illustrating Settle's play *The Empress of Morocco*.

For the Theatre Royal, Drury Lane (No. 5), the position is somewhat different. We have a record of the size of the site and we have a drawing by Wren showing a longitudinal section through a theatre with a length corresponding to that site. But the drawing is only labelled 'Play house' and at some date has been torn across and torn across again, as if discarded. It is, however, a clear design for a Restoration playhouse and we must consider it.

Before we do so, it is worth pointing out that we are

considering a great occasion of innovation. Wren's task was not to plan merely another theatre on lines that had already been established; but to plan a completely new type of building of a sort that had never been required before his time, let alone attempted. He had to *invent* a playhouse. True, he had Davenant's experiments to guide him (and possibly Killigrew's disagreements), but one thing he could not base on was the familiar Elizabethan public playhouse of a few years before, since he had to include scenery.

There is some suggestion, however, that he did in fact consider doing this. We possess a curious plan of his (now at All Souls College, Oxford) that looks like an attempt to roof-over an Elizabethan public playhouse form, and develop it in such a way as to accommodate a stage with scenery. We possess no more than the ground plan; any reconstruction therefore must be very conjectural. But it would appear that the kind of theatre Wren might have built, had this plan ever been executed, might have looked somewhat like Fig. 56. It has an oval disposition of auditorium with the stage in the longer side, and it has seats in the pit, a sort of 'amphitheatre' enclosing the pit, and (presumably) a gallery round the auditorium, for supporting pillars are shown.

It is interesting to speculate upon what contribution this design might have made to the history of stage architecture had it been built. But in fact the other drawing (also at All Souls College) mentioned before, seems to be much closer to what was at length carried out. Here we have a disposition which can be diagrammatized as in Fig. 57. This is really very much nearer in principle to the previous drawing than might at first sight appear. It has an 'oval' (or wide and shallow) pit, a stage along one side and galleries round the auditorium. The *proscaenium* element, however, is particularly interesting.

THE PROSCENIUM AREA

It is of great importance that we should realize how the Restoration theatre men used this considerable 'proscenium' area, that I likened for the moment to a great 'hall' with doors either end—a space into which the audience looked from one side, viewing the action of the players under the light of flickering

Fig. 57. Conjectural reconstruction of Wren's Drury Lane

candles hung from the ceiling, and across which could be seen on the other side a partly obscured, partly illuminated, intriguing and mysterious spectacle of scenery.

The dimness of this whole picture must be stressed. Candles were dear. It is unlikely that there would be every day that glitter of 'all store of light' which made the occasional court performances so brilliant. The impression must commonly have been much more like that we gain from Hogarth's—rather grim—painting of the festivities at the masked ball at Wanstead Assembly, which is almost eerie in its ghoulish lights and louring shadows.

It is important to realize that no playgoer at that time could ever have formed the idea that what he saw in front of him when he went to the theatre could ever come to be compared with an appearance of real life in the world of daylight.

The regard in which scenery was held in the first five London theatres to use it, that we have listed above, must have been, therefore, a totally different regard from that in which we see scenery today. In fact when Sir William Davenant wrote his first play specifically intended to be accompanied with works of perspective in scenes, that is *The Siege of Rhodes*, he did not conceive of the 'scenery' as portraying the visual surroundings of the spot where the action was supposed to take place. He conceived it as a large, painted spectacle accompanying a particular phase in the exposition of his plot. For example, the first three actions in the opening phase of *The Siege* take place, one in the town of Rhodes, one far away in Sicily, and the other in Rhodes again. But the scenery remained the same all through these three

241

'scenes', displaying a map-like, bird's-eye view of the town of Rhodes *seen from a distance*!

To take another side of the Restoration view of the relation between scenery and stage action: In the Dryden-Purcell opera *King Arthur* (Dorset Garden 1691), each act opens without any scene-direction at all! There is merely the entrance of the characters, and their dialogue. Presumably they enter each time by the doors at the side and speak in the 'hall' of the *proscaenium*. Then after these opening speeches we find such a scene-direction as— 'The scene represents a place of heathen worship'; 'Scene, a Deep Wood'; or (very remarkable this) after an exchange of speeches to begin Act IV we have 'Enter Arthur, and Merlin at another Door. *Scene of the Wood continues*'. And after each of these we find the action proceeding *behind* the 'hall' in that farther space flanked by the painted, changeable scenery.

The theatre, then, presented two worlds; one, the frankly-accepted stage world where in Drury Lane or Dorset Garden Playhouse a man dressed as King Arthur came out and exchanged speeches with a man dressed as Conon, Duke of Cornwall, before a listening group of one's friends and contemporaries, and the other a fantastic world, where one saw King Arthur proceed into a magic wood and strike with his sword an enchanted tree that groaned and gushed forth blood.

Again, this candle-lit great hall, with the exciting doors either end and the flat playing space of the old *proscaenium* across it, was made particular use of in still another way in Samuel Tuke's *The Adventures of Five Hours*, Duke's Theatre 1662. Here straightway we have advantage taken of the atmosphere actually present, for the plot is laid to take place at night, in the rooms of strange houses and the streets and gardens outside—and frequently supposed to be in total darkness (the actors miming blindness and failing to see each other exactly as in the brilliant little *scena* of a Fight in the Dark, from the Peking Opera, *The Crossroads*). The most daring use is made of the doors. For instance, two characters pursue each other, with swords drawn, from one room to another, and it is necessary that the action be completely continuous. It would seem that only the moving camera of film-technique could do this. But in that magic 'hall' of the *proscaenium* nothing more is needed than to rush off through one of the doors at one side and immediately rush back through another of the doors on the same side—and the chase from room to room is perfectly represented! And note: the fact that the dim back-scene on the far side of the area has not changed at all *is not of the slightest hindrance to the excitement of the audience!*

So then the compromise effected by the English in order to wed the new scenery of the *scène à l'italienne* with their own tradition of quick-action dramatic playing was to create a stage of two distinct zones, one for each; the one familiar and actual—the boards of the platform in the playhouse flanked by end walls with several doors; and the other away in the distance behind this, more mysterious, less brightly lit, but bearing painted screens. These screens still changed by sliding in grooves like those Inigo Jones had put in for his masques—for the continental system of frame and chariot was scarcely ever employed by the English.

One further Restoration scenic convention remains to be mentioned. Often in the plays a scene in one locality ends, and the next scene in another locality begins, without any exit-direction for the characters to leave the stage. This was of course perfectly in accord with the regard in which the Restoration players held scenery; indeed what better use could be made of the new facility of visibly changing scenery, when a character had to go from one place to another, than to keep the character on the stage and to perform the transformation from spot to spot in his presence by changing the scenery?

It is interesting to see that many authorities have claimed that the particular conventions in the use of scenery that we have noticed above are all signs of a technical crudeness of the age, and a poverty of mind in the players before a new medium with such vast potentialities for verisimilitude! Rather it would seem, in truth, that the real reason for these conventions was that the Restoration theatre men saw well enough the quandaries into which such a development of verisimilitude would lead them, and deliberately chose to keep the new artifice artificial—deferring to it in so far as it delighted their public but strenuously refusing (so far) to truckle to its promise of illusion.

Indeed there was a vociferous faction that scoffed heartily at the whole new paraphernalia of French scenes and Italian tricks. . . . However this may be, the roofed scenic playhouse was established. It had next to expand and to develop.

EARLY LONDON THEATRES

In the first half of the 18th century progress was slow and confined to London (to this statement we should add one particular exception to be considered in a moment). In 1705 Vanbrugh built an *Opera House* in the Haymarket. It was an unwieldy building, out of the English tradition, and was frequently modified and successively rebuilt, until today it is Her Majesty's Theatre. (An excellent history of its chequered career was made by Francis Sheppard with valuable illustrations [58].) In 1714 a new theatre was built in Lincoln's Inn Fields and in 1732 another in Covent Garden (both under Davenant's old patent) whose tradition lives in the present opera house.

Having disposed of these with brief mention we must go back a few years to insert that exception remarked above to the monopoly of theatres by London. The opportunity can be taken to add, first, that in point of fact there was much playing by travelling companies in provincial towns. But supposedly such performances were given in temporary quarters, and the institution of any building specifically for play acting was rare. The case of the little town of Topsham in Devonshire which advertised performances at 'the Playhouse' as early as 1721, is probably a typical example of the taking-over of a room for a short season (or even for only a single performance) and putting on the show there as well as might be. The exception mentioned, however, is more than this; in 1716 the first theatre (at any rate of our present era) was built in America. It was erected in Williamsburg, Virginia, by Levingston. Its presumed foundations have been uncovered by the indefatigable investigators of this historical town, and the Architect's Department there, in conjunction with the present writer, prepared a provisional set of reconstruction-drawings to fit the foundation-remains. A model of the reconstruction is shown in Plate 16. The intention was to embody our present slight knowledge of early 18th-century English theatre interiors, and present as close an approximation of what a 1716 theatre might look like as the evidence allows us to do.

To resume the London story. In 1720 the New or Little Theatre was opened, again in the Haymarket, and another theatre in 1729 in Goodman's Yard, near the Tower of London. And then little followed until the 1760s.

In the 1760s, however, a completely new lease of life was taken. In London, the Lyceum, Astley's, the Pantheon, the King's Concert Rooms (or Regency), the Royal Circus and the Royalty all began their existence within a couple of decades. But equally important was the rise of new theatres in provincial cities. Bath, Bristol and King's Lynn lead the train, and by the '80s and '90s, scarcely a small town in England but had its playhouse. Of these it is instructive to pause on King's Lynn for a particular reason.

King's Lynn

Visiting players had performed at King's Lynn since at least the 16th century. A medieval Guildhall (one of the largest surviving in Britain) had been used; and in 1766 the step was taken of building a complete Georgian playhouse inside this Guildhall of St. George. In 1948 very little survived of this—but that little was informative. There were eight tall wooden posts, six of them united at the top by the remains of a plastered ceiling. All these remnants had to be cleared away for ever when the interior of the hall was converted into a modern concert room. But a detailed survey and record was made by the present writer before the modernization [62].

From marks on these six posts and the ceiling, it was possible to establish that the whole once formed a complete *proscaenium* with its floor, its sides with their doors and boxes, and its ceiling above. Not only this, but other marks on the ancient wooden roof structure of the Guildhall showed the precise extent and shape of the one-time ceiling over the whole Georgian auditorium. And, in short, the model shown in Plate 17 could be made, with very little conjecture, to show how the 18th-century theatre had been laid out. It illustrates, better than any other evidence yet found, the conception outlined above of what we have represented as a 'proscenium hall'. This can be best demonstrated by the diagram in Fig. 58.

In front of the diagram is lightly indicated the scenic area of the stage. In the farthest distance is the auditorium, reaching forward, with a box and a door below and two boxes above, to touch, as it were, the area of the scenery. But between these two sides, and embraced by them, stretches the true players'

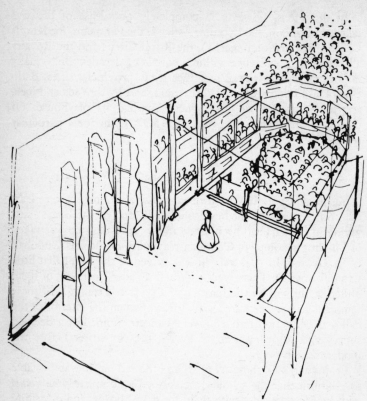

*Fig. 58. The arrangement of the 18th-century playhouse at King's Lynn,
showing close relation of forestage and audience*

area—a considerable space across which an actor could stride
forward to stand at the very brink of the auditorium, or in which
action of considerable complexity could devolve so close to the
audience that they might be said to be on the brink of that action.

Some developmental changes have already come about since
Wren's auditorium of a century before. Chief of these is the
cutting down of the proscenium doors to one a side. But the
front of the forestage still reaches well past them, and takes in
the breadth of a 'stage box' as well.

Two decades later, when the miraculously still-surviving, little
playhouse at Richmond, Yorkshire, was built (in 1788), the
shrinking of the forestage had gone farther; there, the edge

reaches only a few inches beyond the door. Save for this deterioration of forestage depth, Richmond was built on almost the same pattern as King's Lynn. This Georgian pattern was a culminating achievement in theatre design. It was almost a perfect solution to the problem at that time of staging the plays of those days. And as such it spread throughout England—even as far south as Penzance near the tip of Cornwall—an unvarying, competent and happy solution.

It had a further amiable quality. It was a solution also to another problem—one that so worries us today—that of the dual-purpose hall.

Many of these small, provincial 18th-century theatres were used for a part only of the year, when the local travelling company was visiting that part of the circuit. For the rest they were vacant. During such vacant periods *the pit could be floored over*. It should be noticed in Fig. 58 that a line runs round the sloping pit at a level with the lower box fronts. This line was present in all theatres. If a temporary floor is fitted across at its level, the whole of the sloping pit can be concealed and made flat. Not only this, but t is made flat on the same level as the stage—thus the stage-floor and the temporary pit-cover become one large flat area admiirably suited for dances, and ready-equipped with a delicious range of sitting-out boxes, round the sides and above, for non-participating spectators and resting revellers. And to this use the Georgian theatres were frequently put.

The deterioration of the forestage had a particular result of such importance to later history that it will force us soon to recognize a new phase in theatre development. And this is well illustrated at Richmond. The result seems innocuous at first; it merely meant an increase in the number of entrances made through the wings—'in the scenery'—and a decrease in the number made by the proscenium doors.

This change coincides with the rise of the Romantic Movement; and with some reason. For it was an engaging sight to see a rural figure come reflectively into the picture from between the cut-out silhouettes of tree wings—especially as these began to be far more clearly lit with the increase in stage illumination that followed the introduction of gas. With gas, also, the auditorium could be dimmed at a turn of the tap, to help the wonder of the stage.

In a typical play, written for performance by the Richmond company in 1822 (*The Lady's Dream* by George Jefferson), the scenes vary between interiors of lodgings and exteriors showing the countryside. *All* entrances in the exterior scenes were made through the wings. In interior scenes even, most entrances were made through the wings. It is only when a character enters an interior scene *not* as from an adjoining room in the same house, but *as a visitor from the street outside* coming to pay a call, that direction is given to use the proscenium doors! The old function of the 'hall' lingered still. . . .

But you will notice how a feeling for the illusion of verisimilitude is creeping in along with Romanticism. Couple these with brighter-lit scenery whereon the delicate painting can now be clearly shown, and with the auditorium sinking to dimness as a foil to that picture—and you will (alerted by the hints in our approach in this study) scarcely need it to be said that we are within sight of the end of another phase.

Before we leave it we have some loose ends to clear up.

THE CONTINENTAL OPERA HOUSE

The 18th century was the great period of the European Baroque opera house—among the most splendid social buildings the world has ever seen.

The story begins with Aleotti's Teatro Farnese at Parma, 1618, often claimed as the first proscenium-arch theatre. Its influence on the main stream of theatre development is, however, probably less than is claimed, since it was a private court building, not of a form well-adapted for a public theatre, and was only very rarely used for performances.

At Celle in Germany is a little opera house dating from 1670 which well shows the germs of the new style (Plate 10).

The Manoel Theatre in Valletta, Malta, dates from 1731 and remains one of the oldest houses still in use that were originally built as public theatres (Plate 11). It is a gem of the style, and only little altered in later times.

Italy of course produced a wealth of such buildings—a famous example is the San Carlo Opera House at Naples of 1737.

Giuseppe Galli-Bibiena built in 1748 the rich Bayreuth Opera House (Plate 12). At the Castle at Schwetzingen is still to be seen

Fig. 59. A Japanese Kabuki theatre

the theatre of 1752 with its machinery. Cuvilliés' delightful Residenztheater at Munich, now restored, dates from 1752 (Plate 13). From 1766 (the year of the Theatre Royal, Bristol) dates the existing theatre at Krumau, Czechoslovakia. And to the same year again belongs the richest of all from the point of view of surviving contemporary machinery and scenery—the enchanting palace theatre at Drottningholm near Stockholm. In 1770 Gabriel built the astounding Opera House at Versailles with its painted marbling over wood construction—an epitome of the style. The little theatre at Gripsholm Castle, Sweden, followed in 1781; and there were many others throughout Europe. Of these the above survive to recall the fascination of the interiors.

But on the whole these are specialist theatres, and reserved for occasional, princely performances. In some sense they are intrusions into—or extrusions from—the ordinary stream of the professional player's own theatre. The culmination came, perhaps, when state and people banded together to give Paris the world-famous Opera House by Charles Garnier in 1875.

THE KABUKI THEATRE

The *kabuki* stage was originally the same in form as the Noh stage, as a print in Kawatake's *Development of the Japanese Theatrical Art* [34] shows, but in the 18th century it began to develop scenery. The scenery of the *kabuki* stage is highly elaborate, yet for all its vivid effects of house interiors, of boats on the sea, of mountains and gardens, and of every vision of the floating world, it has never become purely naturalistic and has never dropped (especially in the actor's stance, gesture and delivery) a strong element of stylization. The stage opening is immensely wide to Western standards, and the picture through it is of a long, panoramic proportion (Fig. 59). The scene-shifting problem was solved (long before such a thing was discovered in the West) by the system of the revolving stage. There is a considerable number of vivid and informative diagrams of the details and technique of this sort of stage in Shokosai's *Shibai Goya Zue* [59] of which a brief account with some reproductions has been given by the present writer [65].

The main features of divergence, as the Kabuki stage developed away from the Noh stage, were the recession of the acting-area (comparable with the reduction of the Georgian fore-stage), the great expansion in width, the (possibly consequent) shrinking and final disappearance of the *hashi-gakari* (which once existed in the Kabuki theatre as it does in the Noh); and the introduction of an apparently new feature that in some sense took the place of the *hashi-gakari*, this was a long narrow platform from stage to back of auditorium at the level of a seated spectator's shoulder, along which special processional entrances and exits are made. This is the *hana-michi* (*see also* Plate 15). It runs down the theatre near the spectator's-left side. It is sometimes supplemented by a narrower, subsidiary *hana-michi* near the audience's right side.

In the Kabuki stage there seems a happy wedding of stage conventions and full scenery that has been achieved nowhere else in the world. Here it is perfectly consistent to 'come out of the picture' (along the *hana-michi*), or to accept a chorus seated unashamedly in sight on the stage.

SIXTH PHASE

Illusion

Illusion

THE HISTORY OF STAGE ILLUSION

We now have to proceed with even more particular care. We enter the phase when something which is consciously and deliberately isolated by its contemporaries as *stage illusion* comes into the theatre. This was not so before. Any references we have made up to now to 'illusion' in the theatre have been our own comment only; now the word is to be widely used by the people of the time who witnessed that theatre. What did it mean?

Some illustration of the history of this somewhat baffling conception can be given in five references, with a sixth added to them which we must treat at some length as bringing the story into this chapter and into the later 19th century.

In 1425 we have the reference *Tunc descendit in placeam* (Then he descends into the Place). This is the antithesis of illusion; it is fact.

In *c.* 1567 we found the stage reference in *Horestes*: *she speakes over the wall*. This is not precise fact. There was no wall. She spoke over something which served as a wall. How much 'stage illusion' is there here? Surely, scarcely anything at all. It is only a convention being put into practice. And yet in so far as a convention is the use of an agreed symbol to denote something else, so far is it a make-believe—however readily accepted.

Now let us go to a far more abstruse example. In 1623 a certain 'undivided' play was published (that is, a play whose scene-divisions weren't marked) which contained two stage directions close together, one at the end of a particular speech and the other immediately before the next speech by a quite new character. Thus they clearly came between what we should call two different scenes. The text ran:

Now feare I this will give it [his rage] start againe;
Therefore let's follow.   *Exeunt*
                    Enter two Clownes
Clown. Is she to bee buried in Christian buriall, that
        wilfully seekes her owne saluation?

Now what is this? Surprising as it may seem to those unfamiliar
with it, it is the opening of the 'world-famous' Grave Scene from
Hamlet. Yet in the first folio there is nothing about a grave scene,
and no such announcement as 'Scene—a Graveyard'. There is not
a single word at its opening beyond that 'Enter two Clownes'.
Is then the graveyard make-believe? Certainly it is. But is there
an *illusion* of a graveyard? Surely not . . . and yet, what exactly is
the nature of the impression one receives when the first grave-
digger steps into the stage trap and throws up a property skull
and says—'Heres a Scull now: this scul, has laine in the earth
three & twenty year. . . .'?

Is it an illusion of a graveyard?

Is it an unquestioned acknowledgement that one sees an actor
performing a part?

Suppose we decide the latter; suppose we decide illusion has
not yet entered the theatre.

We take the fourth reference. In 1660 and onwards we may
find the direction—*The scene opens and discovers a horrid hell* . . . and
countless variations of that formula. One is prepared to say that
such a scene could not have given an *illusion* of hell. And yet . . . it
did undoubtedly transport the spectator for the moment into the
world of illusions. I ask no more here than to be granted that we
are coming on a strange consequence of using this 'Italian' scenery.

The fifth reference is very simple. In *The Lady's Dream*, 1822
(mentioned above, p. 248) Act IV opens with *A Public Road
with a view of the Hambiton Hills in the distance.* Was this an illusion?
No, surely not! It would only be an illusion if you actually thought
you saw the Hambiton Hills from your seat in the theatre, instead
of a backcloth at the back of the stage. . . . And yet . . .

FENTON AND THE 'DREAM'

Now to our sixth, and current, reference. We come to 1853.
In this year Samuel Phelps presented a revival of *A Midsummer
Night's Dream* at the outlying theatre of Sadler's Wells. Frederick

Fenton painted the scenery, and the following words of his were
preserved from an interview (and this reference we must study
at some length, even to making it the essence of this chapter):

'In those days lighting was a serious difficulty. Very few theatres
were enabled to have gas. When Phelps and Greenwood took the
management into their hands, the lighting of Sadler's Wells was
merely upright side-lights about six lamps to each entrance,
which were placed on angular frames, and revolved to darken
the stage; no lights above. When set pieces were used, a tray of
oil lamps was placed behind them, with coloured glasses for
moon light. For the footlights (or floats) there was a large pipe,
with two vases, one at each end, with a supply of oil to charge
the argand burners on the pipes; it was lowered out between the
acts, to be trimmed as necessity required. . . . But when the Phelps
and Greenwood management was assured, I obtained permission
for the gas to be supplied as a permanent lighting for the theatre,
and it was used for the first time in *A Midsummer Night's Dream*.
With its introduction the smell of oil and sawdust, which was the
prevailing odour of all theatres was finally removed. . . . By
various ingenious devices the moon was seen to rise, to shine
between the boles of the trees, to be partly obscured by passing
clouds, and then to swim, as it were, over and through the trees.
This effect of movement was given by a diorama—that is, two
sets of scenes moving simultaneously. These had cuts and shap-
ings to represent, in the front sets, openings of the woods, spaces
between stumps of trees, and the light parts between the foliage.
The back set of the diorama was similarly treated to produce
various cloud effects. . . . For the first time used, to give a kind of
mist, I sent to Glasgow expressly for a piece of blue nett the same
size as the act drop, without a seam. This, after the first act, was
kept down for the whole of the performance of the Dream, light
being on the stage sufficient to illuminate the actors acting behind
it. The gauze ascended when Oberon and Titania made their
exeunt in the fourth act.'

(This was not, of course, by any means the first time that such
effects had been sought. A Rising Moon had appeared in the
Scene in *The Adventures of Five Hours* (1662); and Garrick's scene
designer, De Loutherbourg, had almost every change on the face
of nature in his *Eidophusikon*. Naturalism is no new thing; only
the presentation of the natural is new.)

The words of this interview with Frederick Fenton were recorded in a curious edition de luxe of *A Midsummer Night's Dream* compiled by J. Moyr Smith in 1892. Compiled, that is to say, by a man who was looking back on the past, on a period some 40 years before. He discusses Fenton's scenery, but with a gentle superiority, as being the early days of something that had gone much farther by his time. For example, he readily admits Fenton's suitability for the work—'Obviously, he was eminently fitted for the delineation of the architectural framework which is necessary to several notable scenes in "A Midsummer Night's Dream".' But he cannot forbear the following qualification:

'In those days, however, strict historical inquiry into the dates of the beginnings of the Greek orders of architecture was not insisted upon, and probably the architecture represented was more closely allied to the age of Pericles than to that of the more primitive Theseus. But it is not to be denied that as stage pictures the scenes gained in richness and beauty by dealing with the fully developed, violet crowned city, rather than with the meagre outlines of the archaic Athens over which Theseus ruled. The dresses of course followed the same rule, and were those of the golden Periclean age instead of the quaint and bespangled robes whose remains have been discovered by Dr. Schliemann.'

There is no escaping the conclusion that this introduction of 'Italian' scenery has involved us in remarkable consequences! What is this particular preoccupation with the difference between the architecture of Theseus' Athens and that of Pericles' Athens? Has it any relation to *A Midsummer Night's Dream*?

Moyr Smith continues with his own impression of this architecture as seen in the show. He says:

'The architectural scenes were, of course, those of Acts I and V. The first scene of Act I represented the palace of Theseus, with a view of the Acropolis of Athens behind. The second scene represented the workshop in which the clowns apportionate the characters of their play; it was divided by a pier and heavy beam; through an opening in the left-hand compartment a glimpse was caught of the open sky and the trees of a suburban garden. The fifth act showed first as a columned hall, with a background of closed curtains, the stage being lighted by Greek candelabra. When the clowns finished their play and Theseus and his train retired, servants came in and put out the lights, and simultaneously the curtains opened. The fluted columns of the hall were partly 'made out' and covered with waxed linen; inside the columns were lengths of gas jets, kept turned down till the curtains opened and the moonlight streamed into the hall; then the gas within the columns was turned up, and the columns had the appearance of being illuminated by the moonlight.

'The opening of the curtains disclosed a terraced garden overlooking Athens. Down the steps and along the terraces trouped Oberon and Titania with their fairy train, all carrying glimmering lights. The fairy song and dance were given, and the curtain fell on the moonlighted palace of Theseus with the slumbering city behind, on the picturesque groups of the fairies arranged on the terraces behind, and on the graceful figures of Oberon, Titania and Puck in front.'

One last quotation before we leave him. This time he refers to that particular item which must have caught the attention of several readers—namely, that vast 'blue nett' that was specially loomed in Glasgow 'to give a kind of mist'.

'In addition to this diaphanous blue nett, other thicknesses of gauze, partly painted, were used occasionally to deepen the misty effect, and to give the illusion necessary at the part where Puck is told by Oberon to:

> *overcast the night;*
> *The starry welkin cover thou anon*
> *With drooping fog as black as Acheron.*

In the scene representing Titania's bower the flowers rose or descended, so as to disclose or conceal the fairy queen as occasion demanded.

'These gauzes vanished, as we have seen, with the exeunt of Oberon and Titania from the wood after the first part of Act IV. Then the day dawned and showed a ravine between pine clad hills; horns were sounded, and Theseus, Hippolyta and their train entered from below, as if coming up the ravine.'

The phrase that it seems to me is outstanding in this detailed account is: *to give the illusion necessary at the part where Puck is told by Oberon . . .* etc. To give the illusion *necessary . . .* How far we seem from *Tunc descendit in placeam*!

Would we be right in supposing that a conscious intention now exists to present the spectator with the effect of a real moon floating in a real night above the genuine Athens? Is this 'scenic illusion'?

It would seem that the story of the whole development of scenic presentation for the next fifty or sixty years is wrapped up in this problem, but, for all that, it is still very difficult to find exactly the right words to define what the illusion was. Illusion was accepted as a function of the stage. But illusion of what? Illusion of 'correctness'? Illusion of reality? But could these schemes be called realistic? It is about this point that we have to be most careful. I think they could not. They certainly took Nature as their model; but Nature is a curious subject to paint. Can a man paint Nature's own image? Or does he paint his own variation or comment on Nature's image—or even merely his own selection from it? And is his work then capable of being classed as naturalism? Or as realism? Scarcely—because such a painting might equally belong to 'impressionism' or 'cubism'.

It is in practice exceptionally difficult to make sure what lies behind Moyr Smith's idea of *the illusion necessary* to a given scene. But for the moment, as historians, we will say no more than that Moyr Smith has left us a fairly clear picture of the scenery in the *Dream*, and that presumably, therefore, it was precisely a scene of that kind which created the illusion necessary at the point where Puck is told by Oberon to overcast the night with fog—it was, in fact, an ingenious simulation of a natural effect seen through the eyes of a typical painter of those times.

It may even be of significance to stress this seeing through the eyes of a painter, and thus to say that scenic illusion consisted in giving the impression that one was looking at a living, or moving, picture. The conception of the scene as 'a painting come to life' was so strong at this time that in 1880 Sir Squire Bancroft, in modernizing his Haymarket Theatre, made the proscenium into 'a massive and elaborately gilded frame complete on all sides', so that the spectator was as before a painting in which the figures spoke and moved. It was said to be 'perfect for illusion' and for artistic pleasure [68]. It would seem then that the illusion sought was the illusion that you were not looking at a stage but at something else.

If however we find it difficult to say at the present moment just what 'scenic illusion' was intended to give the illusion of, let us postpone the question until we can make a closer examination of the aesthetic problem involved. And for one scene-painter at least, towards the end of the great period of theatrical scenepainting, this aesthetic problem was an immensely troubling one, and that was Joseph Harker.

THE RISE AND FALL OF SCENEPAINTING

Before quoting from Harker and trying to settle this difficult matter of the purpose of illusion in the theatre, we should perhaps at this point glance over the peculiar rise of scenepainting in the 19th-century theatre, with which this matter of illusion is so closely wrapped.

It may be fitly introduced with these thoughts of James Boaden [11], first published in 1827:

'But neither tragedy nor comedy ever seemed with me to derive a benefit proportionate to the pains that have been taken in the scenic departments of our stages . . . If the perspective . . . was so accurate that the whole effect should be delusive, and the impression be of actual sky, and land, and building . . . I could understand the object of those who expend so much money on their elaboration—but I confess I am of the opinion, that they should never do more than suggest to the imagination; and that it would not be desirable that the spectator should lose his senses to the point of forgetting that he is in a regular theatre. . . .

'When we have such a being as Mrs. Siddons before us . . . what signifies the order or disorder of the picture of a castle behind her . . . ? I must pity the man who, not being the painter of the canvas, is at leisure to inquire how it is executed.'

Such an opinion, then, was being expressed a full century before the conceptions of Bertolt Brecht.

Just before this date, De Loutherbourg, the Alsatian artist whom Garrick employed and who prompted Gainsborough to enthusiastic ponderings, retired from the stage to perfect his Eidophusikon, and then became a sort of amateur faith-healer and was buried in Chiswick in 1812. He was an exciting innovator in scenery.

This left the way clear for William Capon, who worked for Kemble and produced in 1808 the first scenes designed to 'bring together a selection of Architectural remains in different parts of the kingdom in one point of view so as to form a grand ancient street.'

With Clarkson Stanfield (1793–1867) a seal was set (and a distinguished seal) on the charter which linked the picturesque with the heroic. He was one of the finest storm-cloud painters. (Even poor, worried Ruskin granted him that.)

And then followed William Roxby Beverley (1814–1889) and after him a throng such as England had never known before— the Grieves family, Frederick Lloyds, the Telbin family, Frank O'Connor, Fenton, Hawes Craven, the Harkers. . . .

But the point of this story is not that these were great men at their job (which, on the evidence, is beyond all doubt) but that in every country affected by the *scène à l'italienne* there arose at this time outstanding practitioners of this craft and art. At the Paris Opera House were Ciceri, Philastre and Cambon, Rubé and Chaperon, Carpezat. . . In Germany, Schinkel. . . . In Italy, Sanquirico . . . etc, etc.—all superbly accomplished painters of the picturesque.

There never have been such brilliant scenes as these men painted. In those days, the scenepainter went about in his carriage, wore a top hat, and attended the theatre at night to receive the special calls for himself alone before the curtain from the applauding audience. All this must be visualized to understand Harker's reaction.

Two things grew up to stop all this—two things that were really one. First, the rise of a shattering new conception of the function of painting from the world outside the theatre (at first righteously condemned), and second, an at first very slight and gentle, but growing insidious propagation of the idea that naturalistic scenepainting didn't help theatre.

It is perhaps strange to come thus to the eve of modern times and to realize that half the readers of this statement will hail it, and half bewail it. But we have to reserve our own troubles for the next phase; there were troubles enough here for the last of the great men brought up in the old school, and devastatingly faced by something they could not understand—to see the passing of all they had stood for and made outstanding.

HARKER AND DISILLUSION

Joseph Harker, senior, was one of those men. He was born in 1855, and in 1924 published his life-book, *Studio and Stage*. Mostly this consists of genial reminiscences of the great days he had known and helped to make. But for two solid chapters towards the end he struggles, like Tobias against the Angel, with a force that he cannot understand. Here is a *cri de coeur* if ever there was one—he says (chap. xii) [28]:

'In dealing with this burning question of the advanced movement in scenic art I have tried to take as dispassionate a view as possible. But I am conscious that I have failed . . . I am essentially conservative and intolerant of new ideas . . . I have had a long day in the theatre, and I have no desire to become a bigoted obstructionist . . . abusing those who . . . insist on our believing Nature is unlovely and needs embellishment. . . .

'But what is it—*what is it*—I have asked myself, that stops me from understanding, or even beginning to understand what these ultra-moderns are driving at? What is wrong with Nature? Why must progress lead us into the wilderness?'

What *had* happened?

Let us go back a bit. Contemporary with Fenton there were the revivals at the Princess's Theatre under Charles Kean, and these, through the perspicacity of the manager, have become more widely known to modern students. Kean stood for 'archaeological exactitude' in his revivals of Shakespeare. He also stood for another belief of his time—that art ought to be educational, and such a slip as Fenton's, in getting the wrong sort of Athens to set behind Theseus, was something he spent much money and trouble in avoiding. He was made a Fellow of the Society of Antiquaries.

Then (among all the welter of events in the Victorian world) there emerged another figure with precise ideas of what he wanted of the scenic art—Edward William Godwin, 1833–86. Godwin profoundly influenced Ellen Terry and through her, to some extent, Irving. Godwin made a scholarly series of studies of the informed presentation of Shakespeare's plays, in *The Architect* beginning in 1875. These were reprinted in *The Mask* from 1908. He brought a fresh, informed and intellectual delicacy to the designs for period scenery and costume, and he also instituted one of the first 'open stage' presentations of modern times at Hengler's Circus (now the Palladium) with *Helena in Troas* in 1886.

Following Irving's brilliance came Beerbohm Tree, whom

Ellen Terry persuaded to try a new young designer, arising from this fresh world, and give him an opportunity to set a production of *Macbeth* in 1912. The proposed collaboration failed and Gordon Craig's new vision was rejected for Harker's well-tried one.

But already in the 1890s, Adolphe Appia had been sadly recognizing the failing in his hero, Wagner, of not seeing that realistic scenepainting must fetter poetic vision. Indeed it seems that the greatest controversy at this time raged round the questions: Ought scenepainting to be realistic? Or ought scenepainting *not* to be realistic?

One can feel some sympathy for the uncertainty. If an 18th-century scenepainter had to paint a gate on his scene, then he painted a gate. If, with the rise of the craft of scenepainting in the 19th century and with the increase in the ability of scenepainters to the point of virtuosity, it became possible to paint a gate still more like a gate—or even to paint a gate so that it stood out from the scene in such a way that you took it for a real gate—was not this achievement? Was not this success in the art?

This it was which the painters of the time called 'realism'—whether or not that is a proper use of the term is another matter—and it thus became an extraordinarily puzzling thing when a painter of the new school said (as did Albert Rothenstein in a Symposium on the vexed subject of 'Modern Scenic Art' got up for *The Stage Year Book* of 1914): 'To begin with, let me say at once that I consider any form of realism in the Theatre to be wrong.'

What, then, was to be put in the place of 'realism'?

Whatever it was, it was this, apparently, that worried Harker. But he speaks of it very vaguely. He only implies what is ahead. He says: 'But while I insist that by all means we should have simplicity, with sincerity, in the art of the Theatre, I do not think we need to draw our inspiration from the Noah's Ark of our childhood days, nor seek to encourage the perverted imagination that seeks to destroy all reasonable illusion in illustrating the masterpieces of the Drama.' [28].

From this it seems the new movement had a tendency to 'simplification', that it led to something resembling 'crudeness' or a 'Noah's Ark' quality, that it seemed to be 'perverted', and that it was out to destroy 'reasonable illusion'. It looks as if we are being introduced to the realm of 'stylization'.

We may get a step further by considering four dates:

In 1886 Edward William Godwin died;

In 1899 Appia published *Die Musik und die Inscenierung*;

In 1905 Gordon Craig published the first edition of *The Art of the Theatre*;

And in 1907 Pablo Picasso painted *Les Demoiselles d'Avignon*.

It is true that this painting was then hidden and not reproduced till 1925 nor publicly exhibited till 1937. But the force that produced *Les Demoiselles d'Avignon* in 1907 was the force that overthrew the domination of what was called 'realism' in scene-painting.

With that gone, what is to be done about our problem of the nature of scenic illusion? Is it, or is it not, the illusion of realism? In the same *Stage Year Book* Symposium of 1914, another designer of the new school, Norman Wilkinson, wrote of his own setting for Granville Barker's *Twelfth Night* at the Savoy Theatre the Christmas before: 'There was no attempt at scenic illusion . . .' and 'What one calls a "natural effect" on the stage is got by cheating people, for the moment, into the idea that they are where they are not, and at the Savoy there was no attempt to convince the eye against the judgement of the mind that one was out-of-doors looking at clipped yew hedges and marble canopies.'

Can it be that here Norman Wilkinson has given us the hint we needed to understand finally the intention of the time concerning stage illusion—namely, that the illusion they sought to give was ultimately the illusion that you were not really sitting in a theatre?

At any rate, 'realistic' scenepainting fell farther and farther from favour—save that there still survives a certain sneaking admiration for the brilliance of a job well done. But the question was whether the job done was what the theatre of the times needed. Those times were changing and the last phase of our review is at hand.

The present chapter must not, however, close without some brief reference to an epoch-making event. At the end of the fabulous rise and fall of scenepainting, the whole original *raison d'être* of the *scène à l'italienne*, of course, ceased—simply because without painted scenery the visible changing of scenes became impossible. You cannot change a realistic, built, box-set representing three walls of a room with all its curtains, pictures, fireplace, ornaments, light-fittings, carpet and furniture in a visible scene-change! It was with Irving that the changing of the new built scenery, now become too complicated to be managed in sight, was concealed behind a dropped curtain [61]. This was a remarkable novelty. But all the wonderful system of the continental *chariots* and of the English grooves, with their machinery, had come into existence solely to provide for the *visible* transformation of the scenes. Now it all began to be rooted out and thrown on the rubbish heap to give way to built stuff and braces.

SEVENTH PHASE

Anti-Illusion

SEVENTH PHASE

Anti-Illusion

To force the metaphor of 'The Seven Ages of Theatre' too far would bring us to an unfortunate and incorrect conclusion in our last chapter—namely that the Seventh Age which ends this strange, eventful history is mere oblivion—the decline and ultimate death of the theatre. Happily this is not so. The Seventh Phase brings us up-to-date and indeed the prospects are fair; instead of second childishness, we may well see some promise of renewed youthfulness. But there is one respect in which the metaphor of our title serves us in good stead to the last. For one of the morals of this seventh chapter is that we are forced to learn how the death of a great theatre man does kill *his* theatre.

It is remarkable how much any form of theatre which owes its brilliance to one man owes that brilliance not to his theories, but to his presence. Without him something fails to go on; and no amount of devotion among disciples can further the theories as a living growth. We must turn elsewhere for a fresh beginning.

We have not had occasion to remark this before, because deaths in past theatre never came home to us; we saw only the main stream going on. Davenant's untimely decease before Dorset Garden was completed is, for us now, nothing more than a date in a chart on p. 238. But within our own time we actually experience these bereavements and can remark the great difference in the theatre to be seen on either side of such an event. To take one instance; we can observe the difference between Reinhardt's theatre when he was alive and when he was dead. And it is devastating to discover what has become of that epoch-making, clarion-sounding, Grosses Schauspielhaus now, which seemed in 1919 the promise of a new age in theatre history. There are none of Poelzig's 'stalactites' today in a shell merely vegetating back to its variety days. Here indeed the melancholy Jaques' description of the Seventh Age is a true one.

Before, then, abandoning the fancy we have built our review upon, we can take advantage of it finally to extract the beneficial thought for our understanding of theatre—that it is not the architectural forms that make theatre; nor the splendour or the artistry of the backgrounds; nor the vigour and wisdom of the scripts; any more than it is the most enlightened theories—but it is just one personal thing in the way these things are handled on the stage, and that alone. And that personal thing succeeds or fails not according to its own intentions, but according to the response it evokes in practice from the people present.

In the seventh phase we shall encounter several innovators. Some seem to have the most interesting ideas; some seem to attract a most enthusiastic following; and some achieve the mystery of unforgettable theatre.

In the creative arts the merit of any work of art rests entirely in the beholder. The artist evokes; and there can be no absolute work of art. In the performing arts the 'beholder' is a curiously complicated thing; he is an individual present *on one occasion only* as part of a group of other individuals all influencing each other in the matter of what they behold.

THE PROSCENIUM CONTROVERSY

In the first decades of the 20th century the opposition to the *scène à l'italienne* was concentrated under a new extremist war-cry—'Abolish the proscenium!'

What prompted such a cry?

And what form of theatre could remain if the proscenium were abolished?

The study of the theatre in the present review has shown that the *proscaenium* was, in the 17th century, the stage itself on which the player acted. In fitting it into a roofed playhouse with scenery, this proscaenium became enclosed at the two sides with walls—the proscenium walls. The scenery stood behind the proscenium. Gradually, like shutting a drawer, the proscenium stage was progressively pushed back into the scenic stage to get more spectators into the theatre, and also to make the acting more a 'part of the picture' (in the Italian opera style). What had been the stage proper now became a mere 'fore-stage', and ultimately a twelve-inch 'apron' skirting the scenic stage.

All this sounds very dynamic and very moving; it is like pressing something in with one's thumbs and turning it inside out. And the interested spectators lean forward and press close together to peer more closely at what you are doing. You persevere until suddenly you succeed, and pop!—you have it in the box! At a blow you have created the glass lid, the picture frame, the peep show, the fourth wall. The little, safe, removed, jigging player doing his business in a box of tricks—an illusionist and an illusion in one. (During all this, you have turned the auditorium into a cave of darkness.)

It seems to me, as historian, that it does not matter so much whether the above is a fair description of fact or is a caricature in deliberately belittling terms. What is historically important is that in the early decades of the 20th century some people thought exactly this about the theatre—whether justifiably or not justifiably. And it was this sort of thought that prompted the cry 'Abolish the proscenium!' What was meant was—abolish the effect of the removed and framed peep-show, with its somehow *diminishing* effect on the players.

(It is significant that our phrase for describing an appearance of diminishment is 'to look through the wrong end of the *opera glasses*'—not the wrong end of the field glasses or the binoculars, but of that particular instrument that so vividly increased the impotent-puppet impression which was already present in some degree before the naked eye.)

There is, of course, a certain attractiveness in this little world of the puppet player over which one hangs in darkness sympathizing, with complete immunity, in every tiny naked heart-throb. But it is a question whether one is content to suffer this very often. One wants to feel not so removed. It is not surprising to hear that one of the reasons advanced for the decline of the theatre is that people are now so used to very close spectacles of actors in the cinema and on the television screen, that they feel too distant when they face an *à l'italienne* stage.

It is not until one examines documents of the times that one becomes aware of how rank the contempt was of either party for the other over this conflict about the proscenium 'arch'.

Sean O'Casey gathered together some amusing and significant comments in his essay called 'Pro-Per Proscenium' [47], and referring to the situation as it was in 1936. He makes no pretence at an impartial review, he frankly takes sides against the naturalistic theatre. We may justifiably say that he leads on from the remark of Norman Wilkinson that we quoted on p. 263. His opinion is that 'naturalism, or the exact imitation of life, or the cult of [and he speaks bitterly] real plays for real people, has brought the theatre down very low in the plane of imagination'. He then tells us that he read in one of the greater London weeklies of 1936 the following by a theatre critic:

'. . . The Reinhardt gang has never realized that to venture one inch beyond the proscenium arch destroys the whole illusion so laboriously created. This is the age of the picture stage, and even if you are twelve German producers rolled into one, you cannot put the clock back. You may put something in illusion's place, but that isn't what I want.'

This is an admirably chosen passage to start trouble. One might spend a whole chapter in comment, and O'Casey does in fact make some comment in his essay, but he sums it up simply with the dry question—'And isn't the "this is the age of the picture stage" a funny thing to say?' He returns to the newspaper article and picks on a passage which expresses very well the views of the upholders of the picture frame:

'It is vital to the art of the actor that he shall keep his frame, and that there shall be no point of contact between him and the spectator. A hair's-breadth advance by an actor into the breathing world is utter annihilation.'

'But,' says O'Casey, 'the picture-framed stage is precisely the stage of the time of the sedan chair, the stage-coach, the candle, the linkman, the silk-and-satin-clad ladies and gents that had become wholly separate from the people.' . . .

The Cambridge Festival Theatre

Meanwhile, with some indifference for what O'Casey's critic 'wanted', Terence Gray had re-opened in 1926 an old Georgian playhouse on the outskirts of Cambridge and called it the Festival Theatre, and given it a stage: 'comprising a wide fan of fore-stage with multiple levels gradually merging into the auditorium, a re-

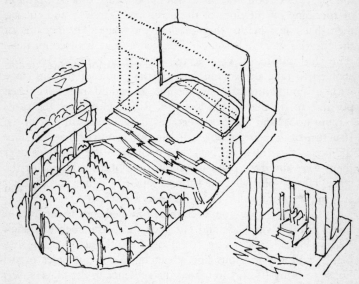

Fig. 60. Diagram of the Festival Theatre, Cambridge, with sketch of a scene-arrangement

volving middle-stage, and a raised and sliding back-stage. . . . This and its cylindrical cyclorama lit with prismatic lighting will make it possible to practise a type of stagecraft never before seen in England.'

This quotation is from the leaflet advertising the first season which (together with *The Festival Theatre Review* No. 1, being the programme of the opening show, Aeschylus's *Oresteia*) have now become interesting theatre documents. In the quotation no direct mention is made of abolishing the proscenium 'arch', though the description of the forestage 'with multiple levels gradually merging into the auditorium' hints strongly at it. In fact, the proscenium *was* abolished. The stage was planned as in Fig. 60.

This diagram is doubly useful for our review because, besides illustrating a new movement, it gives us a chance to show also an old movement in the earlier evolution of the English playhouse auditorium. The Barnwell Theatre (as it was originally named) was built in 1808. In it the dissociation of the stage from the spectators' room was made still more abrupt by a new fashion of rounding-off the lines of the boxes and 'circles', and cutting them back just before they reached the stage. The remains of the theatres at Dorchester, at Wisbech and at Ipswich all illustrate this feature. It was because of it that Terence Gray was enabled to take an axe and slice off the whole of the old stage without mutilating the auditorium. It would not have been possible to do this at, for instance, Richmond; there the proscenium doors and the little balconies above were still part of the structure of the rows of boxes. In the 19th century however (since the boxes were now cut back) the doors and the balconies over them were divorced from the auditorium and made part of the stage, taking somewhat the form of a pair of wings and creating still more the impression of a frame to the scenery.

As the century went on, even these rounded ends to the lines of boxes became cut back and cut back, until the shelf-like affair that we call a 'circle' today, so remote from the actors, came into being; and any gracious line advancing along the sides of the house to bring (if only in token) the audience to the players, was severed.

But we are concerned now with Terence Gray's new stage. He cut off the old stage with its proscenium sides and doors, and built an entirely new stage in the great empty space so left—with *no* frame to it (*see* Fig. 60).

The notion would appear to be to give untrammelled access between scene and spectator; and for such a use and with such a purpose, it seems, the stage was in fact conceived by its designer. But certain impressive diagrammatic sheets representing scene designs and given away with later programmes, show that a significant difficulty arose. Some of these diagrams are accompanied by small photographs illustrating the scene on the stage, and in none of these is the appearance quite the same as in the diagram. In all the photographs two upright screens (shaped like Serlian wings) appear at the sides (*see* side of Fig. 60) and the edge of a border is visible across the top. Thus, though in actual fact the proscenium frame was entirely eliminated in the transformation of the theatre, yet in practice no means was ever found to use scenery adequately on the stage without replacing, for that particular occasion, substitutes for proscenium sides and incorporating the aid of a proscenium top. And on each occasion that is what had to be done.

This is no way alters the fact that some fascinating, stimulating and very modern productions were created on this stage in its seven (or so) years of existence. But the abolition of the proscenium was not effected.

The theatre movement, however, went on. Its progress to the middle of the 20th century can almost be summed up in a paragraph, with two or three points to be elaborated afterwards.

The Little-Theatre, or Art-Theatre, Movement grew and widened. In Russia complete revolution in theatrical technique spread between the Wars, and complete reaction to revolutionary methods followed the Second War. Just as they drew the Georgian Style out of the excesses of the Baroque, so now the British waited till the revolutions had spent their extravagances and then founded the Open Stage and a new school of playwrights. The United States re-discovered the theatre in the round; Germany, the 'epic' theatre; France, the 'illogical' theatre from Jarry to Ionesco.

And Picasso discovered Distortion.

EMOTION AND JUDGEMENT

The first point for elaboration is the old proscenium problem.

As the century wore on the cry to abolish it was repeated, but at the same time the opposition maintained its objections. As late as 1949, Percy Corry [19] rebuked those among the theatre planners who (he said) claimed that 'intimacy' or 'unity' was obstructed by the proscenium arch. He strongly opposes the idea, saying:

'The competent actor finds no technical difficulty in establishing that unity from behind a proscenium arch. It is his job to do so and he is, in fact, aided by the separation of his world of 'realism' from the reality of the auditorium . . . The emotional response is actually heightened by remoteness; a darkened auditorium and concentration on a lighted acting area induce greater emotional sensitivity and help to suspend rational judgement. . . .'

On this remark it is necessary to break in in order to signal the particular matter over which the opposite parties in this struggle come to fiercest blows. *Rational judgement* becomes the first thing that Bertolt Brecht wished to promote in his theatre, and *emotional sensitivity* the first thing he wished to eliminate. Corry says on the one hand:

'A semi-hypnotic state is voluntarily achieved and this helps to preserve the emotional unity between actor and audience. . . . When he [the actor] intrudes into our territory he becomes an obvious performer instead of an illusion in the phenomenal world of the stage.'

Brecht on the other hand, in his postscript to the opera, *The Rise and Fall of the City of Mahagonny*, contrasts the effects of two kinds of theatre; the traditional theatre and the modern theatre as he himself conceives it. One pair of antitheses is that:

The traditional theatre arouses emotions in the spectator (*ermöglicht ihm Gefühle*).	The modern theatre prompts him to make decisions (*erzwingt von ihm Entscheidungen*).

Finer points of meaning here could well take up our consideration for some time; but it does not seem unjust to state the contrast as 'The old theatre induces "emotional sensitivity"; while the new stimulates "rational judgement".'

With reference to this 'trance of emotion' mentioned above, Brecht specifically states in his *Kleines Organon für das Theater*, at Paragraph 47—'. . . the actor . . . since his job is not to put his public into a trance, must not let himself fall into a trance.' (. . . *der Schauspieler . . . nicht beabsichtigend, sein Publikum in Trance zu versetzen, darf er sich selber nicht in Trance versetzen.*)

Here, it seems to me, is the kernel of the whole movement of 'modern' theatre—that is of the advanced theatre of the mid-20th century. It is a refusal to 'dress-up' an essential and pretend it is not there in deference to the demands of some superficial pictorial effect, nor to *palliate facts*. A given element or idea may be of the greatest importance to the meaning of the show; then admit its existence, even though to do so may be to allow the entrance of something that would be out of place in a pleasing, naturalistic painting. (A good example is Brecht's famous argument against *always* hiding the lanterns which give light to the stage.) Such

things may be accepted. They are elements of the show as a scene
on a stage. The fact that they are not elements of, and have
nothing to do with, a naturalistic painting is absolutely neither
here nor there, for the theatre is not any longer out to create the
illusion of showing a living painting. It is out (and this is the
crux) to create the *anti-illusion* that you are sitting in a theatre
watching actors performing. And if they are artists, that means
that you are already witnessing a work of art, without any need
to have it dressed up like one.

Such seems a fair statement of the opposing views. There is
no call to make, at this point, any analysis of whether this view is
'right', or that view 'wrong'. It would be quite foreign to the
whole attitude of this review to do such a thing. But, on the other
hand, what is incumbent upon any reader is to realize that such
divergent views are held at this time.

A more profitable question which must concern us now is—
What kind of a theatre is the anti-illusion phase leading us
towards?

THE NEW THEATRES (1)

ACCEPTING THE PROSCENIUM

There are three kinds. The first is, interestingly enough, the
theatre of the traditional type. Brecht in Berlin made use of the
old, 'late-Victorian', Schiffbauerdamm Theatre, and (apart from
modernizing the stage equipment) has been apparently content
to leave its shape and its atmosphere unchanged. It has a typical,
orthodox proscenium arch. Thus, one way to abolish the proscenium is not to abolish it! There is no need to; because it is
possible to achieve what you want without. What is wanted is to
abolish the idea of the *cutting-off* that we have allowed the proscenium to impose. An example will illustrate this; but it will
have to be in some detail for one of the biggest problems of
contemporary theatre is involved.

In the first place: The cardinal problem about the proscenium-
arch convention is that it creates a line. It is no more than
ordinarily difficult to play *behind* that line; but it is very difficult
indeed to discover in what tone to handle a passage where you
propose to *cross* that line.

Before going any further it is essential to understand how there may arise a genuine need to cross that line, for a curious psychological embarrassment is called up which sets many people utterly against this idea. What is involved here is the *direct address of words to the audience itself*—or even the actual descent of a player from the stage among the spectators.

It must be admitted that this is sometimes very crudely done; but it is done in the name of a 'new' idea called *audience participation*. The professed intention is to 'make the audience feel part of the show'. We know, from our review, that the idea is not a new one but a very old one, so old in fact as almost to be part of the essence of theatre. Compare, for instance, the advance of the Padstow Horse to a woman among the spectators. For this reason it is most important to understand properly. What is it that can go so wrong with such a venerable essential?

One common device for exploiting this idea is to bring one of the performers on to the stage not by any of the orthodox entrances in the scene, nor (of course) by those convenient, impersonal doors in the proscenium of earlier days which had such a valuable function—but down one of the aisles of the auditorium and up a flight of steps over the orchestra rail. Such an entrance through spectators was, in effect, made by Death in *The Castle of Perseverance*, and we suppose it would have been a very significant entrance. Such an entrance too is made (but with a technical difference) every day in the Kabuki theatre when a player enters on the *hana-michi*. Done as we have described it in the orthodox Western theatre, it may have odd consequences, the chief of which is this risk of spreading embarrassment through the spectators.

The reason for this embarrassment is not easy to explain. We can perhaps come nearest with an extreme example: It cannot be to any way of thinking a pleasant thing to come suddenly upon a frantically sobbing woman in a corridor. It has the effect of an outrage. We have frequently to have a frantically sobbing woman (or some figure like her) in a stage play. We can accept her, with some reservations, when she is throned upon the stage and we are enthralled spectators, actually remote but by her artistry intimately related with her event. But not when she is in the audience.

The 'unforeseen' about any theatrical performance comes in here. We are not to know how far she is going to go; she may cling to the nearest figure she sees and beg an actual response from him. This is all right if she is on the stage and the figure is a player who has been rehearsed, and who knows his part and knows her part as well, and of whom there is nothing *unforeseen* demanded. But if she comes into our own seating aisle, our study of the play is interrupted by a too-real need to decide what we ought to do if . . . *not* if we were met by such a frantic woman in real life, for then we should be our human selves according to our natures—but if we are met *now* and suddenly clung to and begged assistance of by an actress made-up and playing a part *in this theatre*, with the event being watched by nine hundred slightly amused, or slightly embarrassed, fellow spectators. Then the situation is entirely different. Our reaction will be a reaction to *that* situation and quite different from the reaction we should have if the event were real. We could not normally avoid embarrassment. The action would be a breach of the conventional courtesy of the theatre.

It can be argued that all this may be true of a wildly wailing woman, but that it is not true, however, of a simple messenger, one not likely to make an appeal upon us, and coming with a letter from a distance to a character on the stage; and that such an action can be made more interesting and immediate if he actually comes in down one of the audience gangways.

But this is very likely to be a false argument for two reasons; the first is that it has always been something of the atmosphere of a stunt in a picture-frame theatre, and will be regarded by the audience as such—they know very well he has not 'come from a distance'!

But the second is far more subtle and important. It is because an actor in his part has still an element of the horrifying, if you go too near. This is not alone because of any item of exaggerated make-up (though that plays a weird part), but because the man himself is strange compared with ordinary men. His mind is working on other than normal lines. He is dedicated to other objects than those to which we dedicate ourselves. He is withdrawn from normal impressions. He is concentrating on another situation than reality; he is concentrating on a fiction. He is not unlike a mad person; he is abnormal; he is a mask; the man himself can no longer be seen. And that (unless he is to some extent removed from us, elevated into another plane, insulated in some sense from us) can be a very uncomfortable thing.

True, much of this style of acting was to be seen in the Middle Ages when the costumed players of Death, Folly or Mankind strode through the crowd of people in the Place, but it must be remembered that it was especially here that the system of 'stytelers', or groups of guardians or interveners, was used. And by them the actor was on the one hand guarded from too great a press of the crowd, but the crowd on the other was guarded from too direct an address from the actor. These stytelers were insulators against the magic-man. The first players we noticed in our review were Wild Men.

But as the picture-frame theatre became established the audience came to watch; they were not asked to 'participate'. And even today a spectator may very legitimately exclaim—'Thank goodness they weren't! I don't want to be asked to participate in anybody's performance! I want to be left entirely alone to watch it and enjoy myself if I can. I don't pay money at the box-office to take on part of the actors' work for them.'

Strangely enough this opinion, though common, is not a consistent one, for the same spectator may be a member of (say) the Players' Theatre Club in Villiers Street, and may quite happily take the Chairman's chaff in good part, and perhaps enjoy heckling him back from his seat. It is true that this may be rather the act of showing-off before your fellow-members at a private club, and part of the game there. But it cannot be denied that there is something of the spirit of theatre about it.

A still more extreme case is seen in the almost hysterical beating of a rhythm by an audience on such occasions as rock and roll demonstrations. This also is 'audience participation' and has its part in the theatre—an important part, capable of an astounding impression of 'catharsis'. But it may become a dangerous power once it is out of hand. In general, one would suppose that audience participation in plays should stop short at the point where a highly-awakened critical attitude is provoked which takes very personal account of the import of the incident on the stage.

If this is so then there is perhaps a kinship between this idea of audience participation and the idea that lay behind Bertolt

Brecht's saying that the modern theatre should tend to 'exact decisions' from its audience.

To return to our question about the proscenium arch and its line, and to the problem of what tone one should take in any passage where one wants to go across that line. Such a passage can be exemplified at once in any *chorus speech*. A chorus or a commentator always goes ill in a picture-frame theatre; an obvious artificiality is at once created because a chorus is meaningless if it pretends to be part of a picture. Its comment must be addressed directly to the audience, and it is hard to find the tone in which to make any direct address if one is behind the 'line'. If one comes out of the picture to do it, then that can be, in a picture-frame theatre, an awkward matter, because it can make the audience suddenly self-conscious in their comfortable darkness and, again, embarrassed.

In a non-picture-frame theatre—that is one where the actor is himself in the auditorium—this awkwardness is much easier to avoid. Direct audience address, whether in comment or chorus or soliloquy, is not artificial in such theatres and does not involve any 'coming out of the picture'. But the root reason for this is not in the form of the theatre alone, it is in the fact that such a theatre makes it much more easy to find the *tone* in which such direct address is comfortable and natural, and indeed exciting.

This tone can be achieved in the picture-frame theatre, and thus we come to the example, led up to on p. 275, of how one form of abolition of the proscenium effect could be achieved by not abolishing the proscenium—and hence could justify our including the traditional picture-frame theatre among the three forms of the theatre of tomorrow. The example is this:

BRECHT'S CHORUS

In Brecht's *Der Kaukasische Kreidekreis*, the introduction is a short naturalistic scene where modern peasants are discussing a local problem. Near its end there enters a Singer from a band of players. He suggests that they play a piece which will have a special relevance to the problem. He asks for refreshment for the troupe first, and all agree to go off with him to a canteen, thus neatly clearing the stage for the play proper. All this is in the picture-frame convention.

The script at this point reads as follows:

THE YOUNG DRIVER (*to the Singer*): How long will it take, Arkadi? Our friend the Expert has to get back to Tiflis tonight.

THE SINGER (*easily*): Oh, there are really two pieces—a couple of hours.

THE YOUNG DRIVER: Couldn't you make it shorter?

THE SINGER: No.

A VOICE: Arkadi's show will take place after food here on the green.

All go cheerfully to eat

THE SINGER (*sitting on the ground in front of his musicians, a black sheepskin wrap over his shoulders, skimming through a well-thumbed little prompt-book with playbills*):
In the olden days . . . etc.

In the Berliner Ensemble presentation of this play, produced by Brecht himself, the two 'musicians' of the script became two women singers in pleasantly-designed, white gowns of a vaguely medieval cut. They walked across the stage, carrying their music-parts, and sat down together on two stools in front of one of the proscenium sides and opened their books (*see* Plate 18).

The interesting problem was this presented. Brecht had broken the rules. He had brought on a chorus in a picture-frame scene, taken them forward across the line of demarcation, and seated them as near to the audience as he could get them. One couldn't avoid them. One couldn't ignore them. They were there for good to sing commentaries throughout the play. The old reaction came at once: this was going to be *awful!* Brecht had committed a major mistake; these women were going to embarrass us throughout.

Brecht handled the situation very simply. He merely made them take their places as if they had never been into a theatre before—but with no trace of self-consciousness. Their reaction was of a certain pleased interest at the auditorium in front of them and the crowd within it. *They looked at us!*

The whole embarrassment was broken down in a trice. These were rather pleasant people! They had a job to do and got on with it; they opened their books and set to work to sing.

When the play was in action they watched it. At exciting

moments they made no pretence of being unfamiliar with it but turned easily to the audience and (one felt) delightedly and sympathetically observed their reactions. And we didn't mind a bit! We enjoyed their enjoying us.

This was something entirely new in theatre. The 'proscenium' had been abolished without abolishing the proscenium. The *tone* of the chorus was so set that they were a part of the show, and at the same time they were the nicest people you could wish to meet. They possessed themselves in peace, and never took the trouble to do a single thing wrong. And they gave us an entirely new experience of the theatre.

The reason why it seemed to me important to quote this example in detail is that it offers us an understandable introduction to something gradually growing in contemporary theatre—the idea of dropping the appearance of performing *before* an audience in favour of the reality of performing deliberately *to* (or *for*) an audience. Instead of the kind of acting which goes to some trouble to further a pretence that the actors are not conscious of the audience, we have acting that very patently and unashamedly remarks their presence and makes much of it—makes it, in fact, what it really is; the very excuse and justification for the performance.

It is the difference between pretending you aren't play-acting and making the most of the fact that you actually are. It is, or would appear to be (for we get to very delicate ground here), an attempt to replace what you're supposed to think by what you really think.

BRECHT'S SCENERY

As in the acting, so this idea of anti-illusion comes into the scenery.

The Caucasian Chalk Circle was one of the most richly set of the Berliner Ensemble shows produced by Brecht. Yet the script contains no explicit scene directions.

The staging was by means of a large, simple, fabric cyclorama enclosing a revolve (Fig. 61). Inside the cyclorama, small light cloths were dropped under the eyes of the audience, and their lower edges made a gay fluttering as they descended. Each bore a simple sketch in line-work for scenery, and fell across the centre

Fig. 61. The river-side scene from Brecht's The Caucasian Chalk Circle
(*director Bertolt Brecht; costumes and scenery Karl von Appen*)

of the revolve; being narrow, they left a portion of the revolve either side. Behind them, set pieces could be built on the farther section of the revolve by stage hands slipping through an opening in the middle of the cyclorama but concealed by the cloth, and the set pieces could be revolved into position round the side of the cloth.

In that delicate scene of Grusche's meeting with the Soldier by the banks of the stream, we saw two rows of reeds running up the stage, and a slight sketch of trees on the little white back-cloth. But in the script we have no more than this:

THE SINGER: As she sat by the stream to wash the clothes she saw his form in the water, and his face was fainter as the months went by . . . (etc.)

By a little stream Grusche is kneeling and washing clothes in the water. . . (etc).

When she turns round the Soldier, Simon Chachava is standing on the far bank in a torn uniform.

Between these three passages some pieces of dialogue occur. But those three passages are the only signs given in the script of any 'scenery' for this very moving and dramatic occasion in the story. There is no thought of indicating an illusionistic picture. Even in a traditional picture-frame theatre, the principle here is to refrain from illusion, but to show actors playing the parts for you on a modern stage. Again we are given a new experience of the theatre.

(It is worth adding that in Brecht's notes drafted for *The Life of Galileo*, but not prepared for publication before his death, No. 1 of them reads [12]: 'The stage decor must not be such that the public believes itself to be in a room in medieval Italy or in the Vatican. The public must remain always clearly aware that it is in a theatre.')

It is this new sense of the theatre that the new theatre architecture has the task of promoting—at any rate so far as concerns plays. To some degree modern opera too can fit into this 'non-illusive' convention, as indeed Brecht had demonstrated in his notes on *The Rise and Fall of the Town of Mahagonny*. But in general, opera still claims the 'Italian' stage, with its frame 'and all which constitutes, even today, the "theatre".'

The longest step forward in modern theatre building in this century so far has been made by Germany, with her close on eighty new theatres in fifteen years. But almost all of them are in the picture-frame tradition, and almost all of them planned for (at least occasional) presentations of grand opera. Relatively few theatres, such as the Smaller House at Mannheim, and that at Gelsenkirchen, and to some extent (even if in atmosphere rather than form) the theatre at Münster, lead towards a new way for plays. In them we may see some move to anti-illusion, to the acceptance, rather than the rejection, of the fact that you are sitting in a theatre. But in Germany as yet these are only occasional and, taking the country as a whole, the first new form of modern theatre, there, is the old Italian form with some variations.

The variations are very considerable for the whole principle of the *scène à l'italienne* has been swept away and been replaced by mostly built, instead of painted, scenery. And for this a new system of stage machinery has been perfected, in power and elaboration far in excess of anything of the sort ever known before. And yet, for all this, the scene is viewed through a frame exactly as the old painted scenes were—and the element of marvellous illusion still dominates (much as it does on the British Stratford-upon-Avon stage).

Outside Germany, however, some countries which Germany has so far outstripped have paused before following her lead, to contemplate other possibilities. Two instances are Norway and

America. Though Norway's interest is still chiefly in picture-frame presentations, she does not see them as committing her to vast machinery plants. Instead, the interest is in travelling ortho-dox theatre of reasonable quality from the capital to small pro-vincial towns. Her newest theatre building is the headquarters of the *Riksteatret* or State Travelling Theatre, at Smestad in the suburbs of Oslo. There, instead of technical luxury, the intention has been to design a sort of ideal adaptation of a provincial hall. On the one hand it serves as a guide for other centres to the best minimum adaptations; on the other as a reasonably equipped rehearsal- and performing-place where the companies can work comfortably, but in surroundings comparable with those they will meet on tour.

Those in America who turn their backs on Broadway look for a new chapter of theatrical life in the medium-small theatre—possibly multi-purpose, possibly adaptable in form—in civic centres. It is in some such new movement that we shall first find the revival of the theatre in the round.

THE NEW THEATRES (2)

ABOLISHING THE STAGE: THE ROUND

Our review has shown that there are two essential forms of theatre to set beside the Italian picture-frame theatre; the first is theatre in a circle—the simplest and oldest—and the second is theatre with a stage and background. Figs. 11 and 32 illustrate basic examples of these. The new modern architectural problem is simply to fit these indoors without violating their essence. Any complication, if it arises, generally comes over the question of the use of scenery because, of course, only the Italian picture-frame theatre was ever designed to accommodate full scenery.

Theatre in the round means three things; the first is obvious—it is a theatre where the audience completely surrounds the action on all sides. The second follows from this but is not so imme-diately obvious—it is a theatre where it is quite impossible to give the effect of a painted picture come to life. The third is that, speaking in general, it is a theatre which has no stage. Thus it can properly be called an *arena theatre*.

The United States of America, stultified on Broadway by the restrictions of site-costs which have helped to commercialize the

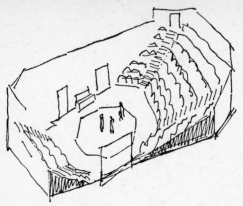

Fig. 62. Diagram of the arrangement of the Teatro Sant' Erasmo in Milan

theatrical adventure as it has never been commercialized before in history, have broken away almost by sheer force of fate to the extremest simplicity in theatre possible. Having been led up the garden by the European allegiance to the *scène à l'italienne*, their reaction has been to leave those there who liked it, and to go back to first principles. For this reason America has become the chief cradle—so far at any rate as number of offspring is concerned—of theatre in the round. Margot Jones's book *Theatre-in-the-Round*, 1951, enthusiastically describes one such venture.

In France, André Villiers not only converted a cabaret hall into the Théâtre en Rond de Paris (*see* Plate 19), but somewhat staggered the theatrical world, after a group of partly successful experiments, by drawing audiences to his presentation in French of *The Caine Mutiny* for a run that lasted season after season. His book [75] is a valuable textbook of the technique.

In Italy, a variant form was instituted at Milan under the name of the Sant' Erasmo Theatre, where the audience sits not fully on all sides but in two sectors facing each other, leaving the acting area at the centre in a sort of waist to the building and capable of being entered direct from doors either side (*see* Fig. 62).

In England, Stephen Joseph has proved an intrepid exponent of the theory and already has established a company for its practice, performing in adapted halls (*see* Plate 20) and presenting new plays written for the form as well as revivals. At Croydon, the young Pembroke Theatre built in an existing hall

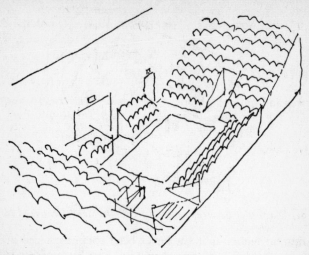

Fig. 63. Diagram of the arrangement of the Pembroke Theatre at Croydon

demonstrates the success possible with completely irregular shape, (*see* Fig. 63).

TERMINOLOGY

A difficulty is threatening over terminology in the theatre in the round. We have seen that the nature of the style is such that, generally speaking, there is no raised stage—the performance taking place on the floor level and the audience being disposed on surrounding slopes like the sides of a saucer. If there is no raised stage, then it is clearly wrong to use the term 'open stage' to include theatre in the round.

On the other hand, because it has the form it has, the word 'arena' is ideally suited to the theatre-in-the-round style, since an arena is a flat space in the middle of a circle of rising seating. But the term 'arena staging' (a contradiction in terms, by the way) is indiscriminately used to cover both open-stage work and theatre in the round. This is careless and unfortunate.

It is unfortunate because the techniques of playing on an open stage and in the round are very different; and if we say of an open-stage show that it is an arena production, or of a theatre-in-the-round show that it is an example of open-stage presentation, then no one is going to know where we are.

I enter an urgent plea that distinction be made here.

Another word capable of much confusion is 'amphitheatre'. We use it correctly when we talk of the Roman circus or amphitheatre, which is an arrangement with seating all round the arena. It is correctly used then because it means 'two theatres' (*amphi* means 'both', as *amphibian* means something that goes *both* in the water and on land); it means two theatres because a *theatron* is a *half* circle (or thereabouts) of seating before a *skene*. Put two 'theatres' face to face, suppressing the *skene*, and you have a circular amphitheatre.

Thus the curious French phrase referring to seating as being *en amphithéâtre* must be read and used carefully; it really means any block of seating sloping up, and perhaps fanning a little, like a *part* of an amphitheatre; that is to say, seating arranged *à la* amphithéâtre, if I may so word it. An example of this meaning is in Brunet's description of Dorset Garden, quoted above on p. 239.

I make these points because it is exceedingly irksome and profitless to discuss a new technique with imperfectly defined terms that mean different things to different people.

THE NEW THEATRES (3)

RESUMING THE OPEN STAGE

Let us have no misunderstanding here; by *open stage* I mean a stage unenclosed by any frame, projecting boldly forward from its background and open to the spectators on three of its sides. In other words the form of the 'booth stage' illustrated in Fig. 32.

This is the third form in the new theatre movement. It would seem that it is more particularly a British contribution—or at least a contribution from the English-speaking world, with its particular heritage of plays based on Speech. By this is meant plays so made that the miraculous organ of Speech takes a particularly important part in the dramatic presentation. In most primitive performances, action plays a greater part than Speech. In all opera, music and singing play a greater part than Speech. In the majority of 18th- and 19th-century European plays, the *scene* as a whole presented on the stage is the vehicle of the drama; and it has come about that stage illusion, and its final state of naturalism, have here so come to subordinate Speech as a vehicle of theatrical presentation that, in the first place, it is almost always restricted to prose, and in the second to prose of a particularly pedestrian, artificial and unevocative kind—the very word used to describe it is 'theatrical'!

The restoration of Speech as an organ to dramatic theatre has passed several phases in the last century. It began with a noble and laborious attempt to revive verse-drama. Little really came to touch the general public (despite such brilliance as Synge's and such understanding as Gordon Bottomley's) until first T. S. Eliot persuaded hearers that plays could be written in verse without one's minding it, and next Christopher Fry persuaded them that words in verse could be a fountain of glittering entertainment. From then onwards many new verse plays were written. Then a reaction came and, going beyond verse, English playwrights began to use the form of General Speech itself as a medium—not restricting to a special form of it ruled by metre and rhyme, but using the spoken word as precisely and evocatively as poetry is used. The genesis of this movement is interesting to watch:

Henrik Ibsen was both a poet and a prose playwright. He made a profound impression upon the young James Joyce, as is shown in Joyce's youthful letter to Ibsen. Joyce later had among his helpers (and incidentally among the writers of *Our Exagmination*) the then unknown Samuel Beckett. Joyce's essays in playwriting were not successful, despite his interest in the sound of words. But in later years, Beckett's *Waiting for Godot* and *Endgame* were to open a new door (albeit a strange door for many). And now, with the assistance of the satire of Anouilh and the illogic of Ionesco, to say nothing of Brecht's revolutionary practical example as poet—and his ideas expressed in the essay *Über reimlose Lyrik mit unregelmässigen Rhythmen* [13]—we see the rising of Harold Pinter, N. F. Simpson, John Arden . . . the tale is merely beginning. All these men are using Speech as an organ of theatre.

For theatre of this sort the open stage was originally created, and for theatre of this sort the open stage is a most promising architectural form today, because of its freedom from restriction —and especially the restriction of illusion. Here poetry is not out of place. In an open-stage theatre, the illusion that you are *not* in a theatre is hard to create; the anti-illusion that that is just where you are and that it is a reality is equally hard to suppress.

It might be worth mentioning that a certain small but vexed

question about seeing opposite spectators comes into consideration here. An objection is raised, both against the theatre in the round and against the side seats in an open-stage arrangement, that the spectator can see beyond the actors a phalanx of other spectators all concentrating on the same stage, and this annoys him. Ask him why; and he replies that *illusion is destroyed* if he can see the actors and the audience at the same time. Ask him if 'illusion' is ever truly maintained if he sees painted canvas behind the actors, and he will reply (rather surprisingly!) 'Yes'. Ask him if at a boxing-contest, or a football match, or a table-tennis tournament, the illusion is destroyed by seeing spectators on the far side of the ring or the pitch or the table, and he will reply 'No' and add 'Of course not! There is no illusion there to destroy.' But enjoyment in the playing is not diminished.

Why then should seeing the spectators on the far side of a stage diminish the enjoyment of a play? Only if one clings to the illusion that it is not a performance on a stage before spectators. Only, that is to say, if one refuses to accept the play for what it is.

There is a growing agreement that to accept the play for what it is is not only no deterrent to the enjoyment of theatre, but is a key to a new appreciation of it. And in practice, to see the actors come out to offer their play on an open stage is to anticipate a session of enjoyment of new facilities and freedoms.

Some of these facilities and freedoms I have discussed in my book on *The Open Stage* [67]. There remains to do here what was not possible there, to survey briefly with illustrative diagrams some of the forms which open-stage practice has taken so far in the modern movement in the British theatre.

MODERN FORMS

One of the earliest came out of John English's creation in 1948 of the so-called Arena Theatre Group at Birmingham, to study the needs of new theatre and to experiment with a form designed to house it most adequately. His theatre was made as shown in Plate 21. It contains two acting-areas, one on a low stage and the other in the form of a strip of floor separating that stage from the audience. This 'peripheral strip' can be entered by doors either side the stage in a background framework, whose centre part, giving on to the stage itself, consists of a 'proscenium

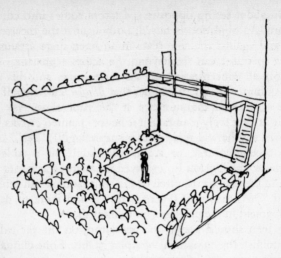

Fig. 64. The Dramatic Studio of the University of Bristol arranged for an open-stage performance

opening' capable of accommodating scenery. The whole stage can be concealed by a curved curtain. The audience is disposed in half a circus. With this theatre John English has worked steadily for sixteen years.

In 1951 the present writer designed for the Department of Drama at the University of Bristol an adaptable studio for theatre practice, one of whose arrangements took the form shown in Fig. 64. This theatre has now had thirteen years of continuous use, and has seen, besides several Elizabethan revivals, the first performance by the Bristol Old Vic Company of John Arden's *The Happy Haven* (production, William Gaskill; costume, Iris Brooke), as well as many other shows both experimental and orthodox; in the round, on the open stage, and in the picture-frame style.

In 1952 and 1953 two simple but significant (though short-lived) experiments were started in London by the Cockpit Theatre Company under Ann Jellicoe and the Theatre Centre under Brian Way respectively. For the first a typical 'small-hall' theatre was taken (Fig. 65 and Plate 23) but used in an unconventional way—the picture-frame stage being disregarded, the proscenium curtains left closed, and the performance given on the floor in front

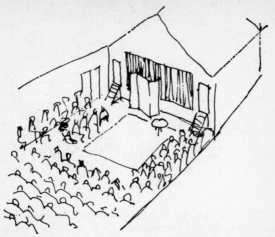

Fig. 65. The theatrical arrangement used by Ann Jellicoe for a production at the Cockpit Theatre Club

of the stage; on some occasions backed by an arrangement of screens. The audience sat on three sides, and the actors entered from the pass-doors in the proscenium sides.

In the Theatre Centre, a studio was used with various dispositions of acting-area and seating, and there in 1955 Peter Coe presented a fully convincing production of J-J. Bernard's *Martine* with a basic lay-out similar to the last Figure.

In 1953 (after some now-famous preliminary essays at the Assembly Rooms, Edinburgh, including *A Satire of the Three Estates*), Sir Tyrone Guthrie and Tanya Moiseiwitsch planned the theatre in Stratford, Ontario, in Canada, as shown in Plate 22.

In 1959, Bernard Miles opened his Mermaid Theatre in London, where a restricted site forced him to exploit a 'principle of frontality' rather than the three-sided embracement of a full open stage. But his venture is equally in the direction of the abolition of a proscenium.

Among specially built new theatres designed to facilitate open stage presentations are the theatre at Chichester and the Nuffield Theatre at Southampton University which was finished in 1964. Figure 66 shows a preliminary sketch for this theatre. The building is so arranged that the open stage can be removed and a normal picture frame stage opened in its place if required.

*Fig. 66. Project for the new adaptable theatre at Southampton University
(designed by Richard Southern with Sir Basil Spence, architect)*

The open-stage form allows of two very different degrees of complication, from the barest simplicity to a mechanical elaboration equalling Brecht's.

It can be used in a perfectly empty hall, with any suitable architectural features drawn into the service of the production, as in the performance by the Bristol University First-year Students of Anouilh's *The Waltz of the Toreadors* in the Dance School at Dartington Hall, Devonshire, in 1960 (*see* Fig. 67 and Plate 24), where the row of long windows down one side was made the basis of a setting, and the natural landscape without, together with the natural evening which fell upon it as the performance advanced, were combined with a not-inadequately furnished stage and the resources of modern spot-lighting to make a unity of picture that was not illusionistic, that never forgot you were looking at a lit stage and the Devonshire hills outside, and that yet was not detrimental to the atmosphere of the play, nor inconsistent with the house of a retired General in the remote French countryside. The generally-difficult problem of the Bedroom Scene was solved by a 'bed thrust on' in the Elizabethan tradition, and the dropping of blinds over the window. . . .

Or the open-stage form can be incorporated in a particular specially-designed theatre, planned to accommodate every kind of setting from the severest expressionism to the most reminiscent naturalism, as is visualized by the group of adventurers at Harlow

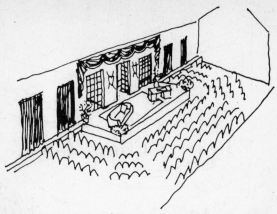

Fig. 67. The open-stage arrangement for Anouilh's The Waltz of the Toreadors *in the Dance School, Dartington Hall (director Richard Southern; costumes Iris Brooke)*

New Town, who proposed to add to their public buildings a small playhouse on the lines shown in Fig. 68.

Indeed, development with the idea of the open-stage form has now gone far enough for us to be able (aided as we are by the approach to theatre history made in this present review) to offer a preliminary formula——

Take any room:

Put a stage against one wall:

Open the four traditional access ways to it in the wall (left, right and centre doors, and an 'above'):

Add the 'booth' or players' rooms behind the stage:

Rake the seating floor:

Provide for a gallery for looking diagonally down on the stage.

And yet after all . . . the history of the theatre is not the history of its forms, but of the impression made on the people in the use of those forms by players. The player is both the nucleus and the vehicle of theatre—and the player alone, now as always. Whether at one side of Europe it is a Leah Deganith leaving the tent of the Ohel in Tel-Aviv for a while to thread two continents, singing and speaking the ancient songs of the Hebrews and modern sketches of the rebirth of Israel; in Paris on Tuesday, Genoa on Friday and a fortnight later in Buenos Aires . . . or whether at the

Fig. 68. Project for a small mechanized open-stage theatre for Harlow, Essex (designer Richard Southern)

other end of Europe we find a man like Emlyn Williams to enchant us for two smooth hours on end with a reincarnation of Dickens, assisted by nothing but a beard and a book, or bring to life again Dylan Thomas and with him several decades of Welsh life in sunlight and lamplight . . . here in the end as in the beginning is one-man theatre, unchanged.

Book List

Book List

1. ALFORD, Violet; 'The Place of Rhythm in the Basque Pastorales' in *The Journal of the English Folk Dance and Song Soc.*, Vol. vii, 1952.

2. ALFORD, Violet; *Pyrenean Festivals*, 1937.

3. ALFORD, Violet; 'Some Hobby Horses of Great Britain' in *The Journal of the English Folk Dance and Song Soc.*, Vol. iii, 1939 (pp. 230, 234).

4. ALLEY, Rewi; *Peking Opera*, Peking 1957.

5. ALTMAN, FREUD, MACGOWAN and MELNITZ; *Theater Pictorial*, Berkeley, 1953.

6. ARLINGTON, L. C.; *The Chinese Drama*, Shanghai 1930.

7. ARMSTRONG, William A.; *The Elizabethan Private Theatres*, Society for Theatre Research Pamphlet No. 6, 1958.

8. BARSACQ, André; 'Lois scéniques' in *La Revue Théâtrale*, No. 5, 1947.

9. *Bauen und Wohnen*, Zürich, Sept. 1958, p. 293.

10. BEARE, W.; *The Roman Stage*, 1950.

11. BOADEN, James; *The Life of Mrs. Siddons*, 1827.

12. BRECHT, Bertolt; *Plays*, Vol. 1, 1959.

13. BRECHT, Bertolt; 'Über reimlose Lyrik mit unregelmässigen Rhythmen' *Versuche* 12, Berlin 1953.

14. BREWER, J. S.; *The Letters and Papers of the Reign of Henry VIII*, 1862.

15. BRIDHYAKORN, Prince, and Dhanit Yupho; *The Khon*, Bangkok 1934.

16. CHAMBERS, E. K.; *The English Folk Play*, Oxford 1933.

BOOK LIST

17. CHAMBERS, E. K.; *The Mediaeval Stage*, Oxford 1903 (Vol. ii, p. 324).

18. COHEN, Gustav; *Le livre de conduite du régisseur et le compte des dépenses pour le Mystère de la Passion*, Strasbourg 1925.

19. CORRY, Percy; 'That "Intimate" Stage' in *Tabs*, Vol. 7, No. 3.

20. CUNNINGHAM, Percy; *Extracts from the Accounts of the Revels at Court*, 1842.

21. DUNCAN, Marion H.; *Harvest Festival Dramas of Tibet*, Alexandria, Va., U.S.A. 1955.

22. EVANS, H. R.; *English Masques*, *n.d.* (*c.* 1897).

23. *Florimene, The Argument of*, 1635.

24. FRAZER, J. G.; *The Golden Bough*, London 1911. (New York, 1911; one volume edition, 1922; paperback, 1960.)

25. GALLOP, Rodney; 'Aerial Dances of the Otomis' in *The Geographical Magazine*, Dec. 1936.

26. GALLOP, Rodney; *A Book of the Basques*, 1930.

27. GRAHAME, Kenneth; *The Golden Age*, 1895.

28. HARKER, Joseph; *Studio and Stage*, 1924.

29. HISS, Philip Hanson; *Bali*, 1941.

30. HOSLEY, Richard; 'The Discovery Space in Shakespeare's Globe' in *Shakespeare Survey*, No. 12, Cambridge 1959.

31. *Illustrated London News*, 26 Dec. 1936.

32. *Illustrated London News*, 5 June 1937.

33. IYER, K. Bharatha; *Kathakali*, 1955.

34. KAWATAKE, Shigetoshi; *Development of Japanese Theatrical Art*, Tokyo 1936.

35. KALVODOVÀ-SIS-VANIS; *Chinese Theatre* (Spring Books, *n.d*)

36. KENNEDY, Peter (ed.); 'The Symondsbury Mumming Play', *Journal of the English Folk Dance and Song Soc.*, Vol. vii, 1952.

37. KITTO, H. D. F.; *The Greeks*, Pelican 1951 (p. 104).

38. LANCASTER, Henry Carrington; *Le Mémoire de Mahelot*, Paris 1920.

39. LAWRENCE, W. J.; *The Elizabethan Playhouse and other studies*, Series 1, Stratford 1912.

40. LAWRENCE, W. J.; *Those Nut-cracking Elizabethans*, 1935.

41. LECLÈRE, Adhémard; *Le théatre cambodgien*, Paris 1911.

42. MEDWALL, H.; *Fulgens and Lucrece* (before 1516), accessible in F. S. Boas's edition of *Five Pre-Shakespearean Comedies*, World's Classics, 1934.

43. MEERWARTH, A.; 'Les *Kathakalis* du Malabar' in *Journal Asiatique* Oct–Dec. 1926.

44. MOTTER, T. H. Vail; *The School Drama in England*, 1929.

45. NAGLER, A. M. (ed.); *Sources of Theatre History*, New York, 1952.

46. NICOLL, Allardyce; *Masks Mimes and Miracles*, 1931.

47. O'CASEY, Sean; *The Green Crow*, 1957. (New York, 1956; paperback, 1958).

48. O'NEILL, P. G; *Early Nō Drama*, 1958 (chap. vii).

49. ORDISH, T. F.; *Early London Theatres*, 1899 (p. 58 *ff*).

50. PICKARD-CAMBRIDGE, Arthur; *The Dramatic Festivals of Athens*, Oxford, 1953.

51. PICKARD-CAMBRIDGE, Arthur; *The Theatre of Dionysus at Athens*, Oxford, 1946.

52. POZZO, Andrea; *Prospettiva dei pittori e architetti*, 1692–1700, Vol. 2 (Fig. 44).

53. RADFORD, Cicely; 'Medieval Actresses', in *Theatre Notebook*, 1953, Vol. 7 (p. 48).

54. RAE, Kenneth and Richard Southern; *An International Vocabulary of Technical Theatre Terms* in eight languages, Brussels, 1959.

55. RAO, Subba and Madhao Achwal; 'A Note on Ancient Indian Theatre' in *Natya*, New Delhi, Winter, 1959–60.

56. REYNOLDS, George Fullmer; *The Staging of Elizabethan Plays*, New York, 1940.

57. REYNOLDS, George Fullmer; ' "Trees" on the stage of Shakespeare' in *Modern Philology*, Vol. 5, 1907.

58. SHEPPARD, Francis; *The Survey of London*, L.C.C., Vols. xxix and xxx, 1960.

59. SHOKOSAI; *Shibai Goya Zue*, 2 Vols. and *Supplement*, 2 Vols., Osaka, 1800.

60. SMITH, J. Moyr; *A Midsummer Night's Dream*, 1892.

61. SOUTHERN, Richard; *Changeable Scenery*, 1952. (New York, 1959.)

62. SOUTHERN, Richard; 'Concerning a Georgian Proscenium Ceiling' in *Theatre Notebook*, Vol. 3 (pp. 6 and 24), 1948.

63. SOUTHERN, Richard; 'He also, was a Scene-painter' in *Life and Letters*, Dec. 1939.

64. SOUTHERN, Richard; 'Inigo Jones and Florimene' in *Theatre Notebook*, Vol. 7 (p. 37), 1953.

65. SOUTHERN, Richard; 'A Japanese Theatre Exhibition' in *Theatre Notebook*, Vol. 6 (p. 83), 1952.

66. SOUTHERN, Richard; *The Medieval Theatre in the Round*, 1957. (New York, 1958.)

67. SOUTHERN, Richard; *The Open Stage*, 1953. (New York, 1959.)

68. SOUTHERN, Richard; 'The Picture-Frame Proscenium of 1880' in *Theatre Notebook*, Vol. v (p. 60), 1951.

69. SOUTHERN, Richard; 'A 17th-century Indoor Stage' in *Theatre Notebook*, Vol. 9 (p. 5), 1954.

70. SOUTHERN, Richard; 'The Staging of 18th-century Designs for Scenery' in *The Journal of the Royal Institute of British Architects*, Vol. 42, 3rd series, No. 18, 1935.

71. *Stage* correspondent; 'The Chinese Stage' in *The Stage Year Book*, 1909.

72. TCHIAO Tch'eng-Tchih; *Le Théâtre chinois d'aujourdhui*, Paris, 1938.

73. TIDDY, R. J. E.; *The Mummers' Play*, Oxford, 1923.

74. *Times, The*; 25 May 1957.

75. VILLIERS, André; *Le Théâtre en Rond*, Paris, 1958.

76. WALEY, Arthur; *The Nō Plays of Japan*, 1921. (New York, 1957.)

77. WICKHAM, Glynne; *Early English Stages 1300 to 1660*, 1959, Vol. 1, 1300 to 1576.

78. WOOLF, H. I.; *Three Tibetan Mysteries*, Routledge, *n.d.*

79. ZOETE, Beryl de, and Walter Spies; *Dance and Drama in Bali*, 1938.

80. ZUNG, Cecilia S. L.; *Secrets of the Chinese Drama*, 1937.

Index

Index

305

INDEX

INDEX

INDEX

INDEX

INDEX

INDEX

INDEX